D1560171

Amplified Bible

Containing the
AMPLIFIED GOSPEL OF JOHN,
PSALMS AND PROVERBS

GRAND RAPIDS, MICHIGAN 49530 USA

TO THE
AMPLIFIED
BIBLE

In 1958 The Lockman Foundation and Zondervan Publishing House issued the first edition of the Amplified New Testament after more than 20,000 hours of research and prayerful study. Some four years later the first of two Old Testament volumes appeared (the Amplified Old Testament, Part Two—Job to Malachi), followed in 1964 by the publication of the Amplified Old Testament, Part One—Genesis to Esther. The next year (1965) the Amplified Bible came out in one volume.

Now, twenty-two years later, Zondervan Bible Publishers and The Lockman Foundation are pleased to present the Amplified Bible, Expanded Edition. The purpose of all the characters in the story of the making of the Amplified Bible is still relevant today: to communicate the Word of God to people and to exalt Jesus Christ. This has been the fourfold aim of the Lockman Foundation from the beginning:

1. That it should be true to the original Hebrew and Greek.
2. That it should be grammatically correct.
3. That it should be understandable to the masses.
4. That it should give the Lord Jesus Christ His proper place, the place which the Word gives Him.

From the days of John Wycliffe (1329–1384) and the first English Bible to the present, translators have worked diligently on English versions designed to faithfully present the Scriptures in contemporary language. The Amplified Bible is not an attempt to duplicate what has already been achieved, nor is it intended to be a substitute for other translations. Its genius lies in its rigorous attempt to go beyond the traditional "word-for-word" concept of translation to bring out the richness of the Hebrew and Greek languages. Its purpose is to reveal, together with the single English word equivalent to each key Hebrew and Greek word, any other clarifying meanings that may be concealed by the traditional translation method. Perhaps for the first time in an English version of the Bible, the full meaning of the key words in the original text is available for the reader. In a sense, the creative use of the amplification merely helps the reader comprehend what the Hebrew and Greek listener instinctively understood (as a matter of course).

Take as an example the Greek word *pisteuo*, which the vast majority of versions render "believe." That simple translation, however hardly does justice to the many meanings contained in the Greek *pisteuo*: "to adhere to, cleave to; to trust, to have faith in; to rely on, to depend on." Consequently, the reader gains understanding through the use of amplification, as in John 11:25: "Jesus said to her, I am [Myself] the Resurrection and the Life. Whoever believes in (adheres to, trusts in, and relies on) Me, although he may die, yet he shall live."

In the words of the apostle Paul, "And we are setting these truths forth in words not taught by human wisdom but taught by the [Holy] Spirit . . . [that His glory may be both manifested and recognized]" (1 Cor 2:13; Phil 1:11).

TO THE
AMPLIFIED
BIBLE

About the Amplified Bible

The story of the Amplified Bible is a remarkable story of faith, hope, and love. It's the story of a woman, a foundation, a committee, and a publisher. Commitment, energy, enthusiasm, giftedness—these are the words that paint the picture, the picture of the making of a translation.

Frances Siewert (Litt. B., B.D., M.A., Litt. D.) was a woman with an intense dedication to the study of the Bible. It was Mrs. Siewert (1881–1967) who laid the foundation of the Amplified Bible, devoting her life to a familiarity with the Bible, with the Hebrew and Greek languages, and with the cultural and archaeological background of Biblical times, which would result in the publication of this unique translation.

Every vision need visionaries willing to follow the cause. The story of this dream is no different. Mrs. Siewert's vision was seen by a California non-profit foundation called The Lockman Foundation, made up of Christian men and women who through their commitment, their expertise, and their financial support undergirded Mrs. Siewert's monumental translation project. The Lockman Foundation's purpose remains today what is was then: to promote Bible translation, Christian evangelism, education, and benevolence.

Commitment, energy, enthusiasm, giftedness—the things visions are made of—describes the efforts of the committee appointed by The Lockman Foundation to carefully review the impressive work of Mrs. Siewert. This Editorial Board, made up of dedicated people, lent credibility and organization to this unprecedented attempt to bring out the richness of the Hebrew and Greek languages within the English text itself.

One chapter yet remained to bring the vision into reality. A publishing house in Grand Rapids, Michigan, on its way to becoming a major religious publishing firm, seized the opportunity to participate in a project which all visionaries involved strongly believed would be used by God to change lives. The Zondervan Publishing House joined the team, and the dream became reality with the publication of the Amplified New Testament in 1958, followed by the two-volume Amplified Old Testament in 1962 and 1964, and the one-volume Amplified Bible in 1965.

Features of the Amplified Bible

The Amplified Bible, Expanded Edition, features the text of the Amplified Bible, with explanatory and devotional footnotes; a reference system contained within the text; a comprehensive bibliography of original sources cited in the footnotes.

THE TEXT OF THE AMPLIFIED BIBLE

The text of the Amplified Bible is easy to understand, and is made even easier to understand by the inclusion of informative footnotes which often alert readers to different textual readings and give insight into Greek grammar and translation. Numerous Bible translation are among the sources cited in the footnotes, as well as some of the greatest lexicographers of all time and some of the best of Bible commentators.

To help readers achieve the greatest possible clarity and understanding in their reading of the text of the Amplified Bible, some explanation of the various markings within the text is necessary:

Parentheses ( ) signify additional phases of meaning included in the original word, phrase, or clause of the original language.

Brackets [ ] contain justified clarifying words or comments not actually expressed in the immediate original text, as well as definitions of Greek names.

Italics point out:
    1. certain familiar passages now recognized as not adequately supported by the original manuscripts. This is the primary use of italics in the New Testament, so that, upon encountering italics, the reader is alerted to a matter of textual readings. Often these will be accompanied by a footnote. See as an example Matthew 16:2–3.
    2. conjunctions such as "and," "or," and the like, not in the original text, but used to connect additional English words indicated in the same original word. In this use, the reader, upon encountering a conjunction in italics, is alerted to the addition of an amplified word or phrase. See as an example Acts 24:3.
    3. words which are not found in the original Greek but implied by it.

Capitals are used:
    1. in names and personal pronouns referring to the Deity. See as an example 1 Peter 2:6.
    2. in proper names of persons, places, specific feasts, topographical names, personifications, and the like. See as an example John 7:2.

Abbreviations may on occasion be encountered in either the text or in the footnotes.
    cf., compare, confer
    ch., chs. chapter, chapters
    e.g. for example
    etc. and so on
    i.e., *that is*
    v., vv. verse, verses
    ff. following
    ft. foot
    c. about
    KJV King James Version
    RV Revised Version
    ASV American Standard Version

THE REFERENCE SYSTEM

The reference system of the Amplified Bible is contained within the text. The Scripture references are placed within brackets at the end of a verse, and are intended to cover any part of the preceding verse to which they apply. If a verse contains more than one Scripture reference, the list of references is in Biblical order. A sensitivity to the prophecy-fulfillment motif is indicated by such references as [Fulfilled in . . .]; [Foretold in . . .].

THE BIBLIOGRAPHY

A comprehensive, though not exhaustive, bibliography of original sources cited in the footnotes is included in the back of the Bible. The bibliography lists basic information such as author or editor/editors, book or periodical title, publisher (and location of publisher), and date of publication. For more information on the bibliography, see the introduction to the bibliography.

TABLE OF CONTENTS

TO THE AMPLIFIED BIBLE

John

THE GOSPEL ACCORDING TO

JOHN

CHAPTER 1

IN THE beginning [before all time] was the Word ([a]Christ), and the Word was with God, and the Word was God [b]Himself. [Isa. 9:6.]

2 He was present originally with God.

3 All things were made *and* came into existence through Him; and without Him was not even one thing made that has come into being.

4 In Him was Life, and the Life was the Light of men.

5 And the Light shines on in the darkness, for the darkness has never overpowered it [put it out or absorbed it or appropriated it, and is unreceptive to it].

6 There came a man sent from God, whose name was John. [Mal. 3:1.]

7 This man came to witness, that he might testify of the Light, that all men might believe in it [adhere to it, trust it, and rely upon it] through him.

8 He was not the Light himself, but came that he might bear witness regarding the Light.

9 There it was—the true Light [was then] coming into the world [the genuine, perfect, steadfast Light] that illumines every person. [Isa. 49:6.]

10 He came into the world, and though the world was made through Him, the world did not recognize Him [did not know Him].

11 He came to that which belonged to Him [to His own—His domain, creation, things, world], and they who were His own did not receive Him *and* did not welcome Him.

12 But to as many as did receive *and* welcome Him, He gave the authority (power, privilege, right) to become the children of God, that is, to those who believe in (adhere to, trust in, and rely on) His name——[Isa. 56:5.]

13 Who owe their birth neither to [c]bloods nor to the will of the flesh [that of physical impulse] nor to the will of man [that of a natural father], but to God. [They are born of God!]

14 And the Word (Christ) became flesh (human, incarnate) and tabernacled (fixed His tent of flesh, lived awhile) among us; and we [actually] saw His glory (His honor, His majesty), such glory as an only begotten son receives from his father, full of grace (favor, loving-kindness) and truth. [Isa. 40:5.]

15 John testified about Him and cried out, This was He of Whom I said, He Who comes after me has priority over me, for He was before me. [He takes rank above me, for He existed before I did. He has advanced before me, because He is my Chief.]

16 For out of His fullness (abundance) we have all received [all had a share and we were all supplied with] one grace after another and spiritual blessing upon spiritual blessing *and* even favor upon favor *and* gift [heaped] upon gift.

17 For while the Law was given through Moses, grace ([d]unearned, undeserved favor and spiritual blessing)

---

a In John's vision (Rev. 19), he sees Christ returning as Warrior-Messiah-King, and "the title by which He is called is The Word of God . . . and Lord of lords" (Rev. 19:13, 16).   b Charles B. Williams, *The New Testament: A Translation in the Language of the People:* "God" appears first in the Greek word order in this phrase, denoting emphasis—so "God Himself."   c Literal translation.   d Richard Trench, *Synonyms of the New Testament.*

and truth came through Jesus Christ.
[Exod. 20:1.]

18 No man has ever seen God at
any time; *the only ^eunique Son, or
^fthe only begotten God, Who is in the
bosom [in the intimate presence] of the
Father, He has declared Him [He has
revealed Him and brought Him out
where He can be seen; He has inter-
preted Him and He has made Him
known]. [Prov. 8:30.]

19 And this is the testimony of John
when the Jews sent priests and Levites
to him from Jerusalem to ask him,
Who are you?

20 He confessed (admitted the
truth) and did not try to conceal it, but
acknowledged, I am not the Christ!

21 They asked him, What then? Are
you Elijah? And he said, I am not! Are
you the Prophet? And he answered,
No! [Deut. 18:15, 18; Mal. 4:5.]

22 Then they said to him, Who are
you? Tell us, so that we may give an
answer to those who sent us. What do
you say about yourself?

23 He said, I am the voice of one
crying aloud in the wilderness [the
voice of one shouting in the desert],
Prepare the way of the Lord [level,
straighten out, the path of the Lord], as
the prophet Isaiah said. [Isa. 40:3.]

24 The messengers had been sent
from the Pharisees.

25 And they asked him, Why then
are you baptizing if you are not the
Christ, nor Elijah, nor the Prophet?

26 John answered them, I [only]
baptize ^gin (with) water. Among you
there stands One Whom you do not
recognize *and* with Whom you are not
acquainted *and of* Whom you know
nothing. [Mal. 3:1.]

27 It is He Who, coming after me,
is preferred before me, the string of

Whose sandal I am not worthy to un-
loose.

28 These things occurred in Betha-
ny (Bethabara) across the Jordan [^hat
the Jordan crossing], where John was
then baptizing.

29 The next day John saw Jesus
coming to him and said, Look! There
is the Lamb of God, Who takes away
the sin of the world! [Exod. 12:3; Isa.
53:7.]

30 This is He of Whom I said, After me comes a Man Who has priority
over me [Who takes rank above me]
because He was before me *and* existed
before I did.

31 And I did not know Him *and* did
not recognize Him [myself]; but it is in
order that He should be made manifest
and be revealed to Israel [be brought
out where we can see Him] that I came
baptizing ⁱin (with) water.

32 John gave further evidence, saying, I have seen the Spirit descending
as a dove out of heaven, and it dwelt
on Him [never to depart].

33 And I did not know Him *nor*
recognize Him, but He Who sent me to
baptize ⁱin (with) water said to me,
Upon Him Whom you shall see the
Spirit descend and remain, that One is
He Who baptizes with the Holy Spirit.

34 And I have seen [that happen—
I actually did see it] and my testimony
is that this is the Son of God!

35 Again the next day John was
standing with two of his disciples,

36 And he looked at Jesus as He
walked along, and said, Look! There is
the Lamb of God!

37 The two disciples heard him say
this, and they followed Him.

38 But Jesus turned, and as He saw
them following Him, He said to them,
What are you looking for? [And what

e James Moulton and George Milligan, *The Vocabulary of the Greek Testament.*   f Marvin Vincent,
Word Studies in the New Testament: This reading is supported by "a great mass of ancient evidence."
g The Greek can be translated "with" or "in;" also in verses 31 and 33. The KJV prefers "with," while the
ASV prefers "in."   h George M. Lamsa, *The New Testament According to the Ancient Text.*   i See
footnote on John 1:26.

is it you wish?] And they answered Him, Rabbi—which translated is Teacher—where are You staying?

39 He said to them, Come and see. So they went and saw where He was staying, and they remained with Him 'that day. It was then about the tenth hour (about four o'clock in the afternoon).

40 One of the two who heard what John said and followed Jesus was Andrew, Simon Peter's brother.

41 He first sought out *and* found his own brother Simon and said to him, We have found (discovered) the Messiah!—which translated is the Christ (the Anointed One).

42 Andrew then led (brought) Simon to Jesus. Jesus looked at him and said, You are Simon son of John. You shall be called Cephas—which translated is Peter [Stone].

43 The next day Jesus desired *and* decided to go into Galilee; and He found Philip and said to him, Join Me as My attendant *and* follow Me.

44 Now Philip was from Bethsaida, of the same city as Andrew and Peter.

45 Philip sought *and* found Nathanael and told him, We have found (discovered) the One Moses in the Law and also the Prophets wrote about—Jesus from Nazareth, the [legal] son of Joseph!

46 Nathanael answered him, [Nazareth!] Can anything good come out of Nazareth? Philip replied, Come and see!

47 Jesus saw Nathanael coming toward Him and said concerning him, See! Here is an Israelite indeed [a true descendant of Jacob], in whom there is no guile *nor* deceit *nor* falsehood *nor* duplicity!

48 Nathanael said to Jesus, How do You know me? [How is it that You know these things about me?] Jesus

answered him, Before [ever] Philip called you, when you were still under the fig tree, I saw you.

49 Nathanael answered, Teacher, You are the Son of God! You are the King of Israel!

50 Jesus replied, Because I said to you, I saw you beneath the fig tree, do you believe in *and* rely on *and* trust in Me? You shall see greater things than this!

51 Then He said to him, I assure you, most solemnly I tell you all, you shall see heaven opened, and the angels of God ascending and descending upon the Son of Man! [Gen. 28:12; Dan. 7:13.]

CHAPTER 2

ON THE third day there was a wedding at Cana of Galilee, and the mother of Jesus was there.

2 Jesus also was invited with His disciples to the wedding.

3 And when the wine was all gone, the mother of Jesus said to Him, They have no more wine!

4 Jesus said to her, [ᵏDear] woman, what is that to you and to Me? [What do we have in common? Leave it to Me.] My time (hour to act) has not yet come. [Eccl. 3:1.]

5 His mother said to the servants, Whatever He says to you, do it.

6 Now there were six waterpots of stone standing there, as the Jewish custom of purification (ceremonial washing) demanded, holding twenty to thirty gallons apiece.

7 Jesus said to them, Fill the waterpots with water. So they filled them up to the brim.

8 Then He said to them, Draw some out now and take it to the manager of the feast [to the one presiding, the superintendent of the banquet]. So they took him some.

---

j George M. Lamsa, *Gospel Light from the Aramaic*: In accordance with Oriental hospitality, the guests would be invited to remain that night also. k G. Abbott-Smith, *Manual Greek Lexicon of the New Testament*: "a term of respect and endearment."

9 And when the manager tasted the water just now turned into wine, not knowing where it came from—though the servants who had drawn the water knew—he called the bridegroom

10 And said to him, Everyone else serves his best wine first, and when people have drunk freely, then he serves that which is not so good; but you have kept back the good wine until now!

11 This, the first of His signs (miracles, wonderworks), Jesus performed in Cana of Galilee, and manifested His glory [by it He displayed His greatness and His power openly], and His disciples believed in Him [adhered to, trusted in, and relied on Him]. [Deut. 5:24; Ps. 72:19.]

12 After that He went down to Capernaum with His mother and brothers and disciples, and they stayed there only a few days.

13 Now the Passover of the Jews was approaching, so Jesus went up to Jerusalem.

14 There He found in the temple [ᶦenclosure] those who were selling oxen and sheep and doves, and the money changers sitting there [also at their stands].

15 And having made a lash (a whip) of cords, He drove them all out of the temple [ᶦenclosure]—both the sheep and the oxen—spilling and scattering the brokers' money and upsetting and tossing around their trays (their stands).

16 Then to those who sold the doves He said, Take these things away (out of here)! Make not My Father's house a house of merchandise (a marketplace, a sales shop)! [Ps. 93:5.]

17 And His disciples remembered that it is written [in the Holy Scriptures], Zeal (the fervor of love) for Your house will eat Me up. [It will be

consumed with jealousy for the honor of Your house.] [Ps. 69:9.]

18 Then the Jews retorted, What sign can ᵐYou show us, seeing You do these things? [What sign, miracle, token, indication can You give us as evidence that You have authority and are commissioned to act in this way?]

19 Jesus answered them, Destroy (undo) this temple, and in three days I will raise it up again.

20 Then the Jews replied, It took forty-six years to build this temple (sanctuary), and will You raise it up in three days?

21 But He had spoken of the temple which was His body.

22 When therefore He had risen from the dead, His disciples remembered that He said this. And so they believed and trusted and relied on the Scripture and the word (message) Jesus had spoken. [Ps. 16:10.]

23 But when He was in Jerusalem during the Passover Feast, many believed in His name [identified themselves with His party] after seeing His signs (wonders, miracles) which He was doing.

24 But Jesus [for His part] did not trust Himself to them, because He knew all [men];

25 And He did not need anyone to bear witness concerning man [needed no evidence from anyone about men], for He Himself knew what was in human nature. [He could read men's hearts.] [I Sam. 16:7.]

CHAPTER 3

NOW THERE was a certain man among the Pharisees named Nicodemus, a ruler (a leader, an authority) among the Jews,

2 Who came to Jesus at night and said to Him, Rabbi, we know and are certain that You have come from God [as] a Teacher; for no one can do these

---

l Richard Trench, *Synonyms of the New Testament*. Son of God, not what the speaker may have thought He was.

m Capitalized because of what He is, the spotless

signs (these wonderworks, these miracles—and produce the proofs) that You do unless God is with him.

3 Jesus answered him, I assure you, most solemnly I tell you, that unless a person is born again (anew, from above), he cannot ever see (know, be acquainted with, and experience) the kingdom of God.

4 Nicodemus said to Him, How can a man be born when he is old? Can he enter his mother's womb again and be born?

5 Jesus answered, I assure you, most solemnly I tell you, unless a man is born of water and the [[n]even] the Spirit, he cannot [ever] enter the kingdom of God. [Ezek. 36:25–27.]

6 What is born of [from] the flesh is flesh [of the physical is physical]; and what is born of the Spirit is spirit.

7 Marvel not [do not be surprised, astonished] at My telling you, You must all be born anew (from above).

8 The wind blows (breathes) where it wills; and though you hear its sound, yet you neither know where it comes from nor where it is going. So it is with everyone who is born of the Spirit.

9 Nicodemus answered by asking, How can all this be possible?

10 Jesus replied, Are you the teacher of Israel, and yet do not know nor understand these things? [Are they strange to you?]

11 I assure you, most solemnly I tell you, We speak only of what we know [we know absolutely what we are talking about]; we have actually seen what we are testifying to [we were eyewitnesses of it]. And still you do not receive our testimony [you reject and refuse our evidence—that of Myself and of all those who are born of the Spirit].

12 If I have told you of things that happen right here on the earth and yet none of you believes Me, how can you

believe (trust Me, adhere to Me, rely on Me) if I tell you of heavenly things?

13 And yet no one has ever gone up to heaven, but there is One Who has come down from heaven—the Son of Man [Himself], [[o]Who is (dwells, has His home) in heaven].

14 And just as Moses lifted up the serpent in the desert [on a pole], so must [so it is necessary that] the Son of Man be lifted up [on the cross], [Num. 21:9.]

15 In order that whoever who believes in Him [who cleaves to Him, trusts Him, and relies on Him] may [[o]not perish, but have eternal life and [actually] live forever!

16 For God so greatly loved and dearly prized the world that He [even] gave up His only begotten ([[p]unique) Son, so that whoever believes in (trusts in, clings to, relies on) Him shall not perish (come to destruction, be lost) but have eternal (everlasting) life.

17 For God did not send the Son into the world in order to judge (to reject, to condemn, to pass sentence on) the world, but that the world might find salvation and be made safe and sound through Him.

18 He who believes in Him [who clings to, trusts in, relies on Him] is not judged [he who trusts in Him never comes up for judgment; for him there is no rejection, no condemnation—he incurs no damnation]; but he who does not believe (cleave to, rely on, trust in Him) is judged already [he has already been convicted and has already received his sentence] because he has not believed in and trusted in the name of the only begotten Son of God. [He is condemned for refusing to let his trust rest in Christ's name.]

19 The [basis of the] judgment (indictment, the test by which men are judged, the ground for the sentence) lies in this: the Light has come into the

n The Greek "kai" ("and") may be rendered "even."
p James Moulton and George Milligan, *The Vocabulary*.
o Some manuscripts add this phrase.

world, and people have loved the darkness rather than *and* more than the Light, for their works (deeds) were evil. [Isa. 5:20.]

20 For every wrongdoer hates (loathes, detests) the Light, and will not come out into the Light *but* shrinks from it, lest his works (his deeds, his activities, his conduct) be exposed *and* reproved.

21 But he who practices truth [who does what is right] comes out into the Light; so that his works may be plainly shown to be what they are—wrought with God [divinely prompted, done with God's help, in dependence upon Him].

22 After this, Jesus and His disciples went into the land (the countryside) of Judea, where He remained with them, and baptized.

23 But John also was baptizing at Aenon near Salim, for there was an abundance of water there, and the people kept coming and being baptized.

24 For John had not yet been thrown into prison.

25 Therefore there arose a controversy between some of John's disciples and a Jew in regard to purification.

26 So they came to John and reported to him, Rabbi, the Man Who was with you on the other side of the Jordan [ᵃat the Jordan crossing]—and to Whom you yourself have borne testimony—notice, here He is baptizing too, and everybody is flocking to Him!

27 John answered, A man can receive nothing [he can claim nothing, he can ʳtake unto himself nothing] except as it has been granted to him from heaven. [A man must be content to receive the gift which is given him from heaven; there is no other source.]

28 You yourselves are my witnesses [you personally bear me out] that I stated, I am not the Christ (the

Anointed One, the Messiah), but I have [only] been sent before Him [in advance of Him, to be His appointed forerunner, His messenger, His announcer]. [Mal. 3:1.]

29 He who has the bride is the bridegroom; but the groomsman who stands by and listens to him rejoices greatly *and* heartily on account of the bridegroom's voice. This then is my pleasure *and* joy, and it is now complete. [S. of Sol. 5:1.]

30 He must increase, but I must decrease. [He must grow more prominent; I must grow less so.] [Isa. 9:7.]

31 He Who comes from above (heaven) is [far] above all [others]; he who comes from the earth belongs to the earth, and talks the language of earth [his words are from an earthly standpoint]. He Who comes from heaven is [far] above all others [far superior to all others in prominence and in excellence].

32 It is to what He has [actually] seen and heard that He bears testimony, and yet no one accepts His testimony [no one receives His evidence as true].

33 Whoever receives His testimony has set his seal of approval to this: God is true. [That man has definitely certified, acknowledged, declared once and for all, and is himself assured that it is divine truth that God cannot lie].

34 For since He Whom God has sent speaks the words of God [proclaims God's own message], God does not give Him His Spirit sparingly *or* by measure, *but* boundless is the gift God makes of His Spirit! [Deut. 18:18.]

35 The Father loves the Son and has given (entrusted, committed) everything into His hand. [Dan. 7:14.]

36 And he who believes in (has faith in, clings to, relies on) the Son has (now possesses) eternal life. But whoever disobeys (is unbelieving to-

ward, refuses to trust in, disregards, is not subject to) the Son will never see (experience) life, but [instead] the 'rath of God abides on him. [God's d₁ pleasure remains on him; His indignation hangs over him continually.] [Hab. 2:4.]

CHAPTER 4

NOW WHEN the Lord knew (learned, became aware) that the Pharisees had been told that Jesus was winning and baptizing more disciples than John—

2 Though Jesus Himself did not baptize, but His disciples—

3 He left Judea and returned to Galilee.

4 It was necessary for Him to go through Samaria.

5 And in doing so, He arrived at a Samaritan town called Sychar, near the tract of land that Jacob gave to his son Joseph.

6 And Jacob's well was there. So Jesus, tired as He was from His journey, sat down [to rest] by the well. It was then about the sixth hour (about noon).

7 Presently, when a woman of Samaria came along to draw water, Jesus said to her, Give Me a drink—

8 For His disciples had gone off into the town to buy food—

9 The Samaritan woman said to Him, How is it that ˢYou, being a Jew, ask me, a Samaritan [and a] woman, for a drink?—For the Jews have nothing to do with the Samaritans—

10 Jesus answered her, If you had only known *and* had recognized God's gift and Who this is that is saying to you, Give Me a drink, you would have asked Him [instead] and He would have given you living water.

11 She said to Him, Sir, You have nothing to draw with [no drawing bucket] and the well is deep; how then can You provide living water? [Where do You get Your living water?]

12 Are You greater than *and* superior to our ancestor Jacob, who gave us this well and who used to drink from it himself, and his sons and his cattle also?

13 Jesus answered her, All who drink of this water will be thirsty again.

14 But whoever takes a drink of the water that I will give him shall never, no never, be thirsty any more. But the water that I will give him shall become a spring of water welling up (flowing, bubbling) [continually] within him unto (into, for) eternal life.

15 The woman said to Him, Sir, give me this water, so that I may never get thirsty nor have to come [continually all the way] here to draw.

16 At this, Jesus said to her, Go, call your husband and come back here.

17 The woman answered, I have no husband. Jesus said to her, You have spoken truly in saying, I have no husband.

18 For you have had five husbands, and the man you are now living with is not your husband. In this you have spoken truly.

19 The woman said to Him, Sir, I see *and* understand that You are a prophet.

20 Our forefathers worshiped on this mountain, but you [Jews] say that Jerusalem is the place where it is necessary *and* proper to worship.

21 Jesus said to her, Woman, believe Me, a time is coming when you will worship the Father neither [merely] in this mountain nor [merely] in Jerusalem.

22 You [Samaritans] do not know what you are worshiping [you worship what you do not comprehend]. We do know what we are worshiping [we worship what we have knowledge of

---

ˢ Capitalized because of what He is, the spotless Son of God, not what the speaker may have thought He was.

and understand], for [after all] salvation comes from [among] the Jews.

23 A time will come, however, indeed it is already here, when the true (genuine) worshipers will worship the Father in spirit and in truth (reality); for the Father is seeking just such people as these as His worshipers.

24 God is a Spirit (a spiritual Being) and those who worship Him must worship *Him* in spirit and in truth (reality).

25 The woman said to Him, I know that Messiah is coming, He Who is called the Christ (the Anointed One); and when He arrives, He will tell us everything we need to know *and* make it clear to us.

26 Jesus said to her, I Who now speak with you am He.

27 Just then His disciples came and they wondered (were surprised, astonished) to find Him talking with a woman [a married woman]. However, not one of them asked Him, What are You inquiring about? *or* What do You want? or, Why do You speak with her?

28 Then the woman left her water jar and went away to the town. And she began telling the people,

29 Come, see a Man Who has told me everything that I ever did! Can this be [is not this] the Christ? [Must not this be the Messiah, the Anointed One?]

30 So the people left the town and set out to go to Him.

31 Meanwhile, the disciples urged Him saying, Rabbi, eat something.

32 But He assured them, I have food (nourishment) to eat of which *you* know nothing *and* have no idea.

33 So the disciples said one to another, Has someone brought Him something to eat?

34 Jesus said to them, My food (nourishment) is to do the will (pleasure) of Him Who sent Me and to accomplish *and* completely finish His work.

35 Do you not say, It is still four

months until harvest time comes? Look! I tell you, raise your eyes and observe the fields *and* see how they are already white for harvesting.

36 Already the reaper is getting his wages [he who does the cutting now has his reward], for he is gathering fruit (crop) unto life eternal, so that he who does the planting and he who does the reaping may rejoice together.

37 For in this the saying holds true, One sows and another reaps.

38 I sent you to reap a crop for which you have not toiled. Other men have labored and you have stepped in to reap the results of their work.

39 Now numerous Samaritans from that town believed in *and* trusted in Him because of what the woman said when she declared *and* testified, He told me everything that I ever did.

40 So when the Samaritans arrived, they asked Him to remain with them, and He did stay there two days.

41 Then many more believed in *and* adhered to *and* relied on Him because of His personal message [what He Himself said].

42 And they told the woman, Now we no longer believe (trust, have faith) just because of what you said; for we have heard Him ourselves [personally], and we know that He truly is the Savior of the world, *the Christ.*

43 But after these two days Jesus went on from there into Galilee—

44 Although He Himself declared that a prophet has no honor in his own country.

45 However, when He came into Galilee, the Galileans also welcomed Him *and* took Him to their hearts eagerly, for they had seen everything *that* He did in Jerusalem during the Feast; for they too had attended the Feast.

46 So Jesus came again to Cana of Galilee, where He had turned the water into wine. And there was a certain royal official whose son was lying ill in Capernaum.

47 Having heard that Jesus had

come back from Judea into Galilee, he went away to meet Him and began to beg Him to come down and cure his son, for he was lying at the point of death.

48 Then Jesus said to him, Unless you see signs and miracles happen, you [people] never will believe (trust, have faith) at all.

49 The king's officer pleaded with Him, Sir, do come down at once before my little child is dead!

50 Jesus answered him, Go in peace; your son will live! And the man put his trust in what Jesus said and started home.

51 But even as he was on the road going down, his servants met him and reported, saying, Your son lives!

52 So he asked them at what time he had begun to get better. They said, Yesterday during the seventh hour (about one o'clock in the afternoon) the fever left him.

53 Then the father knew that it was at that very hour when Jesus had said to him, Your son will live. And he and his entire household believed (adhered to, trusted in, and relied on Jesus).

54 This is the second sign (wonderwork, miracle) that Jesus performed after He had come out of Judea into Galilee.

CHAPTER 5

LATER ON there was a Jewish festival (feast) for which Jesus went up to Jerusalem.

2 Now there is in Jerusalem a pool near the Sheep Gate. This pool in the Hebrew is called Bethesda, having five porches (alcoves, colonnades, doorways).

3 In these lay a great number of sick folk—some blind, some crippled, and some paralyzed (shriveled up)—¹waiting for the bubbling up of the water.

4 *For an angel of the Lord went down at appointed seasons into the pool and moved and stirred up the water; whoever then first, after the stirring up of the water, stepped in was cured of whatever disease with which he was afflicted.*

5 There was a certain man there who had suffered with a deep-seated *and* lingering disorder for thirty-eight years.

6 When Jesus noticed him lying there [helpless], knowing that he had already been a long time in that condition, He said to him, Do you want to become well? [Are you really in earnest about getting well?]

7 The invalid answered, Sir, I have nobody when the water is moving to put me into the pool; but while I am trying to come [into it] myself, somebody else steps down ahead of me.

8 Jesus said to him, Get up! Pick up your bed (sleeping pad) and walk!

9 Instantly the man became well *and* recovered his strength and picked up his bed and walked. But that happened on the Sabbath.

10 So the Jews kept saying to the man who had been healed, It is the Sabbath, and you have no right to pick up your bed [it is not lawful].

11 He answered them, The ᵘMan Who healed me *and* gave me back my strength, He Himself said to me, Pick up your bed and walk!

12 They asked him, Who is the Man Who told you, Pick up your bed and walk?

13 Now the invalid who had been healed did not know who it was, for Jesus had quietly gone away [had passed on unnoticed], since there was a crowd in the place.

14 Afterward, when Jesus found him in the temple, He said to him, See, you are well! Stop sinning or something worse may happen to you.

---

t Many manuscripts omit the last part of verse 3 and all of verse 4.   u Capitalized because of what He is, the spotless Son of God, not what the speaker may have thought He was.

15 The man went away and told the Jews that it was Jesus Who had made him well.

16 For this reason the Jews began to persecute (annoy, torment) Jesus [and sought to kill Him, because He was doing these things on the Sabbath.

17 But Jesus answered them, My Father has worked [even] until now, [He has never ceased working; He is still working] and I, too, must be at [divine] work.

18 This made the Jews more determined than ever to kill Him [to do away with Him]; because He not only was breaking (weakening, violating) the Sabbath, but He actually was speaking of God as being [in a special sense] His own Father, making Himself equal [putting Himself on a level] with God.

19 So Jesus answered them by saying, I assure you, most solemnly I tell you, the Son is able to do nothing of Himself (of His own accord); but He is able to do only what He sees the Father doing, for whatever the Father does is what the Son does in the same way [in His turn].

20 The Father dearly loves the Son and discloses to (shows) Him everything that He Himself does. And He will disclose to Him (let Him see) greater things yet than these, so that you may marvel and be full of wonder and astonishment.

21 Just as the Father raises up the dead and gives them life [makes them live on], even so the Son also gives life to whomever He wills and is pleased to give it.

22 Even the Father judges no one, for He has given all judgment (the last judgment and the whole business of judging) entirely into the hands of the Son,

23 So that all men may give honor (reverence, homage) to the Son just as they give honor to the Father. [In fact]

whoever does not honor the Son does not honor the Father, Who has sent Him.

24 I assure you, most solemnly I tell you, the person whose ears are open to My words [who listens to My message] and believes and trusts in and clings to and relies on Him Who sent Me has (possesses now) eternal life. And he does not come into judgment [does not incur sentence of judgment, will not come under condemnation], but he has already passed over out of death into life.

25 Believe Me when I assure you, most solemnly I tell you, the time is coming and is here now when the dead shall hear the voice of the Son of God and those who hear it shall live.

26 For even as the Father has life in Himself and is self-existent, so He has given to the Son to have life in Himself and be self-existent.

27 And He has given Him authority and granted Him power to execute (exercise, practice) judgment because He is [a Son of man [very man].

28 Do not be surprised and wonder at this, for the time is coming when all those who are in the tombs shall hear His voice,

29 And they shall come out—those who have practiced doing good [will come out] to the resurrection of [new] life, and those who have done evil will be raised for judgment [raised to meet their sentence]. [Dan. 12:2.]

30 I am able to do nothing from Myself [independently, of My own accord—but only as I am taught by God and as I get His orders]. Even as I hear, I judge [I decide as I am bidden to decide. As the voice comes to Me, so I give a decision], and My judgment is right (just, righteous), because I do not seek or consult My own will [I have no desire to do what is pleasing to Myself, My own aim, My own purpose] but

only the will *and* pleasure of the Father Who sent Me.

31 If I alone testify in My behalf, My testimony is not valid *and* cannot be worth anything.

32 There is Another Who testifies concerning Me, and I know *and* am certain that His evidence on My behalf is true and valid.

33 You yourselves have sent [an inquiry] to John and he has been a witness to the truth.

34 But I do not receive [a mere] human witness [the evidence which I accept on My behalf is not from man]; but I simply mention all these things in order that you may be saved (made and kept safe and sound).

35 John was the lamp that kept on burning and shining [to show you the way], and you were willing for a while to delight (sun) yourselves in his light.

36 But I have as My witness something greater (weightier, higher, better) than that of John; for the works that the Father has appointed Me to accomplish *and* finish, the very same works that I am now doing, are a witness *and* proof that the Father has sent Me.

37 And the Father Who sent Me has Himself testified concerning Me. Not one of you has ever given ear to His voice or seen His form (His face—what He is like). [You have always been deaf to His voice and blind to the vision of Him.]

38 And you have not His word (His thought) living in your hearts, because you do not believe *and* adhere to *and* trust in *and* rely on Him Whom He has sent. [That is why you do not keep His message living in you, because you do not believe in the Messenger Whom He has sent.]

39 You search *and* investigate and pore over the Scriptures diligently, because you suppose *and* trust that you have eternal life through them. And these [very Scriptures] testify about Me!

40 And still you are not willing [but refuse] to come to Me, so that you might have life.

41 I receive not glory from men [I crave no human honor, I look for no mortal fame],

42 But I know you and recognize *and* understand that you have not the love of God in you.

43 I have come in My Father's name *and* with His power, and you do not receive Me [your hearts are not open to Me, you give Me no welcome]; but if another comes in his own name *and* his own power *and* with no other authority but himself, you will receive him *and* give him your approval.

44 How is it possible for you to believe [how can you learn to believe], you who [are content to seek and] receive praise *and* honor *and* glory from one another, and yet do not seek the praise *and* honor *and* glory which come from Him Who alone is God?

45 Put out of your minds the thought *and* do not suppose [as some of you are supposing] that I will accuse you before the Father. There is one who accuses you—it is Moses, the very one on whom you have built your hopes [in whom you trust].

46 For if you believed *and* relied on Moses, you would believe *and* rely on Me, for he wrote about Me [personally].

47 But if you do not believe *and* trust his writings, how then will you believe *and* trust My teachings? [How shall you cleave to and rely on My words?]

CHAPTER 6

AFTER THIS, Jesus went to the farther side of the Sea of Galilee—that is, the Sea of Tiberias.

2 And a great crowd was following Him because they had seen the signs (miracles) which He [continually] performed upon those who were sick.

3 And Jesus walked up the moun-

tainside and sat down there with His disciples.

4 Now the Passover, the feast of the Jews, was approaching.

5 Jesus looked up then, and seeing that a vast multitude was coming toward Him, He said to Philip, Where are we to buy bread, so that all these people may eat?

6 But He said this to prove (test) him, for He well knew what He was about to do.

7 Philip answered Him, Two hundred pennies' (forty dollars) worth of bread is not enough that everyone may receive even a little.

8 Another of His disciples, Andrew, Simon Peter's brother, said to Him,

9 There is a little boy here, who has [with him] five barley loaves, and two small fish; but what are they among so many people?

10 Jesus said, Make all the people recline (sit down). Now the ground (a pasture) was covered with thick grass at the spot, so the men threw themselves down, about 5,000 in number.

11 Jesus took the loaves, and when He had given thanks, He distributed ˣto the disciples and the disciples to the reclining people; so also [He did] with the fish, as much as they wanted.

12 When they had all had enough, He said to His disciples, Gather up now the fragments (the broken pieces that are left over), so that nothing may be lost and wasted.

13 So accordingly they gathered them up, and they filled twelve [ʸsmall hand] baskets with fragments left over by those who had eaten from the five barley loaves.

14 When the people saw the sign (miracle) that Jesus had performed, they began saying, Surely and beyond a doubt this is the Prophet Who is to

come into the world! [Deut. 18:15, 18; John 1:21; Acts 3:22.]

15 Then Jesus, knowing that they meant to come and seize Him that they might make Him king, withdrew again to the hillside by Himself alone.

16 When evening came, His disciples went down to the sea,

17 And they took a boat and were going across the sea to Capernaum. It was now dark, and still Jesus had not [yet] come back to them.

18 Meanwhile, the sea was getting rough and rising high because of a great and violent wind that was blowing.

19 [However] when they had rowed three or four miles, they saw Jesus walking on the sea and approaching the boat. And they were afraid (terrified).

20 But Jesus said to them, It is I; be not afraid! [I AM; stop being frightened!] [Exod. 3:14.]

21 Then they were quite willing and glad for Him to come into the boat. And now the boat went at once to the land they had steered toward. [And immediately they reached the shore toward which they had been slowly making their way.]

22 The next day the crowd [that still remained] standing on the other side of the sea realized that there had been only one small boat there, and that Jesus had not gone into it with His disciples, but that His disciples had gone away by themselves.

23 But now some other boats from Tiberias had come in near the place where they ate the bread after the Lord had given thanks.

24 So the people, finding that neither Jesus nor His disciples were there, themselves got into the small boats and came to Capernaum looking for Jesus.

25 And when they found Him on

x Some manuscripts add this phrase.   y G. Abbott-Smith, Manual Greek Lexicon. See also footnote on Matt. 14:20.

the other side of the lake, they said to Him, Rabbi! When did You come here?

26 Jesus answered them, I assure you, most solemnly I tell you, you have been searching for Me, not because you saw the miracles *and* signs but because you were fed with the loaves *and* were filled *and* satisfied.

27 Stop toiling *and* doing *and* producing for the food that perishes *and* decomposes [in the using], but strive *and* work *and* produce rather for the [lasting] food which endures [continually] unto life eternal; the Son of Man will give (furnish) you that, for God the Father has authorized *and* certified Him *and* put His seal of endorsement upon Him.

28 They then said, What are we to do, that we may [habitually] be working the works of God? [What are we to do to carry out what God requires]?

29 Jesus replied, This is the work (service) that God asks of you: that you believe in the One Whom He has sent [that you cleave to, trust, rely on, and have faith in His Messenger].

30 Therefore they said to Him, What sign (miracle, wonderwork) will 'You perform then, so that we may see it and believe *and* rely on *and* adhere to You? What [supernatural] work have You [to show what You can do]?

31 Our forefathers ate the manna in the wilderness; as the Scripture says, He gave them bread out of heaven to eat. [Exod. 16:15; Neh. 9:15; Ps. 78:24.]

32 Jesus then said to them, I assure you, most solemnly I tell you, Moses did not give you the Bread from heaven [what Moses gave you was not the Bread from heaven], but it is My Father Who gives you the true heavenly Bread.

33 For the Bread of God is He Who comes down out of heaven and gives life to the world.

34 Then they said to Him, Lord, give us this bread always (all the time)!

35 Jesus replied, I am the Bread of Life. He who comes to Me will never be hungry, and he who believes in *and* cleaves to *and* trusts in *and* relies on Me will never thirst any more (at any time).

36 But [as] I told you, although you have seen Me, still you do not believe *and* trust *and* have faith.

37 All whom My Father gives (entrusts) to Me will come to Me; and the one who comes to Me I will most certainly not cast out [I will never, no never, reject one of them who comes to Me].

38 For I have come down from heaven not to do My own will *and* purpose but to do the will *and* purpose of Him Who sent Me.

39 And this is the will of Him Who sent Me, that I should not lose any of all that He has given Me, but that I should give new life *and* raise [them all] up at the last day.

40 For this is My Father's will *and* His purpose, that everyone who sees the Son and believes in *and* cleaves to *and* trusts in *and* relies on Him should have eternal life, and I will raise him up [from the dead] at the last day.

41 Now the Jews murmured *and* found fault with *and* grumbled about Jesus because He said, I am [Myself] the Bread that came down from heaven.

42 They kept asking, Is not this Jesus, the 'Son of Joseph, Whose father and mother we know? How then can He say, I have come down from heaven?

43 So Jesus answered them, Stop grumbling *and* saying things against Me to one another.

44 No one is able to come to Me unless the Father Who sent Me attracts and draws him and gives him the desire to come to Me, and [then] I will raise him up [from the dead] at the last day.

45 It is written in [the book of] the Prophets, And they shall all be taught of God [have Him in person for their Teacher]. Everyone who has listened to and learned from the Father comes to Me—[Isa. 54:13.]

46 Which does not imply that anyone has seen the Father [not that anyone has ever seen Him] except He [Who was with the Father] Who comes from God; He [alone] has seen the Father.

47 I assure you, most solemnly I tell you, he who believes in Me [who adheres to, trusts in, relies on, and has faith in Me] has (now possesses) eternal life.

48 I am the Bread of Life [that gives life—the Living Bread].

49 Your forefathers ate the manna in the wilderness, and [yet] they died.

50 [But] this is the Bread that comes down from heaven, so that [any]one may eat of it and never die.

51 I [Myself] am this Living Bread that came down from heaven. If anyone eats of this Bread, he will live forever; and also the Bread that I shall give for the life of the world is My flesh (body).

52 Then the Jews angrily contended with one another, saying, How is He able to give us His flesh to eat?

53 And Jesus said to them, I assure you, most solemnly I tell you, you cannot have any life in you unless you eat the flesh of the Son of Man and drink His blood [unless you appropriate His life and the saving merit of His blood].

54 He who feeds on My flesh and drinks My blood [has (possesses) now] eternal life, and I will raise him up [from the dead] on the last day.

55 For My flesh is true and genuine food, and My blood is true and genuine drink.

56 He who feeds on My flesh and drinks My blood dwells continually in Me, and I [in like manner dwell continually] in him.

57 Just as the living Father sent Me and I live by (through, because of) the Father, even so whoever continues to feed on Me [whoever takes Me for his food and is nourished by Me] shall [in his turn] live through and because of Me.

58 This is the Bread that came down from heaven. It is not like the manna which our forefathers ate, and yet died; he who takes this Bread for his food shall live forever.

59 He said these things in a synagogue while He was teaching at Capernaum.

60 When His disciples heard this, many of them said, This is a hard and difficult and strange saying (an offensive and unbearable message). Who can stand to hear it? [Who can be expected to listen to such teaching?]

61 But Jesus, knowing within Himself that His disciples were complaining and protesting and grumbling about it, said to them: Is this a stumbling block and an offense to you? [Does this upset and displease and shock and scandalize you?]

62 What then [will be your reaction] if you should see the Son of Man ascending to [the place] where He was before?

63 It is the Spirit Who gives life [He is the Life-giver]; the flesh conveys no benefit whatever [there is no profit in it]. The words (truths) that I have been speaking to you are spirit and life.

64 But [still] some of you fail to believe and trust and have faith. For Jesus knew from the first who did not believe and had no faith and who would betray Him and be false to Him.

65 And He said, This is why I told you that no one can come to Me unless

it is granted him [unless he is enabled to do so] by the Father.

66 After this, many of His disciples drew back (returned to their old associations) and no longer accompanied Him.

67 Jesus said to the Twelve, Will you also go away? [And do you too desire to leave Me?]

68 Simon Peter answered, Lord, to whom shall we go? You have the words (the message) of eternal life.

69 And we have learned to believe and trust, and [more] we have come to know [surely] that You are the Holy One of God, the Christ (the Anointed One), the Son of the living God.

70 Jesus answered them, Did I not choose you, the Twelve? And [yet] one of you is a devil (of the evil one and a false accuser).

71 He was speaking of Judas, the son of Simon Iscariot, for he was about to betray Him, [although] he was one of the Twelve.

CHAPTER 7

AFTER THIS, Jesus went from place to place in Galilee, for He would not travel in Judea because the Jews were seeking to kill Him.

2 Now the Jewish Feast of Tabernacles was drawing near.

3 So His brothers said to Him, Leave here and go into Judea, so that [a]Your disciples [there] may see the works that You do. [This is no place for You.]

4 For no one does anything in secret when he wishes to be conspicuous and secure publicity. If You [must] do these things [if You must act like this], show Yourself openly and make Yourself known to the world!

5 For [even] His brothers did not believe in or adhere to or trust in or rely on Him either.

6 Whereupon Jesus said to them,

My time (opportunity) has not come yet; but any time is suitable for you and your opportunity is ready any time [is always here].

7 The world cannot [be expected to] hate you, but it does hate Me because I denounce it for its wicked works and reveal that its doings are evil.

8 Go to the Feast yourselves. I am not [yet] going up to the Festival, because My time is not ripe. [My term is not yet completed; it is not time for Me to go.]

9 Having said these things to them, He stayed behind in Galilee.

10 But afterward, when His brothers had gone up to the Feast, He went up also, not publicly [not with a caravan], but by Himself quietly and as if He did not wish to be observed.

11 Therefore the Jews kept looking for Him at the Feast and asking, Where can He be? [Where is that Fellow?]

12 And there was among the mass of the people much whispered discussion and hot disputing about Him. Some were saying, He is good! [He is a good Man!] Others said, No, He misleads and deceives the people [gives them false ideas!]

13 But no one dared speak out boldly about Him for fear of [the leaders of] the Jews.

14 When the Feast was already half over, Jesus went up into the temple [[b]court] and began to teach.

15 The Jews were astonished. They said, How is it that this Man has learning [is so versed in the sacred Scriptures and in theology] when He has never studied?

16 Jesus answered them by saying, My teaching is not My own, but His Who sent Me.

17 If any man desires to do His will (God's pleasure), he will know (have the needed illumination to recognize,

---

a Capitalized because of what He is, the spotless Son of God, not what the speaker may have thought He was.   b Richard Trench, *Synonyms of the New Testament.*

and can tell for himself) whether the teaching is from God or whether I am speaking from Myself *and* of My own accord *and* on My own authority.

18 He who speaks on his own authority seeks to win honor for himself. [He whose teaching originates with himself seeks his own glory.] But He Who seeks the glory *and* is eager for the honor of Him Who sent Him, He is true; and there is no unrighteousness *or* falsehood *or* deception in Him.

19 Did not Moses give you the Law? And yet not one of you keeps the Law. [If that is the truth] why do you seek to kill Me [for not keeping it]?

20 The crowd answered Him, You are possessed by a demon! [You are raving!] Who seeks to kill You?

21 Jesus answered them, I did one work, and you all are astounded. [John 5:1–9.]

22 Now Moses established circumcision among you—though it did not originate with Moses but with the previous patriarchs—and you circumcise a person [even] on the Sabbath day.

23 If, to avoid breaking the Law of Moses, a person undergoes circumcision on the Sabbath day, have you any cause to be angry with (indignant with, bitter against) Me for making a man's whole body well on the Sabbath?

24 Be honest in your judgment *and* do not decide at a glance (superficially and by appearances); but judge fairly *and* righteously.

25 Then some of the Jerusalem people said, Is not this the Man they seek to kill?

26 And here He is speaking openly, and they say nothing to Him! Can it be possible that the rulers have discovered *and* know that this is truly the Christ?

27 No, we know where this Man comes from; when the Christ arrives, no one is to know from what place He comes.

28 Whereupon Jesus called out as He taught in the temple [´porches], Do you know Me, and do you know where I am from? I have not come on My own authority *and* of My own accord *and* as self-appointed, but the One Who sent Me is true (real, genuine, steadfast); and Him you do not know!

29 I know Him [Myself] because I come from His [very] presence, and it was He [personally] Who sent Me.

30 Therefore they were eager to arrest Him, but no one laid a hand on Him, for His hour (time) had not yet come.

31 And besides, many of the multitude believed in Him [adhered to Him, trusted in Him, relied on Him]. And they kept saying, When the Christ comes, will He do [can He be expected to do] more miracles *and* produce more proofs *and* signs than what this Man has done?

32 The Pharisees learned how the people were saying these things about Him under their breath; and the chief priests and Pharisees sent attendants (guards) to arrest Him.

33 Therefore Jesus said, For a little while I am [still] with you, and then I go back to Him Who sent Me.

34 You will look for Me, but you will not [be able to] find Me; where I am, you cannot come.

35 Then the Jews said among themselves, Where does this Man intend to go that we shall not find Him? Will He go to the Jews who are scattered in the Dispersion among the Greeks, and teach the Greeks?

36 What does this statement of His mean, You will look for Me and not be able to find Me, and, Where I am, you cannot come?

37 Now on the final and most important day of the Feast, Jesus stood, and He cried in a loud voice, If any

c Richard Trench, *Synonyms of the New Testament.*

man is thirsty, let him come to Me and drink!

38 He who believes in Me [who cleaves to *and* trusts in *and* relies on Me] as the Scripture has said, From his innermost being shall flow [continuously] springs *and* rivers of living water.

39 But He was speaking here of the Spirit, Whom those who believed (trusted, had faith) in Him were afterward to receive. For the [Holy] Spirit had not yet been given, because Jesus was not yet glorified (raised to honor).

40 Listening to those words, some of the multitude said, This is certainly *and* beyond doubt the Prophet! [Deut. 18:15, 18; John 1:21; 6:14; Acts 3:22.]

41 Others said, This is the Christ (the Messiah, Anointed One)! But some said, Why! Does the Christ come out of Galilee?

42 Does not the Scripture tell us that the Christ will come from the offspring of David and from Bethlehem, the village where David lived? [Ps. 89:3, 4; Mic. 5:2.]

43 So there arose a division *and* dissension among the people concerning Him.

44 Some of them wanted to arrest Him, but no one [ventured and] laid hands on Him.

45 Meanwhile the attendants (guards) had gone back to the chief priests and Pharisees, who asked them, Why have you not brought Him here with you?

46 The attendants replied, Never has a man talked as this Man talks! [No mere man has ever spoken as He speaks!]

47 The Pharisees said to them, Are you also deluded *and* led astray? [Are you also swept off your feet?]

48 Has any of the authorities or of the Pharisees believed in Him?

49 As for this multitude (rabble) that does not know the Law, they are contemptible *and* doomed *and* accursed!

50 Then Nicodemus, who came to Jesus before at night and was one of them, asked,

51 Does our Law convict a man without giving him a hearing and finding out what he has done?

52 They answered him, Are you too from Galilee? Search [the Scriptures yourself], and you will see that no prophet comes (will rise to prominence) from Galilee.

53 [d]And they went [back], each to his own house.

CHAPTER 8

BUT JESUS went to the Mount of Olives.

2 Early in the morning (at dawn), He came back into the temple [[e]court], and the people came to Him in crowds. He sat down and was teaching them,

3 When the scribes and Pharisees brought a woman who had been caught in adultery. They made her stand in the middle of the court and put the case before Him.

4 Teacher, they said, This woman has been caught in the very act of adultery.

5 Now Moses in the Law commanded us that such [women—offenders] shall be stoned to death. But what do You say [to do with her—what is Your sentence]? [Deut. 22:22–24.]

6 This they said to try (test) Him, hoping they might find a charge on which to accuse Him. But Jesus

---

d John 7:53 to 8:11 is absent from most of the older manuscripts, and those that have it sometimes place it elsewhere. The story may well be authentic. Indeed, Christ's response of compassion and mercy is so much in keeping with His character that we accept it as authentic, and feel that to omit it would be most unfortunate.   e Richard Trench, *Synonyms of the New Testament.*

stooped down and wrote on the ground with His finger.

7 However, when they persisted with their question, He raised Himself up and said, Let him who is without sin among you be the first to throw a stone at her.

8 Then He bent down and went on writing on the ground with His finger.

9 They listened to Him, and then they began going out, conscience-stricken, one by one, from the oldest down to the last one of them, till Jesus was left alone, with the woman standing there before Him in the center of the court.

10 When Jesus raised Himself up, He said to her, Woman, where are your accusers? Has no man condemned you?

11 She answered, No one, Lord! And Jesus said, I do not condemn you either. Go on your way and from now on sin no more.

12 Once more Jesus addressed the crowd. He said, I am the Light of the world. He who follows Me will not be walking in the dark, but will have the Light which is Life.

13 Whereupon the Pharisees told Him, You are testifying on Your own behalf; Your testimony is not valid *and* is worthless.

14 Jesus answered, Even if I do testify on My own behalf, My testimony is true *and* reliable *and* valid, for I know where I came from and where I am going; but you do not know where I come from or where I am going.

15 You [set yourselves up to] judge according to the flesh (by what you *see*). [You condemn by *external*, human standards.] I do not [set Myself up to] judge *or* condemn *or* sentence anyone.

16 Yet even if I do judge, My judgment is true [My decision is right]; for I am not alone [in making it], but

[there are two of Us] I and the Father, Who sent Me.

17 In your [own] Law it is written that the testimony (evidence) of two persons is reliable *and* valid. [Deut. 19:15.]

18 I am One [of the Two] bearing testimony concerning Myself; and My Father, Who sent Me, He also testifies about Me.

19 Then they said to Him, Where is this *f* Father of Yours? Jesus answered, You know My Father as little as you know Me. If you knew Me, you would know My Father also.

20 Jesus said these things in the treasury while He was teaching in the temple [* g* court]; but no one ventured to arrest Him, because His hour had not yet come.

21 Therefore He said again to them, I am going away, and you will be looking for Me, and you will die in (under the curse of) your sin. Where I am going, it is not possible for you to come.

22 At this the Jews began to ask among themselves, Will He kill Himself? Is that why He says, Where I am going, it is not possible for you to come?

23 He said to them, You are from below; I am from above. You are of this world (of this earthly order); I am not of this world.

24 That is why I told you that you will die in (under the curse of) your sins; for if you do not believe that I am He [Whom I claim to be—if you do not adhere to, trust in, and rely on Me], you will die in your sins.

25 Then they said to Him, Who are You anyway? Jesus replied, [Why do I even speak to you!] I am exactly what I have been telling you from the first.

26 I have much to say about you and to judge *and* condemn. But He

---

f Capitalized because of Who He is, the everlasting Father, not who the speaker may have thought He was. **g** Richard Trench, *Synonyms of the New Testament.*

Who sent Me is true (reliable), and I tell the world [only] the things that I have heard from Him.

27 They did not perceive (know, understand) that He was speaking to them about the Father.

28 So Jesus added, When you have lifted up the Son of Man [on the cross], you will realize (know, understand) that I am He [for Whom you look] and that I do nothing of Myself (of My own accord or on My own authority), but I say [exactly] what My Father has taught Me.

29 And He Who sent Me is ever with Me; My Father has not left Me alone, for I always do what pleases Him.

30 As He said these things, many believed in Him [trusted, relied on, and adhered to Him].

31 So Jesus said to those Jews who had believed in Him, If you abide in My word [hold fast to My teachings and live in accordance with them], you are truly My disciples.

32 And you will know the Truth, and the Truth will set you free.

33 They answered Him, We are Abraham's offspring (descendants) and have never been in bondage to anybody. What do You mean by saying, You will be set free?

34 Jesus answered them, I assure you, most solemnly I tell you, Whoever commits and practices sin is the slave of sin.

35 Now a slave does not remain in a household permanently (forever); the son [of the house] does remain forever.

36 So if the Son liberates you [makes you free men], then you are really and unquestionably free.

37 [Yes] I know that you are Abraham's offspring; yet you plan to kill Me, because My word has no entrance (makes no progress, does not find any place) in you.

38 I tell the things which I have seen and learned at My Father's side, and your actions also reflect what you have heard and learned from your father.

39 They retorted, Abraham is our father. Jesus said, If you were [truly] Abraham's children, then you would do the works of Abraham [follow his example, do as Abraham did].

40 But now [instead] you are wanting and seeking to kill Me, a Man Who has told you the truth which I have heard from God. This is not the way Abraham acted.

41 You are doing the works of your [own] father. They said to Him, We are not illegitimate children and born out of fornication; we have one Father, even God.

42 Jesus said to them, If God were your Father, you would love Me and respect Me and welcome Me gladly, for I proceeded (came forth) from God [out of His very presence]. I did not even come on My own authority or of My own accord (as self-appointed); but He sent Me.

43 Why do you misunderstand what I say? It is because you are unable to hear what I am saying. [You cannot bear to listen to My message; your ears are shut to My teaching.]

44 You are of your father, the devil, and it is your will to practice the lusts and gratify the desires [which are characteristic] of your father. He was a murderer from the beginning and does not stand in the truth, because there is no truth in him. When he speaks a falsehood, he speaks what is natural to him, for he is a liar [himself] and the father of lies and of all that is false.

45 But because I speak the truth, you do not believe Me [do not trust Me, do not rely on Me, or adhere to Me].

46 Who of you convicts Me of wrongdoing or finds Me guilty of sin? Then if I speak truth, why do you not believe Me [trust Me, rely on, and adhere to Me]?

47 Whoever is of God listens to God. [Those who belong to God hear

the words of God.] This is the reason that you do not listen [to those words, to Me]: because you do not belong to God *and* are not of God *or* in harmony with Him.

48 The Jews answered Him, Are we not right when we say You are a Samaritan and that You have a demon [that You are under the power of an evil spirit]?

49 Jesus answered, I am not possessed by a demon. On the contrary, I honor *and* reverence My Father and you dishonor (despise, vilify, and scorn) Me.

50 However, I am not in search of honor for Myself. [I do not seek and am not aiming for My own glory.] There is One Who [looks after that; He] seeks [My glory], and He is the Judge.

51 I assure you, most solemnly I tell you, if anyone observes My teaching [lives in accordance with My message, keeps My word], he will by no means ever see *and* experience death.

52 The Jews said to Him, Now we know that You are under the power of a demon (*h*insane). Abraham died, and also the prophets, yet You say, If a man keeps My word, he will never taste of death into all eternity.

53 Are You greater than our father Abraham? He died, and all the prophets died! Who do You make Yourself out to be?

54 Jesus answered, If I were to glorify Myself (magnify, praise, and honor Myself), I would have no real glory, for My glory would be nothing *and* worthless. [My honor must come to Me from My Father.] It is My Father Who glorifies Me [Who extols Me, magnifies, and praises Me], of Whom you say that He is your God.

55 Yet you do not know Him *or* recognize Him *and* are not acquainted with Him, but I know Him. If I should say that I do not know Him, I would be

a liar like you. But I know Him and keep His word [obey His teachings, am faithful to His message].

56 Your forefather Abraham was extremely happy at the hope *and* prospect of seeing My day (My incarnation); and he did see it and was delighted. [Heb. 11:13.]

57 Then the Jews said to Him, You are not yet fifty years old, and have You seen Abraham?

58 Jesus replied, I assure you, most solemnly I tell you, before Abraham was born, I AM. [Exod. 3:14.]

59 So they took up stones to throw at Him, but Jesus, by mixing with the crowd, concealed Himself and went out of the temple [*i*enclosure].

CHAPTER 9

AS HE passed along, He noticed a man blind from his birth.

2 His disciples asked Him, Rabbi, who sinned, this man or his parents, that he should be born blind?

3 Jesus answered, It was not that this man or his parents sinned, but he was born blind in order that the workings of God should be manifested (displayed and illustrated) in him.

4 We must work the works of Him Who sent Me *and* be busy with His business while it is daylight; night is coming on, when no man can work.

5 As long as I am in the world, I am the world's Light.

6 When He had said this, He spat on the ground and made clay (mud) with His saliva, and He spread it [as ointment] on the man's eyes.

7 And He said to him, Go, wash in the Pool of Siloam—which means Sent. So he went and washed, and came back seeing.

8 When the neighbors and those who used to know him by sight as a beggar saw him, they said, Is not this the man who used to sit and beg?

9 Some said, It is he. Others said,

No, but he looks very much like him. But he said, Yes, I am the man.

10 So they said to him, How were your eyes opened?

11 He replied, The Man called Jesus made mud and smeared it on my eyes and said to me, Go to Siloam and wash. So I went and washed, and I obtained my sight!

12 They asked him, Where is He? He said, I do not know.

13 Then they conducted to the Pharisees the man who had formerly been blind.

14 Now it was on the Sabbath day that Jesus mixed the mud and opened the man's eyes.

15 So now again the Pharisees asked him how he received his sight. And he said to them, He smeared mud on my eyes, and I washed, and now I see.

16 Then some of the Pharisees said, This Man [Jesus] is not from God, because He does not observe the Sabbath. But others said, How can a man who is a sinner (a bad man) do such signs *and* miracles? So there was a difference of opinion among them.

17 Accordingly they said to the blind man again, What do you say about Him, seeing that He opened your eyes? And he said, He is [He must be] a prophet!

18 However, the Jews did not believe that he had [really] been blind and that he had received his sight until they called (summoned) the parents of the man.

19 They asked them, Is this your son, whom you reported as having been born blind? How then does he see now?

20 His parents answered, We know that this is our son, and that he was born blind.

21 But as to how he can now see, we do not know; or who has opened

his eyes, we do not know. He is of age. Ask him; let him speak for himself *and* give his own account of it.

22 His parents said this because they feared [the leaders of] the Jews; for the Jews had already agreed that if anyone should acknowledge Jesus to be the Christ, he should be expelled *and* excluded from the synagogue.

23 On that account his parents said, He is of age; ask him.

24 So the second time they summoned the man who had been born blind, and said to him, Now give God the glory (praise). This *j*Fellow we know is only a sinner (a wicked person).

25 Then he answered, I do not know whether He is a sinner *and* wicked or not. But one thing I do know, that whereas I was blind before, now I see.

26 So they said to him, What did He [actually] do to you? How did He open your eyes?

27 He answered, I already told you and you would not listen. Why do you want to hear it again? Can it be that you wish to become His disciples also?

28 And they stormed at him [they jeered, they sneered, they reviled him] and retorted, You are His disciple yourself, but we are the disciples of Moses.

29 We know for certain that God spoke with Moses, but as for this Fellow, we know nothing about where He hails from.

30 The man replied, Well, this is astonishing! Here a Man has opened my eyes, and yet you do not know where He comes from. [That is amazing!]

31 We know that God does not listen to sinners; but if anyone is Godfearing *and* a worshiper of Him and does His will, He listens to him.

32 Since the beginning of time it

j Capitalized because of what He is, the spotless Son of God, not what the speaker may have thought He was.

has never been heard that anyone opened the eyes of a man born blind.

33 If this Man were not from God, He would not be able to do anything like this.

34 They retorted, You were wholly born in sin [from head to foot]; and do you [presume to] teach us? So they cast him out [threw him clear outside the synagogue].

35 Jesus heard that they had put him out, and meeting him He said, Do you believe in and adhere to the Son of Man [k]or the Son of God?

36 He answered, Who is He, Sir? Tell me, that I may believe in and adhere to Him.

37 Jesus said to him, You have seen Him; [in fact] He is talking to you right now.

38 He called out, Lord, I believe! [I rely on, I trust, I cleave to You!] And he worshiped Him.

39 Then Jesus said, I came into this world for judgment [as a Separator, in order that there may be [l]separation between those who believe on Me and those who reject Me], to make the sightless see and to make those who see become blind.

40 Some Pharisees who were near, hearing this remark, said to Him, Are we also blind?

41 Jesus said to them, If you were blind, you would have no sin; but because you now claim to have sight, your sin remains. [If you were blind, you would not be guilty of sin; but because you insist, We do see clearly, you are unable to escape your guilt.]

CHAPTER 10

I ASSURE you, most solemnly I tell you, he who does not enter by the door into the sheepfold, but climbs up some other way (elsewhere, from some other quarter) is a thief and a robber.

2 But he who enters by the door is the shepherd of the sheep.

3 The watchman opens the door for this man, and the sheep listen to his voice and heed it; and he calls his own sheep by name and brings (leads) them out.

4 When he has brought his own sheep outside, he walks on before them, and the sheep follow him because they know his voice.

5 They will never [on any account] follow a stranger, but will run away from him because they do not know the voice of strangers or recognize their call.

6 Jesus used this parable (illustration) with them, but they did not understand what He was talking about.

7 So Jesus said again, I assure you, most solemnly I tell you, that I Myself am the Door [f]for the sheep.

8 All others who came [as such] before Me are thieves and robbers, but the [true] sheep did not listen to and obey them.

9 I am the Door; anyone who enters in through Me will be saved (will live). He will come in and he will go out [freely], and will find pasture.

10 The thief comes only in order to steal and kill and destroy. I came that they may have and enjoy life, and have it in abundance (to the full, till it [m]overflows).

11 I am the Good Shepherd. The Good Shepherd risks and lays down His [own] life for the sheep. [Ps. 23.]

12 But the hired servant (he who merely serves for wages) who is neither the shepherd nor the owner of the sheep, when he sees the wolf coming, deserts the flock and runs away. And the wolf chases and snatches them and scatters them [the flock].

13 Now the hireling flees because he merely serves for wages and is not

k Many ancient manuscripts read "the Son of God." l Marvin Vincent, Word Studies.
m Alexander Souter, Pocket Lexicon of the Greek New Testament.

himself concerned about the sheep [cares nothing for them].

14 I am the Good Shepherd; and I know *and* recognize My own, and My own know *and* recognize Me—

15 Even as [truly as] the Father knows Me and I also know the Father—and I am giving My [very own] life *and* laying it down on behalf of the sheep.

16 And I have other sheep [beside these] that are not of this fold. I must bring *and* ⁿimpel those also; and they will listen to My voice *and* heed My call, and so there will be [they will become] one flock under one Shepherd. [Ezek. 34:23.]

17 For this [reason] the Father loves Me, because I lay down My [own] life—to take it back again.

18 No one takes it away from Me. On the contrary, I lay it down voluntarily. [I put it from Myself.] I am authorized *and* have power to lay it down (to resign it) and I am authorized *and* have power to take it back again. These are the instructions (orders) which I have received [as My charge] from My Father.

19 Then a fresh division of opinion arose among the Jews because of His saying these things.

20 And many of them said, He has a demon and He is mad (insane—He raves, He rambles). Why do you listen to Him?

21 Others argued, These are not the thoughts *and* the language of one possessed. Can a demon-possessed person open blind eyes?

22 After this the Feast of Dedication [of the reconsecration of the temple] was taking place at Jerusalem. It was winter,

23 And Jesus was walking in Solomon's Porch in the temple area.

24 So the Jews surrounded Him and began asking Him, How long are You going to keep us in doubt *and* suspense? If You are really the Christ (the Messiah), tell us so plainly *and* openly.

25 Jesus answered them, I have told you so, yet you do not believe Me [you do not trust Me *and* rely on Me]. The very works that I do by the power of My Father *and* in My Father's name bear witness concerning Me [they are My credentials and evidence in support of Me].

26 But you do not believe *and* trust *and* rely on Me because you do not belong to My fold [you are no sheep of Mine].

27 The sheep that are My own hear *and* are listening to My voice; and I know them, and they follow Me.

28 And I give them eternal life, and they shall never lose it *or* perish throughout the ages. [To all eternity they shall never by any means be destroyed.] And no one is able to snatch them out of My hand.

29 My Father, Who has given them to Me, is greater *and* mightier than all [else]; and no one is able to snatch [them] out of the Father's hand.

30 I and the Father are One.

31 Again the Jews °brought up stones to stone Him.

32 Jesus said to them, My Father has enabled Me to do many good deeds. [I have shown many acts of mercy in your presence.] For which of these do you mean to stone Me?

33 The Jews replied, We are not going to stone You for a good act, but for blasphemy, because You, a mere ᵖMan, make Yourself [out to be] God.

34 Jesus answered, Is it not written in your Law, I said, You are gods? [Ps. 82:6.]

35 So men are called gods [by the Law], men to whom God's message came—and the Scripture cannot be set

n G. Abbott-Smith, *Manual Greek Lexicon*.   o Marvin Vincent, *Word Studies*.   p Capitalized because of what He is, the spotless Son of God, not what the speaker may have thought He was.

aside or cancelled or broken or annulled—

36 [If that is true] do you say of the One Whom the Father consecrated and dedicated and set apart for Himself and sent into the world, You are blaspheming, because I said, I am the Son of God?

37 If I am not doing the works [performing the deeds] of My Father, then do not believe Me [do not adhere to Me and trust Me and rely on Me].

38 But if I do them, even though you do not believe Me or have faith in Me, [at least] believe the works and have faith in what I do, in order that you may know and understand [clearly] that the Father is in Me, and I am in the Father [One with Him].

39 They sought again to arrest Him, but He escaped from their hands.

40 He went back again across the Jordan to the locality where John was when he first baptized, and there He remained.

41 And many came to Him, and they kept saying, John did not perform a [single] sign or miracle, but everything John said about this Man was true.

42 And many [people] there became believers in Him. [They adhered to and trusted in and relied on Him.]

CHAPTER 11

NOW A certain man named Lazarus was ill. He was of Bethany, the village where Mary and her sister Martha lived.

2 This Mary was the one who anointed the Lord with perfume and wiped His feet with her hair. It was her brother Lazarus who was [now] sick.

3 So the sisters sent to Him, saying, Lord, he whom You love [so well] is sick.

4 When Jesus received the message, He said, This sickness is not to end in death; but [on the contrary] it is to honor God and to promote His glory, that the Son of God may be glorified through (by) it.

5 Now Jesus loved Martha and her sister and Lazarus. [They were His dear friends, and He held them in loving esteem.]

6 Therefore [even] when He heard that Lazarus was sick, He still stayed two days longer in the same place where He was.

7 Then after that interval He said to His disciples, Let us go back again to Judea.

8 The disciples said to Him, Rabbi, the Jews only recently were intending and trying to stone You, and are You [thinking of] going back there again?

9 Jesus answered, Are there not twelve hours in the day? Anyone who walks about in the daytime does not stumble, because he sees [by] the light of this world.

10 But if anyone walks about in the night, he does stumble, because there is no light in him [the light is lacking to him].

11 He said these things, and then added, Our friend Lazarus is at rest and sleeping; but I am going there that I may awaken him out of his sleep.

12 The disciples answered, Lord, if he is sleeping, he will recover.

13 However, Jesus had spoken of his death, but they thought that He referred to falling into a refreshing and natural sleep.

14 So then Jesus told them plainly, Lazarus is dead,

15 And for your sake I am glad that I was not there; it will help you to believe (to trust and rely on Me). However, let us go to him.

16 Then Thomas, who was called the Twin, said to his fellow disciples, Let us go too, that we may die [be killed] along with Him.

17 So when Jesus arrived, He found that he [Lazarus] had already been in the tomb four days.

18 Bethany was near Jerusalem, only about two miles away,

19 And a considerable number of the Jews had gone out to see Martha and Mary to console them concerning their brother.

20 When Martha heard that Jesus was coming, she went to meet Him, while Mary remained sitting in the house.

21 Martha then said to Jesus, Master, if You had been here, my brother would not have died.

22 And even now I know that whatever You ask from God, He will grant it to You.

23 Jesus said to her, Your brother shall rise again.

24 Martha replied, I know that he will rise again in the resurrection at the last day.

25 Jesus said to her, I am [Myself] the Resurrection and the Life. Whoever believes in (adheres to, trusts in, and relies on) Me, although he may die, yet he shall live;

26 And whoever continues to live and believes in (has faith in, cleaves to, and relies on) Me shall never [actually] die at all. Do you believe this?

27 She said to Him, Yes, Lord, I have believed [I do believe] that You are the Christ (the Messiah, the Anointed One), the Son of God, [even He] Who was to come into the world. [It is for Your coming that the world has waited.]

28 After she had said this, she went back and called her sister Mary, privately whispering to her, The Teacher is close at hand and is asking for you.

29 When she heard this, she sprang up quickly and went to Him.

30 Now Jesus had not yet entered the village, but was still at the same spot where Martha had met Him.

31 When the Jews who were sitting with her in the house and consoling her saw how hastily Mary had arisen and gone out, they followed her, supposing that she was going to the tomb to pour out her grief there.

32 When Mary came to the place where Jesus was and saw Him, she dropped down at His feet, saying to Him, Lord, if You had been here, my brother would not have died.

33 When Jesus saw her sobbing, and the Jews who came with her [also] sobbing, He was deeply moved in spirit and troubled. [He chafed in spirit and sighed and was disturbed.]

34 And He said, Where have you laid him? They said to Him, Lord, come and see.

35 Jesus wept.

36 The Jews said, See how [tenderly] He loved him!

37 But some of them said, Could not He Who opened a blind man's eyes have prevented this man from dying?

38 Now Jesus, again sighing repeatedly *and* deeply disquieted, approached the tomb. It was a cave (a hole in the rock), and a boulder lay against [the entrance to close] it.

39 Jesus said, Take away the stone. Martha, the sister of the dead man, exclaimed, But Lord, by this time he [is decaying and] throws off an offensive odor, for he has been dead four days!

40 Jesus said to her, Did I not tell you *and* ᑫpromise you that if you would believe *and* rely on Me, you would see the glory of God?

41 So they took away the stone. And Jesus lifted up His eyes and said, Father, I thank You that You have heard Me.

42 Yes, I know You always hear *and* listen to Me, but I have said this on account of *and* for the benefit of the people standing around, so that they may believe that You did send Me [that You have made Me Your Messenger].

43 When He had said this, He shouted with a loud voice, Lazarus, come out!

ᑫ Charles B. Williams, *The New Testament: A Translation.*

44 And out walked the man who had been dead, his hands and feet wrapped in burial cloths (linen strips), and with a [burial] napkin bound around his face. Jesus said to them, Free him of the burial wrappings and let him go.

45 Upon seeing what Jesus had done, many of the Jews who had come with Mary believed in Him. [They trusted in Him and adhered to Him and relied on Him.]

46 But some of them went back to the Pharisees and told them what Jesus had done.

47 So the chief priests and Pharisees called a meeting of the council (the Sanhedrin) and said, What are we to do? For this Man performs many signs (evidences, miracles).

48 If we let Him alone to go on like this, everyone will believe in Him *and* adhere to Him, and the Romans will come and suppress *and* destroy *and* take away our [holy] place and our nation ['our temple and city and our civil organization].

49 But one of them, Caiaphas, who was the high priest that year, declared, You know nothing at all!

50 Nor do you understand *or* reason out that it is expedient *and* better for your own welfare that one man should die on behalf of the people than that the whole nation should perish (be destroyed, ruined).

51 Now he did not say this simply of his own accord [he was not self-moved]; but being the high priest that year, he prophesied that Jesus was to die for the nation, [Isa. 53:8.]

52 And not *only for the nation* but *also* for the purpose of uniting into one body the children of God who have been scattered far and wide. [Isa. 49:6.]

53 So from that day on they took counsel *and* plotted together how they might put Him to death.

54 For that reason Jesus no longer appeared publicly among the Jews, but left there and retired to the district that borders on the wilderness (the desert), to a village called Ephraim, and there He stayed with the disciples.

55 Now the Jewish Passover was at hand, and many from the country went up to Jerusalem in order that they might purify *and* consecrate themselves before the Passover.

56 So they kept looking for Jesus and questioned among themselves as they were standing about in the temple ['area], What do you think? Will He not come to the Feast at all?

57 Now the chief priests and Pharisees had given orders that if anyone knew where He was, he should report it to them, so that they might arrest Him.

CHAPTER 12

SO SIX days before the Passover Feast, Jesus came to Bethany, where Lazarus was, who had died and whom He had raised from the dead.

2 So they made Him a supper; and Martha served, but Lazarus was one of those at the table with Him.

3 Mary took a pound of ointment of pure liquid nard [a rare perfume] that was very expensive, and she poured it on Jesus' feet and wiped them with her hair. And the whole house was filled with the fragrance of the perfume.

4 But Judas Iscariot, the one of His disciples who was about to betray Him, said,

5 Why was this perfume not sold for 300 denarii [a year's wages for an ordinary workman] and that [money] given to the poor (the destitute)?

6 Now he did not say this because he cared for the poor but because he was a thief; and having the bag (the money box, the purse of the Twelve), he took for himself what was put into it [pilfering the collections].

r Marvin Vincent, *Word Studies.*   s Richard Trench, *Synonyms of the New Testament.*

7 But Jesus said, Let her alone. It was [intended] that she should keep it for the time of My preparation for burial. [She has kept it that she might have it for the time of My 'embalming.]

8 You always have the poor with you, but you do not always have Me.

9 Now a great crowd of the Jews heard that He was at Bethany, and they came there, not only because of Jesus but that they also might see Lazarus, whom He had raised from the dead.

10 So the chief priests planned to put Lazarus to death also,

11 Because on account of him many of the Jews were going away [were withdrawing from and leaving the Judeans] and believing in and adhering to Jesus.

12 The next day a vast crowd of those who had come to the Passover Feast heard that Jesus was coming to Jerusalem.

13 So they took branches of palm trees and went out to meet Him. And as they went, they kept shouting, Hosanna! Blessed is He and praise to Him Who comes in the name of the Lord, even the King of Israel! [Ps. 118:26.]

14 And Jesus, having found a young donkey, rode upon it, [just] as it is written in the Scriptures,

15 Do not fear, O Daughter of Zion! Look! Your King is coming, sitting on a donkey's colt! [Zech. 9:9.]

16 His disciples did not understand and could not comprehend the meaning of these things at first; but when Jesus was glorified and exalted, they remembered that these things had been written about Him and had been done to Him.

17 The group that had been with Jesus when He called Lazarus out of the tomb and raised him from among the dead kept telling it [bearing witness] to others.

18 It was for this reason that the crowd went out to meet Him, because they had heard that He had performed this sign (proof, miracle).

19 Then the Pharisees said among themselves, You see how futile your efforts are and how you accomplish nothing. See! The whole world is running after Him!

20 Now among those who went up to worship at the Feast were some Greeks.

21 These came to Philip, who was from Bethsaida in Galilee, and they made this request, Sir, we desire to see Jesus.

22 Philip came and told Andrew; then Andrew and Philip together [went] and told Jesus.

23 And Jesus answered them, The time has come for the Son of Man to be glorified and exalted.

24 I assure you, most solemnly I tell you, Unless a grain of wheat falls into the earth and dies, it remains [just one grain; it never becomes more but lives] by itself alone. But if it dies, it produces many others and yields a rich harvest.

25 Anyone who loves his life loses it, but anyone who hates his life in this world will keep it to life eternal. [Whoever has no love for, no concern for, no regard for his life here on earth, but despises it, preserves his life forever and ever.]

26 If anyone serves Me, he must continue to follow Me ["to cleave steadfastly to Me, conform wholly to My example in living and, if need be, in dying] and wherever I am, there will My servant be also. If anyone serves Me, the Father will honor him.

27 Now My soul is troubled and distressed, and what shall I say? Father, save Me from this hour [of trial and agony]? But it was for this very purpose that I have come to this hour [that I might undergo it].

28 [Rather, I will say,] Father, glo-

t Marvin Vincent, *Word Studies*.   u Joseph Thayer, *A Greek-English Lexicon*.

rify (honor and extol) Your [own] name! Then there came a voice out of heaven saying, I have already glorified it, and I will glorify it again.

29 The crowd of bystanders heard the sound and said that it had thundered; others said, An angel has spoken to Him!

30 Jesus answered, This voice has not come for My sake, but for your sake.

31 Now the judgment (crisis) of this world is coming on [sentence is now being passed on this world]. Now the ruler (evil genius, prince) of this world shall be cast out (expelled).

32 And I, if and when I am lifted up from the earth [on the cross], will draw and attract all men [Gentiles as well as Jews] to Myself.

33 He said this to signify in what manner He would die.

34 At this the people answered Him, We have learned from the Law that the Christ is to remain forever; how then can You say, The Son of Man must be lifted up [on the cross]? Who is this Son of Man? [Ps. 110:4.]

35 So Jesus said to them, You will have the Light only a little while longer. Walk while you have the Light [keep on living by it], so that darkness may not overtake and overcome you. He who walks about in the dark does not know where he goes [he is drifting].

36 While you have the Light, believe in the Light [have faith in it, hold to it, rely on it], that you may become sons of the Light and be filled with Light. Jesus said these things, and then He went away and hid Himself from them (was lost to their view).

37 Even though He had done so many miracles before them (right before their eyes), yet they still did not trust in Him and failed to believe in Him—

38 So that what Isaiah the prophet said was fulfilled: Lord, who has believed our report and our message? And to whom has the arm (the power) of the Lord been shown (unveiled and revealed)? [Isa. 53:1.]

39 Therefore they could not believe [they were unable to believe]. For Isaiah has also said,

40 He has blinded their eyes and hardened and benumbed their [callous, degenerated] hearts [He has made their minds dull], to keep them from seeing with their eyes and understanding with their hearts and minds and repenting and turning to Me to heal them.

41 Isaiah said this because he saw His glory and spoke of Him. [Isa. 6:9, 10.]

42 And yet [in spite of all this] many even of the leading men (the authorities and the nobles) believed and trusted in Him. But because of the Pharisees they did not confess it, for fear that [if they should acknowledge Him] they would be expelled from the synagogue;

43 For they loved the approval and the praise and the glory that come from men [instead of and] more than the glory that comes from God. [They valued their credit with men more than their credit with God.]

44 But Jesus loudly declared, The one who believes in Me does not [only] believe in and trust and rely on Me, but [in believing in Me he believes] in Him Who sent Me.

45 And whoever sees Me sees Him Who sent Me.

46 I have come as a Light into the world, so that whoever believes in Me [whoever cleaves to and trusts in and relies on Me] may not continue to live in darkness.

47 If anyone hears My teachings and fails to observe them [does not keep them, but disregards them], it is not I who judges him. For I have not come to judge and to condemn and to pass sentence and to inflict penalty on the world, but to save the world.

48 Anyone who rejects Me and persistently sets Me at naught, refusing to

accept My teachings, has his judge [however]; for the [very] message that I have spoken will itself judge *and* convict him at the last day.

49 This is because I have never spoken on My own authority *or* of My own accord *or* as self-appointed, but the Father Who sent Me has Himself given Me orders [concerning] what to say and what to tell. [Deut. 18:18, 19.]

50 And I know that His commandment is (means) eternal life. So whatever I speak, I am saying [exactly] what My Father has told Me to say *and* in accordance with His instructions.

CHAPTER 13

[N[OW] BEFORE the Passover Feast began, Jesus knew (was fully aware) that the time had come for Him to leave this world *and* return to the Father. And as He had loved those who were His own in the world, He loved them to the last *and* [v]to the highest degree.

2 So [it was] during supper, Satan having already put the thought of betraying Jesus in the heart of Judas Iscariot, Simon's son,

3 [That] Jesus, knowing (fully aware) that the Father had put everything into His hands, and that He had come from God and was [now] returning to God,

4 Got up from supper, took off His garments, and taking a [servant's] towel, He fastened it around His waist.

5 He poured water into the washbasin and began to wash the disciples' feet and to wipe them with the [servant's] towel with which He was girded.

6 When He came to Simon Peter, [Peter] said to Him, Lord, are my feet to be washed by You? [Is it for You to wash my feet?]

7 Jesus said to him, You do not understand now what I am doing, but you will understand later on.

8 Peter said to Him, You shall never wash my feet! Jesus answered him, Unless I wash you, you have no part with ([w]in) Me [you have no share in companionship with Me].

9 Simon Peter said to Him, Lord, [wash] not only my feet, but my hands and my head too!

10 Jesus said to him, Anyone who has bathed needs only to wash his feet, but is clean all over. And you [My disciples] are clean, but not all of you.

11 For He knew who was going to betray Him; that was the reason He said, Not all of you are clean.

12 So when He had finished washing their feet and had put on His garments and had sat down again, He said to them, Do you understand what I have done to you?

13 You call Me the Teacher (Master) and the Lord, and you are right in doing so, for that is what I am.

14 If I then, your Lord and Teacher (Master), have washed your feet, you ought [it is your duty, you are under obligation, you owe it] to wash one another's feet.

15 For I have given you this as an example, so that you should do [in your turn] what I have done to you.

16 I assure you, most solemnly I tell you, A servant is not greater than his master, and no one who is sent is superior to the one who sent him.

17 If you know these things, blessed *and* happy *and* [x]to be envied are you if you practice them [if you act accordingly and really do them].

18 I am not speaking of *and* I do not mean all of you. I know whom I have chosen; but it is that the Scripture may

---

[v] Saint John Chrysostom, cited by Joseph Thayer, *A Greek-English Lexicon.*   [w] Origen (the greatest theologian of the early Greek Church); Adam Clarke, *The Holy Bible with A Commentary*; and others so interpret this passage. Notice the "in Me" emphasis in John 15, especially in verses 4-9, words spoken concerning the same subject, and on the same evening.   [x] Alexander Souter, *Pocket Lexicon.*

be fulfilled, He who eats *My bread with Me* has raised up his heel against Me. [Ps. 41:9.]

19 I tell you this now before it occurs, so that when it does take place you may be persuaded *and* believe that I am He [Who I say I am—the Christ, the Anointed One, the Messiah].

20 I assure you, most solemnly I tell you, he who receives *and* welcomes *and* takes into his heart any messenger of Mine receives Me [in just that way]; and he who receives *and* welcomes *and* takes Me into his heart receives Him Who sent Me [in that same way].

21 After Jesus had said these things, He was troubled (disturbed, agitated) in spirit and said, I assure you, most solemnly I tell you, one of you will deliver Me up [one of you will be false to Me and betray Me]!

22 The disciples kept looking at one another, puzzled as to whom He could mean.

23 One of His disciples, whom Jesus loved [whom He esteemed and delighted in], was reclining [next to Him] on Jesus' bosom.

24 So Simon Peter motioned to him to ask of whom He was speaking.

25 Then leaning back against Jesus' breast, he asked Him, Lord, who is it?

26 Jesus answered, It is the one to whom I am going to give this morsel (bit) of food after I have dipped it. So when He had dipped the morsel of bread [into the dish], He gave it to Judas, Simon Iscariot's son.

27 Then after [he had taken] the bit of food, Satan entered into *and* took possession of [Judas]. Jesus said to him, What you are going to do, do ˢmore swiftly than you seem to intend *and* ᵃmake quick work of it.

28 But nobody reclining at the table knew why He spoke to him *or* what He meant by telling him this.

29 Some thought that, since Judas had the money box (the purse), Jesus was telling him, Buy what we need for the Festival, or that he should give something to the poor.

30 So after receiving the bit of bread, he went out immediately. And it was night.

31 When he had left, Jesus said, Now is the Son of Man glorified! [Now He has achieved His glory, His honor, His exaltation!] And God has been glorified through *and* in Him.

32 And if God is glorified through *and* in Him, God will also glorify Him in Himself, and He will glorify Him at once *and* not delay.

33 [Dear] little children, I am to be with you only a little longer. You will look for Me and, as I told the Jews, so I tell you now: you are not able to come where I am going.

34 I give you a new commandment: that you should love one another. Just as I have loved you, so you too should love one another.

35 By this shall all [men] know that you are My disciples, if you love one another [if you keep on showing love among yourselves].

36 Simon Peter said to Him, Lord, where are You going? Jesus answered, You are not able to follow Me now where I am going, but you shall follow Me afterwards.

37 Peter said to Him, Lord, why cannot I follow You now? I will lay down my life for You.

38 Jesus answered, Will you [really] lay down your life for Me? I assure you, most solemnly I tell you, before a rooster crows, you will deny Me [completely disown Me] three times.

CHAPTER 14

DO NOT let your hearts be troubled (distressed, agitated). You be-

y Many ancient manuscripts read "with Me."   z Joseph Thayer, *A Greek-English Lexicon.*
a Charles B. Williams, *The New Testament: A Translation.*

lieve in *and* adhere to *and* trust in *and* rely on God; believe in *and* adhere to *and* trust in *and* rely also on Me.

2 In My Father's house there are many dwelling places (homes). If it were not so, I would have told you; for I am going away to prepare a place for you.

3 And when (if) I go and make ready a place for you, I will come back again and will take you to Myself, that where I am you may be also.

4 And [to the place] where I am going, you know the way.

5 Thomas said to Him, Lord, we do not know where You are going, so how can we know the way?

6 Jesus said to him, I am the Way and the Truth and the Life; no one comes to the Father except by (through) Me.

7 If you had known Me [had learned to recognize Me], you would also have known My Father. From now on, you know Him and have seen Him.

8 Philip said to Him, Lord, show us the Father [cause us to see the Father—that is all we ask]; then we shall be satisfied.

9 Jesus replied, Have I been with all of you for so long a time, and do you not recognize *and* know Me yet, Philip? Anyone who has seen Me has seen the Father. How can you say then, Show us the Father?

10 Do you not believe that I am in the Father, and that the Father is in Me? What I am telling you I do not say on My own authority *and* of My own accord; but the Father Who lives continually in Me does the (ᵇHis) works (His own miracles, deeds of power).

11 Believe Me that I am in the Father and the Father in Me; or else believe Me for the sake of the [very] works themselves. [If you cannot trust Me, at least let these works that I do in My Father's name convince you.]

12 I assure you, most solemnly I tell you, if anyone steadfastly believes in Me, he will himself be able to do the things that I do; and he will do even greater things than these, because I go to the Father.

13 And I will do [I Myself will grant] whatever you ask in My Name [as ᶜpresenting all that I AM], so that the Father may be glorified *and* extolled in (through) the Son. [Exod. 3:14.]

14 [Yes] I will grant [I Myself will do for you] whatever you shall ask in My Name [as ᶜpresenting all that I AM].

15 If you [really] love Me, you will keep (obey) My commands.

16 And I will ask the Father, and He will give you another Comforter (Counselor, Helper, Intercessor, Advocate, Strengthener, and Standby), that He may remain with you forever—

17 The Spirit of Truth, Whom the world cannot receive (welcome, take to its heart), because it does not see Him or know *and* recognize Him. But you know *and* recognize Him, for He lives with you [constantly] and will be in you.

18 I will not leave you as orphans [comfortless, desolate, bereaved, forlorn, helpless]; I will come [back] to you.

19 Just a little while now, and the world will not see Me any more, but you will see Me; because I live, you will live also.

20 At that time [when that day comes] you will know [for yourselves] that I am in My Father, and you [are] in Me, and I [am] in you.

21 The person who has My commands and keeps them is the one who [really] loves Me; and whoever [really] loves Me will be loved by My Father, and I [too] will love him and will show (reveal, manifest) Myself to

b Several ancient manuscripts read "His works."   c Hermann Cremer, *Biblico-Theological Lexicon.*

him. [I will let Myself be clearly seen by him and make Myself real to him.]

22 Judas, not Iscariot, asked Him, Lord, how is it that You will reveal Yourself [make Yourself real] to us and not to the world?

23 Jesus answered, If a person [really] loves Me, he will keep My word [obey My teaching]; and My Father will love him, and We will come to him and make Our home (abode, special dwelling place) with him.

24 Anyone who does not [really] love Me does not observe *and* obey My teaching. And the teaching which you hear *and* heed is not Mine, but [comes] from the Father Who sent Me.

25 I have told you these things while I am still with you.

26 But the Comforter (Counselor, Helper, Intercessor, Advocate, Strengthener, Standby), the Holy Spirit, Whom the Father will send in My name [in My place, to represent Me and act on My behalf], He will teach you all things. And He will cause you to recall (will remind you of, bring to your remembrance) everything I have told you.

27 Peace I leave with you; My [own] peace I now give *and* bequeath to you. Not as the world gives do I give to you. Do not let your hearts be troubled, neither let them be afraid. [Stop allowing yourselves to be agitated and disturbed; and do not permit yourselves to be fearful and intimidated and cowardly and unsettled.]

28 You heard Me tell you, I am going away and I am coming [back] to you. If you [really] loved Me, you would have been glad, because I am going to the Father; for the Father is greater *and* mightier than I am.

29 And now I have told you [this] before it occurs, so that when it does take place you may believe *and* have faith in *and* rely on Me.

30 I will not talk with you much more, for the prince (evil genius, ruler) of the world is coming. And he has no claim on Me. [He has nothing in common with Me; there is nothing in Me that belongs to him, and he has no power over Me.]

31 But [*Satan is coming and] I do as the Father has commanded Me, so that the world may know (be convinced) that I love the Father and that I do only what the Father has instructed Me to do. [I act in full agreement with His orders.] Rise, let us go away from here.

CHAPTER 15

I AM the True Vine, and My Father is the Vinedresser.

2 Any branch in Me that does not bear fruit [that stops bearing] He cuts away (trims off, takes away); and He cleanses *and* repeatedly prunes every branch that continues to bear fruit, to make it bear more *and* richer *and* more excellent fruit.

3 You are cleansed *and* pruned already, because of the word which I have given you [the teachings I have discussed with you].

4 Dwell in Me, and I will dwell in you. [Live in Me, and I will live in you.] Just as no branch can bear fruit of itself without abiding in (being vitally united to) the vine, neither can you bear fruit unless you abide in Me.

5 I am the Vine; you are the branches. Whoever lives in Me and I in him bears much (abundant) fruit. However, apart from Me [cut off from vital union with Me] you can do nothing.

6 If a person does not dwell in Me, he is thrown out like a [broken-off] branch, and withers; such branches are gathered up and thrown into the fire, and they are burned.

7 If you live in Me [abide vitally united to Me] and My words remain in

d Marvin Vincent, *Word Studies.*

you *and* continue to live in your hearts, ask whatever you will, and it shall be done for you.

8 When you bear (produce) much fruit, My Father is honored *and* glorified, and you show *and* prove yourselves to be true followers of Mine.

9 I have loved you, [just] as the Father has loved Me; abide in My love [*continue in His love with Me].

10 If you keep My commandments [if you continue to obey My instructions], you will abide in My love *and* live on in it, just as I have obeyed My Father's commandments and live on in His love.

11 I have told you these things, that My joy *and* delight may be in you, and that your joy *and* gladness may be of full measure *and* complete *and* overflowing.

12 This is My commandment: that you love one another [just] as I have loved you.

13 No one has greater love [no one has shown stronger affection] than to lay down (give up) his own life for his friends.

14 You are My friends if you keep on doing the things which I command you to do.

15 I do not call you servants (slaves) any longer, for the servant does not know what his master is doing (working out). But I have called you My friends, because I have made known to you everything that I have heard from My Father. [I have revealed to you everything that I have learned from Him.]

16 You have not chosen Me, but I have chosen you and I have appointed you [I have planted you], that you might go and bear fruit *and* keep on bearing, and that your fruit may be lasting [that it may remain, abide], so that whatever you ask the Father in My Name [as *presenting all that I AM], He may give it to you.

17 This is what I command you: that you love one another.

18 If the world hates you, know that it hated Me before it hated you.

19 If you belonged to the world, the world would treat you with affection *and* would love you as its own. But because you are not of the world [no longer one with it], but I have chosen (selected) you out of the world, the world hates (detests) you.

20 Remember that I told you, A servant is not greater than his master [is not superior to him]. If they persecuted Me, they will also persecute you; if they kept My word *and* obeyed My teachings, they will also keep *and* obey yours.

21 But they will do all this to you [inflict all this suffering on you] because of [your bearing] My name *and* on My account, for they do not know *or* understand the One Who sent Me.

22 If I had not come and spoken to them, they would not be guilty of sin [would be blameless]; but now they have no excuse for their sin.

23 Whoever hates Me also hates My Father.

24 If I had not done (accomplished) among them the works which no one else ever did, they would not be guilty of sin. But [the fact is] now they have both seen [these works] and have hated both Me and My Father.

25 But [this is so] that the word written in their Law might be fulfilled, They hated Me without a cause. [Ps. 35:19; 69:4.]

26 But when the Comforter (Counselor, Helper, Advocate, Intercessor, Strengthener, Standby) comes, Whom I will send to you from the Father, the Spirit of Truth Who comes (proceeds) from the Father, He [Himself] will testify regarding Me.

27 But you also will testify *and* be My witnesses, because you have been with Me from the beginning.

e Hermann Cremer, *Biblico-Theological Lexicon.*

CHAPTER 16

I HAVE told you all these things, so that you should not be offended (taken unawares and falter, or be caused to stumble and fall away). [I told you to keep you from being scandalized and repelled.]

2 They will put you out of (expel you from) the synagogues; but an hour is coming when whoever kills you will think and claim that he has offered service to God.

3 And they will do this because they have not known the Father or Me.

4 But I have told you these things now, so that when their time occur you will remember that I told you of them. I did not say these things to you from the beginning, because I was with you.

5 But now I am going to Him Who sent Me, yet none of you asks Me, Where are You going?

6 But because I have said these things to you, sorrow has filled your hearts [taken complete possession of them].

7 However, I am telling you nothing but the truth when I say it is profitable (good, expedient, advantageous) for you that I go away. Because if I do not go away, the Comforter (Counselor, Helper, Advocate, Intercessor, Strengthener, Standby) will not come to you [into close fellowship with you]; but if I go away, I will send Him to you [to be in close fellowship with you].

8 And when He comes, He will convict and convince the world and bring demonstration to it about sin and about righteousness (uprightness of heart and right standing with God) and about judgment:

9 About sin, because they do not believe in Me [trust in, rely on, and adhere to Me];

10 About righteousness (uprightness of heart and right standing with God), because I go to My Father, and you will see Me no longer;

11 About judgment, because the ruler (evil genius, prince) of this world [Satan] is judged and condemned and sentence already is passed upon him.

12 I have still many things to say to you, but you are not able to bear them or to take them upon you or to grasp them now.

13 But when He, the Spirit of Truth (the Truth-giving Spirit) comes, He will guide you into all the Truth (the whole, full Truth). For He will not speak His own message [on His own authority]; but He will tell whatever He hears [from the Father; He will give the message that has been given to Him], and He will announce and declare to you the things that are to come [that will happen in the future].

14 He will honor and glorify Me, because He will take of (receive, draw upon) what is Mine and will reveal (declare, disclose, transmit) it to you.

15 Everything that the Father has is Mine. That is what I meant when I said that He [the Spirit] will take the things that are Mine and will reveal (declare, disclose, transmit) it to you.

16 In a little while you will no longer see Me, and again after a short while you will see Me.

17 So some of His disciples questioned among themselves, What does He mean when He tells us, In a little while you will no longer see Me, and again after a short while you will see Me, and, Because I go to My Father?

18 What does He mean by a little while? We do not know or understand what He is talking about.

19 Jesus knew that they wanted to ask Him, so He said to them, Are you wondering and inquiring among yourselves what I meant when I said, In a little while you will no longer see Me, and again after a short while you will see Me?

20 I assure you, most solemnly I tell you, that you shall weep and grieve, but the world will rejoice. You

will be sorrowful, but your sorrow will be turned into joy.

21 A woman, when she gives birth to a child, has grief (anguish, agony) because her time has come. But when she has delivered the child, she no longer remembers her pain (trouble, anguish) because she is so glad that a man (a child, a human being) has been born into the world.

22 So for the present you are also in sorrow (in distress and depressed); but I will see you again and [then] your hearts will rejoice, and no one can take from you your joy (gladness, delight).

23 And when that time comes, you will ask nothing of Me [you will need to ask Me no questions]. I assure you, most solemnly I tell you, that My Father will grant you whatever you ask in My Name [as ᶠpresenting all that I AM]. [Exod. 3:14.]

24 Up to this time you have not asked a [single] thing in My Name [as ᶠpresenting all that I AM]; but now ask and keep on asking and you will receive, so that your joy (gladness, delight) may be full and complete.

25 I have told you these things in parables (veiled language, allegories, dark sayings); the hour is now coming when I shall no longer speak to you in figures of speech, but I shall tell you about the Father in plain words and openly (without reserve).

26 At that time you will ask (pray) in My Name; and I am not saying that I will ask the Father on your behalf [for it will be unnecessary].

27 For the Father Himself [tenderly] loves you because you have loved Me and have believed that I came out from the Father.

28 I came out from the Father and have come into the world; again, I am leaving the world and going to the Father.

29 His disciples said, Ah, now You are speaking plainly to us and not in parables (veiled language and figures of speech)!

30 Now we know that You are acquainted with everything and have no need to be asked questions. Because of this we believe that you [really] came from God.

31 Jesus answered them, Do you now believe? [Do you believe it at last?]

32 But take notice, the hour is coming, and it has arrived, when you will all be dispersed and scattered, every man to his own home, leaving Me alone. Yet I am not alone, because the Father is with Me.

33 I have told you these things, so that in Me you may have [perfect] peace and confidence. In the world you have tribulation and trials and distress and frustration; but be of good cheer [take courage; be confident, certain, undaunted]! For I have overcome the world. [I have deprived it of power to harm you and have conquered it for you.]

CHAPTER 17

WHEN JESUS had spoken these things, He lifted up His eyes to heaven and said, Father, the hour has come. Glorify and exalt and honor and magnify Your Son, so that Your Son may glorify and extol and honor and magnify You.

2 [Just as] You have granted Him power and authority over all flesh (all humankind), [now glorify Him] so that He may give eternal life to all whom You have given Him.

3 And this is eternal life: [it means] to know (to perceive, recognize, become acquainted with, and understand) You, the only true and real God, and [likewise] to know Him, Jesus [as the] Christ (the Anointed One, the Messiah), Whom You have sent.

4 I have glorified You down here

ᶠ Hermann Cremer, Biblico-Theological Lexicon.

on the earth by completing the work that You gave Me to do.

5 And now, Father, glorify Me along with Yourself and restore Me to such majesty and honor in Your presence as I had with You before the world existed.

6 I have manifested Your Name [I have revealed Your very Self, Your real Self] to the people whom You have given Me out of the world. They were Yours, and You gave them to Me, and they have obeyed and kept Your word.

7 Now [at last] they know and understand that all You have given Me belongs to You [is really and truly Yours].

8 For the [uttered] words that You gave Me I have given them; and they have received and accepted [them] and have come to know positively and in reality [to believe with absolute assurance] that I came forth from Your presence, and they have believed and are convinced that You did send Me.

9 I am praying for them. I am not praying (requesting) for the world, but for those You have given Me, for they belong to You.

10 All [things that are] Mine are Yours, and all [things that are] Yours belong to Me; and I am glorified in (through) them. [They have done Me honor; in them My glory is achieved.]

11 And [now] I am no more in the world, but these are [still] in the world, and I am coming to You. Holy Father, keep in Your Name [ᵍin the knowledge of Yourself] those whom You have given Me, that they may be one as We [are one].

12 While I was with them, I kept and preserved them in Your Name [ᵍin the knowledge and worship of You]. Those You have given Me I guarded and protected, and not one of them has perished or is lost except the son of perdition [Judas Iscariot—the

one who is now doomed to destruction, destined to be lost], that the Scripture might be fulfilled. [Ps. 41:9; John 6:70.]

13 And now I am coming to You; I say these things while I am still in the world, so that My joy may be made full and complete and perfect in them [that they may experience My delight fulfilled in them, that My enjoyment may be perfected in their own souls, that they may have My gladness within them, filling their hearts].

14 I have given and delivered to them Your word (message) and the world has hated them, because they are not of the world [do not belong to the world], just as I am not of the world.

15 I do not ask that You will take them out of the world, but that You will keep and protect them from the evil one.

16 They are not of the world (worldly, belonging to the world), [just] as I am not of the world.

17 Sanctify them [purify, consecrate, separate them for Yourself, make them holy] by the Truth; Your Word is Truth.

18 Just as You sent Me into the world, I also have sent them into the world.

19 And so for their sake and on their behalf I sanctify (dedicate, consecrate) Myself, that they also may be sanctified (dedicated, consecrated, made holy) in the Truth.

20 Neither for these alone do I pray [it is not for their sake only that I make this request], but also for all those who will ever come to believe in (trust in, cling to, rely on) Me through their word and teaching,

21 That they all may be one, [just] as You, Father, are in Me and I in You, that they also may be one in Us, so that the world may believe and be convinced that You have sent Me.

22 I have given to them the glory

and honor which You have given Me, that they may be one [even] as We are one:

23 I in them and You in Me, in order that they may become one *and* perfectly united, that the world may know *and* [definitely] recognize that You sent Me and that You have loved them [even] as You have loved Me.

24 Father, I desire that they also whom You have entrusted to Me [as Your gift to Me] may be with Me where I am, so that they may see My glory, which You have given Me [Your love gift to Me]; for You loved Me before the foundation of the world.

25 O just *and* righteous Father, although the world has not known You *and* has failed to recognize You *and* has never acknowledged You, I have known You [continually]; and these men understand *and* know that You have sent Me.

26 I have made Your Name known to them *and* revealed Your character *and* Your very [h]Self, and I will continue to make [You] known, that the love which You have bestowed upon Me may be in them [felt in their hearts] and that I [Myself] may be in them.

CHAPTER 18

HAVING SAID these things, Jesus went out with His disciples beyond (across) the winter torrent of the Kidron [in the ravine]. There was a garden there, which He and His disciples entered.

2 And Judas, who was betraying Him *and* delivering Him up, also knew the place, because Jesus had often retired there with His disciples.

3 So Judas, obtaining *and* taking charge of the band of soldiers and some guards (attendants) of the high priests and Pharisees, came there with lanterns and torches and weapons.

4 Then Jesus, knowing all that was about to befall Him, went out to them

and said, Whom are you seeking? [Whom do you want?]

5 They answered Him, Jesus the Nazarene. Jesus said to them, I am He. Judas, who was betraying Him, was also standing with them.

6 When Jesus said to them, I am He, they went backwards (drew back, lurched backward) and fell to the ground.

7 Then again He asked them, Whom are you seeking? And they said, Jesus the Nazarene.

8 Jesus answered, I told you that I am He. So, if you want Me [if it is only I for Whom you are looking], let these men go their way.

9 Thus what He had said was fulfilled *and* verified, Of those whom You have given Me, I have not lost even one. [John 6:39; 17:12.]

10 Then Simon Peter, who had a sword, drew it and struck the high priest's servant and cut off his right ear. The servant's name was Malchus.

11 Therefore, Jesus said to Peter, Put the sword [back] into the sheath! The cup which My Father has given Me, shall I not drink it?

12 So the troops and their captain and the guards (attendants) of the Jews seized Jesus and bound Him,

13 And they brought Him first to Annas, for he was the father-in-law of Caiaphas, who was the high priest that year.

14 It was Caiaphas who had counseled the Jews that it was expedient *and* for their welfare that one man should die for (instead of, in behalf of) the people. [John 11:49, 50.]

15 Now Simon Peter and another disciple were following Jesus. And that disciple was known to the high priest, and so he entered along with Jesus into the court of the palace of the high priest;

16 But Peter was standing outside at the door. So the other disciple, who

---

[h] Joseph Thayer, *A Greek-English Lexicon.*

was known to the high priest, went out and spoke to the maid who kept the door and brought Peter inside.

17 Then the maid who in charge at the door said to Peter, You are not also one of the disciples of this [i]Man, are you? He said, I am not!

18 Now the servants and the guards (the attendants) had made a fire of coals, for it was cold, and they were standing and warming themselves. And Peter was with them, standing and warming himself.

19 Then the high priest questioned Jesus about His disciples and about His teaching.

20 Jesus answered him, I have spoken openly to the world. I have always taught in a synagogue and in the temple [area], where the Jews [habitually] congregate (assemble); and I have spoken nothing secretly.

21 Why do you ask Me? Ask those who have heard [Me] what I said to them. See! They know what I said.

22 But when He said this, one of the attendants who stood by struck Jesus, saying, Is that how [i]You answer the high priest?

23 Jesus replied, If I have said anything wrong [if I have spoken abusively, if there was evil in what I said] tell what was wrong with it. But if I spoke rightly *and* properly, why do you strike Me?

24 Then Annas sent Him bound to Caiaphas the high priest.

25 But Simon Peter [still] was standing and was warming himself. They said to him, You are not also one of His disciples, are you? He denied it *and* said, I am not!

26 One of the high priest's servants, a relative of the man whose ear Peter cut off, said, Did I not see you in the garden with Him?

27 And again Peter denied it. And immediately a rooster crowed.

28 Then they brought Jesus from Caiaphas into the Praetorium (judgment hall, governor's palace). And it was early. They themselves did not enter the Praetorium, that they might not be defiled (become ceremonially unclean), but might be fit to eat the Passover [supper].

29 So Pilate went out to them and said, What accusation do you bring against this [i]Man?

30 They retorted, If He were not an evildoer (criminal), we would not have handed Him over to you.

31 Pilate said to them, Take Him yourselves and judge *and* sentence *and* punish Him according to your [own] law. The Jews answered, It is not lawful for us to put anyone to death.

32 This was to fulfill the word which Jesus had spoken to show (indicate, predict) by what manner of death He was to die. [John 12:32–34.]

33 So Pilate went back again into the judgment hall and called Jesus and asked Him, Are You the King of the Jews?

34 Jesus replied, Are you saying this of yourself [on your own initiative], or have others told you about Me?

35 Pilate answered, Am I a Jew? Your [own] people *and* nation and their chief priests have delivered You to me. What have You done?

36 Jesus answered, My kingdom (kingship, royal power) belongs not to this world. If My kingdom were of this world, My followers would have been fighting to keep Me from being handed over to the Jews. But as it is, My kingdom is not from here (this world); [it has no such origin or source.]

37 Pilate said to Him, Then You are a King? Jesus answered, You say it! [You speak correctly!] For I am a King. [Certainly I am a King!] This is why I was born, and for this I have

i Capitalized because of what He is, the spotless Son of God, not what the speaker may have thought He was.

come into the world, to bear witness to the Truth. Everyone who is of the Truth [who is a friend of the Truth, who belongs to the Truth] hears *and* listens to My voice.

38 Pilate said to Him, What is Truth? On saying this he went out to the Jews again and told them, I find no fault in Him.

39 But it is your custom that I release one [prisoner] for you at the Passover. So shall I release for you the King of the Jews?

40 Then they all shouted back again, Not Him [not this Man], but Barabbas! Now Barabbas was a robber.

CHAPTER 19

SO THEN Pilate took Jesus and scourged (flogged, whipped) Him.

2 And the soldiers, having twisted together a crown of thorns, put it on His head, and threw a purple cloak around Him.

3 And they kept coming to Him and saying, Hail, King of the Jews! [Good health to you! Peace to you! Long life to you, King of the Jews!] And they struck Him with the palms of their hands. [Isa. 53:3, 5, 7.]

4 Then Pilate went out again and said to them, See, I bring Him out to you, so that you may know that I find no fault (crime, cause for *accusation*) in Him.

5 So Jesus came out wearing the thorny crown and purple cloak, and Pilate said to them, See, [here is] the ʲMan!

6 When the chief priests and attendants (guards) saw Him, they cried out, Crucify Him! Crucify Him! Pilate said to them, Take Him yourselves and crucify Him, for I find no fault (crime) in Him.

7 The Jews answered him, We have a law, and according to that law He

should die, because He has claimed *and* made Himself out to be the Son of God.

8 So, when Pilate heard this said, he was more alarmed *and* awestricken *and* afraid than before.

9 He went into the judgment hall again and said to Jesus, Where are You from? [To what world do You belong?] But Jesus did not answer him.

10 So Pilate said to Him, Will You not speak [even] to me? Do You not know that I have power (authority) to release You and I have power to crucify You?

11 Jesus answered, You would not have any power *or* authority whatsoever against (over) Me if it were not given you from above. For this reason the sin *and* guilt of the one who delivered Me over to you is greater.

12 Upon this, Pilate wanted (sought, was anxious) to release Him, but the Jews kept shrieking, If you release this Man, you are no friend of Caesar! Anybody who makes himself [out to be] a king sets himself up against Caesar [is a rebel against the emperor]!

13 Hearing this, Pilate brought Jesus out and sat down on the judgment seat at a place called the Pavement [the Mosaic Pavement, the Stone Platform]—in Hebrew, Gabbatha.

14 Now it was the day of Preparation for the Passover, and it was about the sixth hour (about twelve o'clock noon). He said to the Jews, See, [here is] your King!

15 But they shouted, Away with Him! Away with Him! Crucify Him! Pilate said to them, Crucify your King? The chief priests answered, We have no king but Caesar!

16 Then he delivered Him over to them to be crucified.

17 And they took Jesus *and* led [Him] away; so He went out, bearing

---

ʲ Capitalized because of what He is, the spotless Son of God, not what the speaker may have thought He was.

His own cross, to the spot called The Place of the Skull—in Hebrew it is called Golgotha.

18 There they crucified Him, and with Him two others—one on either side and Jesus between them. [Isa. 53:12.]

19 And Pilate also wrote a title (an inscription on a placard) and put it on the cross. And the writing was: Jesus the Nazarene, the King of the Jews.

20 And many of the Jews read this title, for the place where Jesus was crucified was near the city, and it was written in Hebrew, in Latin, [and] in Greek.

21 Then the chief priests of the Jews said to Pilate, Do not write, The King of the Jews, but, He said, I am King of the Jews.

22 Pilate replied, What I have written, I have written.

23 Then the soldiers, when they had crucified Jesus, took His garments and made four parts, one share for each soldier, and also the tunic (the long shirtlike undergarment). But the tunic was seamless, woven [in one piece] from the top throughout.

24 So they said to one another, Let us not tear it, but let us cast lots to decide whose it shall be. This was to fulfill the Scripture, They parted My garments among them, and for My clothing they cast lots. So the soldiers did these things. [Ps. 22:18.]

25 But by the cross of Jesus stood His mother, His mother's sister, Mary the [wife] of Clopas, and Mary Magdalene.

26 So Jesus, seeing His mother *there, and the disciple whom He loved* standing near, said to His mother, [kDear] woman, See, [here is] your son!

27 Then He said to the disciple, See, [here is] your mother! And from that hour, the disciple took her into his own [keeping, own home].

28 After this, Jesus, knowing that all was now finished (ended), said in fulfillment of the Scripture, I thirst. [Ps. 69:21.]

29 A vessel (jar) full of sour wine (vinegar) was placed there, so they put a sponge soaked in the sour wine on [a stalk, reed of] hyssop, and held it to [His] mouth.

30 When Jesus had received the sour wine, He said, It is finished! And He bowed His head and gave up His spirit.

31 Since it was the day of Preparation, in order to prevent the bodies from hanging on the cross on the Sabbath—for that Sabbath was a very solemn *and* important one—the Jews requested Pilate to have the legs broken and the bodies taken away.

32 So the soldiers came and broke the legs of the first one, and of the other who had been crucified with Him.

33 But when they came to Jesus and they saw that He was already dead, they did not break His legs.

34 But one of the soldiers pierced His side with a spear, and immediately blood and water came (flowed) out.

35 And he who saw it (the eyewitness) gives this evidence, and his testimony is true; and he knows that he tells the truth, that you may believe also.

36 For these things took place, that the Scripture might be fulfilled (verified, carried out), Not one of His bones shall be broken; [Exod. 12:46; Num. 9:12; Ps. 34:20.]

37 And again another *Scripture* says, They shall look on Him Whom they have pierced. [Zech. 12:10.]

38 And after this, Joseph of Arimathea—a disciple of Jesus, but secretly for fear of the Jews—asked Pilate to let him take away the body of Jesus. And Pilate granted him permission. So he came and took away His body.

k G. Abbott-Smith, *Manual Greek Lexicon*: "A term of respect and endearment."

39 And Nicodemus also, who first had come to Jesus by night, came bringing a mixture of myrrh and aloes, [weighing] about a hundred pounds.

40 So they took Jesus' body and bound it in linen cloths with the spices (aromatics), as is the Jews' customary way to prepare for burial.

41 Now there was a garden in the place where He was crucified, and in the garden a new tomb, in which no one had ever [yet] been laid.

42 So there, because of the Jewish day of Preparation [and] since the tomb was near by, they laid Jesus.

CHAPTER 20

NOW ON the first day of the week, Mary Magdalene came to the tomb early, while it was still dark, and saw that the stone had been removed (lifted out of the groove across the entrance of) the tomb.

2 So she ran and went to Simon Peter and the other disciple, whom Jesus [tenderly] loved, and said to them, They have taken away the Lord out of the tomb, and we do not know where they have laid Him!

3 Upon this, Peter and the other disciple came out and they went toward the tomb.

4 And they came running together, but the other disciple outran Peter and arrived at the tomb first.

5 And stooping down, he saw the linen cloths lying there, but he did not enter.

6 Then Simon Peter came up, following him, and went into the tomb and saw the linen cloths lying there;

7 But the burial napkin (kerchief) which had been around Jesus' head, was not lying with the other linen cloths, but was [still] ¹ rolled up (wrapped round and round) in a place by itself.

8 Then the other disciple, who had reached the tomb first, went in too; and he saw and was convinced *and* believed.

9 For as yet they did not know (understand) the statement of Scripture that He must rise again from the dead. [Ps. 16:10.]

10 Then the disciples went back again to their homes (lodging places).

11 But Mary remained standing outside the tomb sobbing. As she wept, she stooped down [and looked] into the tomb.

12 And she saw two angels in white sitting there, one at the head and one at the feet, where the body of Jesus had lain.

13 And they said to her, Woman, why are you sobbing? She told them, Because they have taken away my Lord, and I do not know where they have laid Him.

14 On saying this, she turned around and saw Jesus standing [there], but she did not know (recognize) that it was Jesus.

15 Jesus said to her, Woman, why are you crying [so]? For Whom are you looking? Supposing that it was the gardener, she replied, Sir, if you carried Him away from here, tell me where you have put Him and I will take Him away.

16 Jesus said to her, Mary! Turning around she said to Him in Hebrew, Rabboni!—which means Teacher *or* Master.

17 Jesus said to her, Do not cling to Me [do not hold Me], for I have not yet ascended to the Father. But go to My brethren and tell them, I am ascending to My Father and your Father, and to My God and your God.

18 Away came Mary Magdalene, bringing the disciples news (word) that she had seen the Lord and that He had said these things to her.

19 Then on that same first day of

¹ Marvin Vincent, *Word Studies.*

the week, when it was evening, though the disciples were behind closed doors for fear of the Jews, Jesus came and stood among them and said, Peace to you!

20 So saying, He showed them His hands and His side. And when the disciples saw the Lord, they were filled with joy (delight, exultation, ecstasy, rapture).

21 Then Jesus said to them again, Peace to you! [Just] as the Father has sent Me forth, so I am sending you.

22 And having said this, He breathed on them and said to them, Receive the Holy Spirit!

23 [Now having received the Holy Spirit, and being ^m led and directed by Him] if you forgive the sins of anyone, they are forgiven; if you retain the sins of anyone, they are retained.

24 But Thomas, one of the Twelve, called the Twin, was not with them when Jesus came.

25 So the other disciples kept telling him, We have seen the Lord! But he said to them, Unless I see in His hands the marks made by the nails and put my finger into the nail prints, and put my hand into His side, I will never believe [it].

26 Eight days later His disciples were again in the house, and Thomas was with them. Jesus came, though they were behind closed doors, and stood among them and said, Peace to you!

27 Then He said to Thomas, Reach out your finger here, and see My hands; and put out your hand and place [it] in My side. Do not be faithless *and incredulous,* but [stop your unbelief and] believe!

28 Thomas answered Him, My Lord and my God!

29 Jesus said to him, Because you have seen Me, *Thomas,* do you now believe (trust, have faith)? Blessed *and*

happy *and* ^n to be envied are those who have never seen Me and yet have believed *and* adhered to *and* trusted *and* relied on Me.

30 There are also many other signs *and* miracles which Jesus performed in the presence of the disciples which are not written in this book.

31 But these are written (recorded) in order that you may believe that Jesus is the Christ (the Anointed One), the Son of God, and that through believing *and* cleaving to *and* trusting *and* relying upon Him you may have life through (in) His name [^n through Who He is]. [Ps. 2:7, 12.]

CHAPTER 21

AFTER THIS, Jesus let Himself be seen *and* revealed [Himself] again to the disciples, at the Sea of Tiberias. And He did it in this way:

2 There were together Simon Peter, and Thomas, called the Twin, and Nathanael from Cana of Galilee, also the sons of Zebedee, and two others of His disciples.

3 Simon Peter said to them, I am going fishing! They said to him, And we are coming with you! So they went out and got into the boat, and throughout that night they caught nothing.

4 Morning was already breaking when Jesus came to the beach and stood there. However, the disciples did not know that it was Jesus.

5 So Jesus said to them, ^n Boys (children), you do not have any meat (fish), do you? [Have you caught anything to eat along with your bread?] They answered Him, No!

6 And He said to them, Cast the net on the right side of the boat and you will find [some]. So they cast the net, and now they were not able to haul it in for such a big catch (mass, quantity) of fish [was in it].

---

m Matthew Henry, *Commentary on the Holy Bible.*
o Hermann Cremer, *Biblico-Theological Lexicon.*

n Alexander Souter, *Pocket Lexicon.*

7 Then the disciple whom Jesus loved said to Peter, It is the Lord! Simon Peter, hearing him say that it was the Lord, put (girded) on his upper garment (his fisherman's coat, his outer tunic)—for he was stripped [for work]—and sprang into the sea.

8 And the other disciples came in the small boat, for they were not far from shore, only some hundred yards away, dragging the net full of fish.

9 When they got out on land (the beach), they saw a fire of coals there and fish lying on it [cooking], and bread.

10 Jesus said to them, Bring some of the fish which you have just caught.

11 So Simon Peter went aboard and hauled the net to land, full of large fish, 153 of them; and [though] there were so many of them, the net was not torn.

12 Jesus said to them, Come [and] have breakfast. But none of the disciples ventured *or* dared to ask Him, Who are You? because they [well] knew that it was the Lord.

13 Jesus came and took the bread and gave it to them, and so also [with] the fish.

14 This was now the third time that Jesus revealed Himself (appeared, was manifest) to the disciples after He had risen from the dead.

15 When they had eaten, Jesus said to Simon Peter, Simon, son of John, do you love Me more than these [others do—with reasoning, intentional, spiritual devotion, as one loves the Father]? He said to Him, Yes, Lord, You know that I love You [that I have deep, instinctive, personal affection for You, as for a close friend]. He said to him, Feed My lambs.

16 Again He said to him the second time, Simon, son of John, do you love Me [with reasoning, intentional, spiritual devotion, as one loves the Father]? He said to Him, Yes, Lord, You know

that I love You [that I have a deep, instinctive, personal affection for You, as for a close friend]. He said to him, Shepherd (tend) My sheep.

17 He said to him the third time, Simon, son of John, do you love Me [with a deep, instinctive, personal affection for Me, as for a close friend]? Peter was grieved (was saddened and hurt) that He should ask him the third time, Do you love Me? And he said to Him, Lord, You know everything; You know that I love You [that I have a deep, instinctive, personal affection for You, as for a close friend]. Jesus said to him, Feed My sheep.

18 I assure you, most solemnly I tell you, when you were young you girded yourself [put on your own belt or girdle] and you walked about wherever you pleased to go. But when you grow old you will stretch out your hands, and someone else will put a girdle around you and carry you where you do not wish to go.

19 He said this to indicate by what kind of death Peter would glorify God. And after this, He said to him, Follow Me!

20 But Peter turned and saw the disciple whom Jesus loved, following—the one who also had leaned back on His breast at the supper and had said, Lord, who is it that is going to betray You?

21 When Peter saw him, he said to Jesus, Lord, what about this man?

22 Jesus said to him, If I want him to stay (survive, live) until I come, what is that to you? [What concern is it of yours?] You follow Me!

23 So word went out among the brethren that this disciple was not going to die; yet Jesus did not say to him that he was not going to die, but, If I want him to stay (survive, live) till I come, what is that to you?

24 It is this same disciple who is bearing witness to these things and who has recorded (written) them; and

we [well] know that his testimony is true.

25 And there are also many other things which Jesus did. If they should be all recorded one by one [in detail], I suppose that even the world itself could not contain (have room for) the books that would be written.

Psalms

THE
PSALMS

BOOK ONE

PSALM 1[a]

BLESSED (HAPPY, fortunate, prosperous, and enviable) is the man who walks *and* lives not in the counsel of the ungodly [following their advice, their plans and purposes], nor stands [submissive and inactive] in the path where sinners walk, nor sits down [to relax and rest] where the scornful [and the mockers] gather.

2 But his delight *and* desire are in the law of the Lord, and on His law (the precepts, the instructions, the teachings of God) he habitually meditates (ponders and studies) by day and by night. [Rom. 13:8–10; Gal. 3:1–29; II Tim. 3:16.]

3 And he shall be like a tree firmly planted [and tended] by the streams of water, ready to bring forth its fruit in its season; its leaf also shall not fade *or* wither; and everything he does shall prosper [and come to maturity]. [Jer. 17:7, 8.]

4 Not so the wicked [those disobedient and living without God are not so]. But they are like the chaff [worthless, dead, without substance] which the wind drives away.

5 Therefore the wicked [those disobedient and living without God] shall not stand [justified] in the judgment, nor [b] sinners in the congregation of the righteous [those who are upright and in right standing with God].

6 For the Lord knows *and* is fully acquainted with the way of the righteous, but the way of the ungodly [those living outside God's will] shall perish (end in ruin and come to nought).

PSALM 2

WHY DO the nations assemble with commotion [uproar and confusion of voices], and why do the people imagine (meditate upon and devise) an empty scheme?

2 The kings of the earth take their places; the rulers take counsel together against the Lord and His Anointed One (the Messiah, the Christ). *They say,* [Acts 4:25–27.]

3 Let us break Their bands [of restraint] asunder and cast Their cords [of control] from us.

4 He Who sits in the heavens laughs; the Lord has them in derision [and in supreme contempt He mocks them].

5 He speaks to them in His deep anger and troubles (terrifies and confounds) them in His displeasure *and* fury, *saying,*

6 Yet have I anointed (installed and placed) My King [firmly] on My holy hill of Zion.

7 I will declare the decree of the Lord: He said to Me, You are My Son; this day [I declare] I have begotten You. [Heb. 1:5; 3:5, 6; II Pet. 1:17, 18.]

a This has been called "The Preface Psalm" because in some respects it may be considered "the text upon which the whole of the Psalms make up a divine sermon." It opens with a benediction, "Blessed," as does our Lord's Sermon on the Mount (Matt. 5:3).   b Charles Haddon Spurgeon (*The Treasury of David*) said, "Sinners cannot live in heaven. They would be out of their element. Sooner could a fish live upon a tree than the wicked in paradise." The only way they will ever be able to endure heaven is to be born again and become new creatures with pure hearts able fully to enjoy the presence of God, His holy angels, and the redeemed.

8 Ask of Me, and I will give You the nations as Your inheritance, and the uttermost parts of the earth as Your possession.

9 You shall break them with a rod of iron; You shall dash them in pieces like potters' ware. [Rev. 12:5; 19:15.]

10 Now therefore, O you kings, act wisely; be instructed *and* warned, O you rulers of the earth.

11 Serve the Lord with reverent awe *and* worshipful fear; rejoice *and* be in high spirits with trembling [lest you displease Him].

12 Kiss the Son [pay homage to Him in purity], lest He be angry and you perish in the way, for soon shall His wrath be kindled. O blessed (happy, fortunate, and to be envied) are all those who seek refuge *and* put their trust in Him!

PSALM 3

A Psalm of David. When he fled
from Absalom his son.

LORD, HOW they are increased who trouble me! Many are they who rise up against me.

2 Many are saying of me, There is no help for him in God. Selah [pause, and calmly think of that]!

3 But You, O Lord, are a shield for me, my glory, and the lifter of my head.

4 With my voice I cry to the Lord, and He hears and answers me out of His holy hill. Selah [pause, and calmly think of that]!

5 I lay down and slept; I wakened again, for the Lord sustains me.

6 *I will not be afraid of ten thousands of people who have set themselves against me round about.*

7 Arise, O Lord; save me, O my God! For You have struck all my enemies on the cheek; You have broken the teeth of the ungodly.

8 Salvation belongs to the Lord; May Your blessing be upon Your peo-ple. Selah [pause, and calmly think of that]!

PSALM 4

To the Chief Musician; on stringed
instruments. A Psalm of David.

ANSWER ME when I call, O God of my righteousness (uprightness, justice, and right standing with You)! You have freed me when I was hemmed in *and* enlarged me when I was in distress; have mercy upon me and hear my prayer.

2 O you sons of men, how long will you turn my honor *and* glory into shame? How long will you love vanity *and* futility *and* seek after lies? Selah [pause, and calmly think of that]!

3 But know that the Lord has set apart for Himself [and given distinction to] him who is godly [the man of loving-kindness]. The Lord listens *and* heeds when I call to Him.

4 Be angry [or stand in awe] and sin not; commune with your own hearts upon your beds and be silent (sorry for the things you say in your hearts). Selah [pause, and calmly think of that]! [Eph. 4:26.]

5 Offer just *and* right sacrifices; trust (lean on and be confident) in the Lord.

6 Many say, Oh, that we might see some good! Lift up the light of Your countenance upon us, O Lord.

7 You have put more joy *and* rejoicing in my heart than [they know] when their wheat and new wine have yielded abundantly.

8 In peace I *will* both lie down and sleep, for You, Lord, alone make me dwell in safety *and* confident trust.

PSALM 5

To the Chief Musician; on wind
instruments. A Psalm of David.

LISTEN TO my words, O Lord, give heed to my sighing *and* groaning.

2 Hear the sound of my cry, my

King and my God, for to You do I pray.

3 In the morning You hear my voice, O Lord; in the morning I prepare [a prayer, a sacrifice] for You and watch *and* wait [for You to speak to my heart].

4 For You are not a God Who takes pleasure in wickedness; neither will the evil [man] so much as dwell [temporarily] with You.

5 Boasters can have no standing in Your sight; You abhor all evildoers.

6 You will destroy those who speak lies; the Lord abhors [and rejects] the bloodthirsty and deceitful man.

7 But as for me, I will enter Your house through the abundance of Your steadfast love *and* mercy; I will worship toward *and* at Your holy temple in reverent fear *and* awe of You.

8 Lead me, O Lord, in Your righteousness because of my enemies; make Your way level (straight and right) before my face.

9 For there is nothing trustworthy *or* steadfast *or* truthful in their talk; their heart is destruction [or a destructive chasm, a yawning gulf]; their throat is an open sepulcher; they flatter and make smooth with their tongue. [Rom. 3:13.]

10 Hold them guilty, O God; let them fall by their own designs *and* counsels; cast them out because of the multitude of their transgressions, for they have rebelled against You.

11 But let all those who take refuge *and* put their trust in You rejoice; let them ever sing *and* shout for joy, because You make a covering over them *and* defend them; let those also who love Your name be joyful in You *and* be in high spirits.

12 For You, Lord, will bless the [uncompromisingly] righteous [him who is upright and in right standing with You]; as with a shield You will surround him with goodwill (pleasure and favor).

PSALM 6

To the Chief Musician; on stringed instruments, set [possibly] an octave below. A Psalm of David.

O LORD, rebuke me not in Your anger nor discipline *and* chasten me in Your hot displeasure.

2 Have mercy on me *and* be gracious to me, O Lord, for I am weak (faint and withered away); O Lord, heal me, for my bones are troubled.

3 My [inner] self [as well as my body] is also exceedingly disturbed *and* troubled. But You, O Lord, how long [until You return and speak peace to me]?

4 Return [to my relief], O Lord, deliver my life; save me for the sake of Your steadfast love *and* mercy.

5 For in death there is no remembrance of You; in Sheol (the place of the dead) who will give You thanks?

6 I am weary with my groaning; all night I soak my pillow with tears, I drench my couch with my weeping.

7 My eye grows dim because of grief; it grows old because of all my enemies.

8 Depart from me, all you workers of iniquity, for the Lord has heard the voice of my weeping. [Matt. 7:23; Luke 13:27.]

9 The Lord has heard my supplication; the Lord receives my prayer.

10 Let all my enemies be ashamed and sorely troubled; let them turn back *and* be put to shame suddenly.

PSALM 7

An Ode of David, [probably] in a wild, irregular, enthusiastic strain, which he sang to the Lord concerning the words of Cush, a Benjamite.

O LORD my God, in You I take refuge *and* put my trust; save me from all those who pursue *and* persecute me, and deliver me,

2 Lest my foe tear my life [from my body] like a lion, dragging *me* away while there is none to deliver.

3 O Lord my God, if I have done this, if there is wrong in my hands,

4 If I have paid back with evil him who was at peace with me or without cause have robbed him who was my enemy,

5 Let the enemy pursue my life and take it; yes, let him trample my life to the ground and lay my honor in the dust. Selah [pause, and calmly think of that]!

6 Arise, O Lord, in Your anger; lift up Yourself against the rage of my enemies; and awake [and stir up] for me the justice and vindication [that] You have commanded.

7 Let the assembly of the peoples be gathered about You, and return on high over them.

8 The Lord judges the people; judge me, O Lord, and do me justice according to my righteousness [my rightness, justice, and right standing with You] and according to the integrity that is in me.

9 Oh, let the wickedness of the wicked come to an end, but establish the [uncompromisingly] righteous [those upright and in harmony with You]; for You, Who try the hearts and emotions and thinking powers, are a righteous God. [Rev. 2:23.]

10 My defense and shield depend on God, Who saves the upright in heart.

11 God is a righteous Judge, yes, a God Who is indignant every day.

12 If a man does not turn and repent, [God] will whet His sword; He has strung and bent His [huge] bow and made it ready [by treading it with His foot].

13 He has also prepared for him deadly weapons; He makes His arrows fiery shafts.

14 Behold, [the wicked man] conceives iniquity and is pregnant with mischief and gives birth to lies.

15 He made a pit and hollowed it out and has fallen into the hole which

he made [before the trap was completed].

16 His mischief shall fall back in return upon his own head, and his violence come down [with the loose dirt] upon his own scalp.

17 I will give to the Lord the thanks due to His rightness and justice, and I will sing praise to the name of the Lord Most High.

PSALM 8

To the Chief Musician; set
to a Philistine lute, or [possibly]
to a particular Hittite tune. A Psalm
of David.

O LORD, our Lord, how excellent (majestic and glorious) is Your name in all the earth! You have set Your glory on [or above] the heavens.

2 Out of the mouths of babes and unweaned infants You have established strength because of Your foes, that You might silence the enemy and the avenger. [Matt. 21:15, 16.]

3 When I view and consider Your heavens, the work of Your fingers, the moon and the stars, which You have ordained and established,

4 What is man that You are mindful of him, and the son of [earthborn] man that You care for him?

5 Yet You have made him but a little lower than God [or heavenly beings], and You have crowned him with glory and honor.

6 You made him to have dominion over the works of Your hands; You have put all things under his feet: [I Cor. 15:27; Eph. 1:22, 23; Heb. 2:6–8.]

7 All sheep and oxen, yes, and the beasts of the field,

8 The birds of the air, and the fish of the sea, and whatever passes along the paths of the seas.

9 O Lord, our Lord, how excellent (majestic and glorious) is Your name in all the earth!

PSALM 9

To the Chief Musician; set
for [possibly] soprano voices.
A Psalm of David.

I WILL praise You, O Lord, with
my whole heart; I will show forth
(recount and tell aloud) all Your marvelous works *and* wonderful deeds!

2 I will rejoice in You and be in
high spirits; I will sing praise to Your
name, O Most High!

3 When my enemies turned back,
they stumbled and perished before
You.

4 For You have maintained my
right and my cause; You sat on the
throne judging righteously.

5 You have rebuked the nations,
You have destroyed the wicked; You
have blotted out their name forever
and ever.

6 The enemy have been cut off *and*
have vanished in everlasting ruins,
You have plucked up *and* overthrown
their cities; the very memory of them
has perished *and* vanished.

7 But the Lord shall remain *and*
continue forever; He has prepared *and*
established His throne for judgment.
[Heb. 1:11.]

8 And He will judge the world in
righteousness (rightness and equity);
He will minister justice to the peoples
in uprightness. [Acts 17:31.]

9 The Lord also will be a refuge
and a high tower for the oppressed, a
refuge *and* a stronghold in times of
trouble (high cost, destitution, and desperation).

10 And they who know Your name
[who have experience and acquain-
tance with Your mercy] will lean on
and confidently put their trust in You,
for You, Lord, have not forsaken those
who seek (inquire of and for) You [on
the authority of God's Word and the
right of their necessity]. [Ps. 42:1.]

11 Sing praises to the Lord, Who
dwells in Zion! Declare among the
peoples His doings!

12 For He Who avenges the blood
[of His people shed unjustly] remembers them; He does not forget the cry
of the afflicted (the poor and the humble).

13 Have mercy upon me *and* be
gracious *to me*, O Lord; consider how
I am afflicted by those who hate me,
You Who lift me up from the gates of
death,

14 That I may show forth (recount
and tell aloud) all Your praises! In the
gates of the Daughter of Zion I will
rejoice in Your salvation *and* Your
saving help.

15 The nations have sunk down in
the pit that they made; in the net which
they hid is their own foot caught.

16 The Lord has made Himself
known; He executes judgment; the
wicked are snared in the work of their
own hands. Higgaion [meditation].
Selah [pause, and calmly think of
that]!

17 The wicked shall be turned back
[headlong into premature death] into
Sheol (the place of the departed spirits
of the wicked), even all the nations
that forget *or* are forgetful of God.

18 For the needy shall not always
be forgotten, and the expectation *and*
hope of the meek *and* the poor shall
not perish forever.

19 Arise, O Lord! Let not man prevail; let the nations be judged before
You.

20 Put them in fear [make them realize their frail nature], O Lord, that
the nations may know themselves to
be but men. Selah [pause, and calmly
think of that]!

PSALM 10

W HY DO You stand afar off,
O Lord? Why do You hide
Yourself, [veiling Your eyes] in times
of trouble (distress and desperation)?

2 The wicked in pride *and* arrogance hotly pursue *and* persecute the
poor; let them be taken in the schemes
which they have devised.

3 For the wicked *man* boasts (sings the praises) of his own heart's desire, and the one greedy for gain curses *and* spurns, yes, renounces *and* despises the Lord.

4 The wicked one in the pride of his countenance will not seek, inquire for, *and* yearn for God; all his thoughts are that there is no God [so He never punishes].

5 His ways are grievous [or persist] at all times; Your judgments [Lord] are far above *and* on high out of his sight [so he never thinks about them]; as for all his foes, he sniffs *and* sneers at them.

6 He thinks in his heart, I shall not be moved; for throughout all generations I shall not come to want *or* be in adversity.

7 His mouth is full of cursing, deceit, oppression (fraud); under his tongue are trouble and sin (mischief and iniquity).

8 He sits in ambush in the villages; in hiding places he slays the innocent; he watches stealthily for the poor [the helpless and unfortunate].

9 He lurks in secret places like a lion in his thicket; he lies in wait that he may seize the poor [the helpless and the unfortunate]; he seizes the poor when he draws him into his net.

10 [The prey] is crushed, sinks down; and the helpless falls by his mighty [claws].

11 [The foe] thinks in his heart, God has quite forgotten; He has hidden His face; He will never see [my deed].

12 Arise, O Lord! O God, lift up *Your* hand; forget not the humble [patient and crushed].

13 Why does the wicked [man] condemn (spurn and renounce) God? Why has he thought in his heart, You will not call to account?

14 You have seen it; yes, You note trouble and grief (vexation) to requite it with Your hand. The unfortunate commits himself to You; You are the helper of the fatherless.

15 Break the arm of the wicked man; and as for the evil man, search out his wickedness until You find no more.

16 The Lord is King forever and ever; the nations will perish out of His land.

17 O Lord, You have heard the desire *and* the longing of the humble *and* oppressed; You will prepare *and* strengthen *and* direct their hearts, You will cause Your ear to hear,

18 To do justice to the fatherless and the oppressed, so that man, who is of the earth, may not terrify them any more.

PSALM 11

To the Chief Musician *or* Choir Leader. [A Psalm] of David.

IN THE Lord I take refuge [and put my trust]; how can you say to me, Flee like a bird to your mountain?

2 For see, the wicked are bending the bow; they make ready their arrow upon the string, that they [furtively] in darkness may shoot at the upright in heart.

3 If the foundations are destroyed, what can the [unyieldingly] righteous do, *or* what has He [the Righteous One] wrought *or* accomplished?

4 The Lord is in His holy temple; the Lord's throne is in heaven. His eyes behold; His eyelids test *and* prove the children of men. [Acts 7:49; Rev. 4:2.]

5 The Lord tests *and* proves the [unyieldingly] righteous, but His soul abhors the wicked and him who loves violence. [James 1:12.]

6 Upon the wicked He will rain quick burning coals *or* snares; fire, brimstone, and a [dreadful] scorching wind shall be the portion of their cup.

7 For the Lord is [rigidly] righteous, He loves righteous deeds; the upright shall behold His face, *or* He beholds the upright.

PSALM 12

To the Chief Musician; set [possibly]
an octave below. A Psalm of David.

HELP, LORD! For principled *and*
godly people are here no more;
faithfulness *and* the faithful vanish
from among the sons of men.

2 To his neighbor each one speaks
words without use *or* worth *or* truth;
with flattering lips and double heart
[deceitfully] they speak.

3 May the Lord cut off all flattering
lips *and* the tongues that speak proud
boasting,

4 Those who say, With our tongues
we prevail; our lips are our own [to
command at our will]—who is lord
and master over us?

5 Now will I arise, says the Lord,
because the poor are oppressed, because of the groans of the needy; I will
set him in safety *and* in the salvation
for which he pants.

6 The words *and* promises of the
Lord are pure words, like silver refined
in an earthen furnace, purified seven
times over.

7 You will keep them and preserve
them, O Lord; You will guard *and*
keep us from this [evil] generation forever.

8 The wicked walk *or* prowl about
on every side, as vileness is exalted
[and baseness is rated high] among the
sons of men.

PSALM 13

To the Chief Musician. A Psalm
of David.

HOW LONG will You forget me,
O Lord? Forever? How long will
You hide Your face from me?

2 How long must I lay up cares
within me and have sorrow in my heart
day after day? How long shall my enemy exalt himself over me?

3 Consider and answer me, O Lord
my God; lighten the eyes [of my faith
to behold Your face in the pitchlike

darkness], lest I sleep the sleep of
death,

4 Lest my enemy say, I have prevailed over him, *and* those that trouble
me rejoice when I am shaken.

5 But I have trusted, leaned on, *and*
been confident in Your mercy *and* loving-kindness; my heart shall rejoice
and be in high spirits in Your salvation.

6 I will sing to the Lord, because
He has dealt bountifully with me.

PSALM 14

To the Chief Musician. [A Psalm]
of David.

THE [empty-headed] fool has said
in his heart, There is no God. They
are corrupt, they have done abominable deeds; there is none that does good
or right. [Rom. 3:10.]

2 The Lord looked down from
heaven upon the children of men to see
if there were any who understood,
dealt wisely, *and* sought after God, inquiring for *and* of Him *and* requiring
Him [of vital necessity].

3 They are all gone aside, they have
all together become filthy; there is
none that does good *or* right, no, not
one. [Rom. 3:11, 12.]

4 Have all the workers of iniquity
no knowledge, who eat up my people
as they eat bread and who do not call
on the Lord?

5 There they shall be in great fear
[literally—dreading a dread], for God
is with the generation of the [uncom-
promisingly] righteous (those upright
and in right standing with Him).

6 You [evildoers] would put to
shame *and* confound the plans of the
poor *and* patient, but the Lord is his
safe refuge.

7 Oh, that the salvation of Israel
would come out of Zion! When the
Lord shall restore the fortunes of His
people, then Jacob shall rejoice *and*
Israel shall be glad. [Rom. 11:25–27.]

PSALM 15
A Psalm of David.

LORD, WHO shall dwell [temporarily] in Your tabernacle? Who shall dwell [permanently] on Your holy hill?

2 He who walks and lives uprightly and blamelessly, who works rightness and justice and speaks and thinks the truth in his heart,

3 He who does not slander with his tongue, nor does evil to his friend, nor takes up a reproach against his neighbor;

4 In whose eyes a vile person is despised, but he who honors those who fear the Lord (who revere and worship Him); who swears to his own hurt and does not change;

5 [He who] does not put out his money for ᶜinterest [to one of his own people] and who will not take a bribe against the innocent. He who does these things shall never be moved. [Exod. 22:25, 26.]

PSALM 16
A Poem of David; [probably] intended to record memorable thoughts.

KEEP and protect me, O God, for in You I have found refuge, and in You do I put my trust and hide myself.

2 I say to the Lord, You are my Lord; I have no good beside or beyond You.

3 As for the godly (the saints) who are in the land, they are the excellent, the noble, and the glorious, in whom is all my delight.

4 Their sorrows shall be multiplied who choose another god; their drink offerings of blood will I not offer or take their names upon my lips.

5 The Lord is my chosen and assigned portion, my cup; You hold and maintain my lot.

6 The lines have fallen for me in pleasant places; yes, I have a good heritage.

7 I will bless the Lord, Who has given me counsel; yes, my heart instructs me in the night seasons.

8 I have set the Lord continually before me; because He is at my right hand, I shall not be moved.

9 Therefore my heart is glad and my glory [my inner self] rejoices; my body too shall rest and confidently dwell in safety.

10 For You will not abandon me to Sheol (the place of the dead), neither will You suffer Your holy one [Holy One] to see corruption. [Acts 13:35.]

11 You will show me the path of life; in Your presence is fullness of joy, at Your right hand there are pleasures forevermore. [Acts 2:25–28, 31.]

PSALM 17
A Prayer of David.

HEAR THE right (my righteous cause), O Lord; listen to my shrill, piercing cry! Give ear to my prayer, that comes from unfeigned and guileless lips.

2 Let my sentence of vindication come from You! May Your eyes behold the things that are just and upright.

3 You have proved my heart; You have visited me in the night; You have tried me and find nothing [no evil purpose in me]; I have purposed that my mouth shall not transgress.

4 Concerning the works of men, by the word of Your lips I have avoided

---

c "Israel was originally not a mercantile people, and the law aimed at an equal diffusion of wealth, not at enriching some while others were poor. The spirit of the law still is obligatory—not to take advantage of a brother's distress to lend at interest ruinous to him—but the letter of the law is abrogated, and a loan at moderate interest is often of great service to the poor. Hence, it is referred to by our Lord in parables, apparently as a lawful as well as recognized usage. (Matt. 25:27; Luke 19:23)" (A.R. Fausset, *Bible Encyclopedia and Dictionary*).

the ways of the violent (the paths of the destroyer).

5 My steps have held closely to Your paths [to the tracks of the One Who has gone before]; my feet have not slipped.

6 I have called upon You, O God, for You will hear me; incline Your ear to me *and* hear my speech.

7 Show Your marvelous loving-kindness, O You Who save by Your right hand those who trust *and* take refuge in You from those who rise up against them.

8 Keep *and* guard me as the pupil of Your eye; hide me in the shadow of Your wings

9 From the wicked who despoil *and* oppress me, my deadly adversaries who surround me.

10 They are enclosed in their own prosperity *and* have shut up their hearts to pity; with their mouths they make exorbitant claims *and* proudly *and* arrogantly speak.

11 They track us down in each step we take; now they surround us; they set their eyes to cast us to the ground.

12 Like a lion greedy *and* eager to tear his prey, and as a young lion lurking in hidden places.

13 Arise, O Lord! Confront *and* forestall them, cast them down! Deliver my life from the wicked by Your sword,

14 From men by Your hand, O Lord, from men of *this* world [these poor moths of the night] whose portion in life is idle *and* vain. Their bellies are filled with Your hidden treasure [what You have stored up]; their children are satiated, and they leave the rest [of their] wealth to their babes.

15 As for me, I will continue beholding Your face in righteousness (rightness, justice, and right standing with You); I shall be fully satisfied, when I awake [to find myself] beholding Your form [and having sweet communion with You].

PSALM 18

To the Chief Musician. [A Psalm]
of David the servant of the Lord, who
spoke the words of this song to the
Lord on the day when the
Lord delivered him from the hand of all his
enemies and from the hand of Saul.
And he said:

I LOVE You fervently *and* devotedly, O Lord, my Strength.

2 The Lord is my Rock, my Fortress, and my Deliverer; my God, my keen *and* firm Strength in Whom I will trust *and* take refuge, my Shield, and the Horn of my salvation, my High Tower. [Heb. 2:13.]

3 I will call upon the Lord, Who is to be praised; so shall I be saved from my enemies. [Rev. 5:12.]

4 The cords *or* bands of death surrounded me, and the streams of ungodliness *and* the torrents of ruin terrified me.

5 The cords of Sheol (the place of the dead) surrounded me; the snares of death confronted *and* came upon me.

6 In my distress [when seemingly closed in] I called upon the Lord and cried to my God; He heard my voice out of His temple (heavenly dwelling place), and my cry came before Him, into His [very] ears.

7 Then the earth quaked and rocked, the foundations also of the mountains trembled; they moved *and* were shaken because He was indignant *and* angry.

8 There went up smoke from His nostrils; and lightning out of His mouth devoured; coals were kindled by it.

9 He bowed the heavens also and came down; and thick darkness was under His feet.

10 And He rode upon a cherub [a storm] and flew [swiftly]; yes, He sped on with the wings of the wind.

11 He made darkness His secret hiding place; as His pavilion (His canopy) round about Him were dark waters *and* thick clouds of the skies.

12 Out of the brightness before Him there broke forth through His thick clouds hailstones and coals of fire.

13 The Lord also thundered from the heavens, and the Most High uttered His voice, amid hailstones and coals of fire.

14 And He sent out His arrows and scattered them; and He flashed forth lightnings and put them to rout.

15 Then the beds of the sea appeared and the foundations of the world were laid bare at Your rebuke, O Lord, at the blast of the breath of Your nostrils.

16 He reached from on high, He took me; He drew me out of many waters.

17 He delivered me from my strong enemy and from those who hated and abhorred me, for they were too strong for me.

18 They confronted and came upon me in the day of my calamity, but the Lord was my stay and support.

19 He brought me forth also into a large place; He was delivering me because He was pleased with me and delighted in me.

20 The Lord rewarded me according to my righteousness (my conscious integrity and sincerity with Him); according to the cleanness of my hands has He recompensed me.

21 For I have kept the ways of the Lord and have not wickedly departed from my God.

22 For all His ordinances were before me, and I put not away His statutes from me.

23 I was upright before Him and blameless with Him, ever [on guard] to keep myself free from my sin and guilt.

24 Therefore has the Lord recompensed me according to my righteousness (my uprightness and right standing with Him), according to the cleanness of my hands in His sight.

25 With the kind and merciful You will show Yourself kind and merciful, with an upright man You will show Yourself upright,

26 With the pure You will show Yourself pure, and with the perverse You will show Yourself contrary.

27 For You deliver an afflicted and humble people but will bring down those with haughty looks.

28 For You cause my lamp to be lighted and to shine; the Lord my God illumines my darkness.

29 For by You I can run through a troop, and by my God I can leap over a wall.

30 As for God, His way is perfect! The word of the Lord is tested and tried; He is a shield to all those who take refuge and put their trust in Him.

31 For who is God except the Lord? Or who is the Rock save our God,

32 The God who girds me with strength and makes my way perfect?

33 He makes my feet like hinds' feet [able to stand firmly or make progress on the dangerous heights of testing and trouble]; He sets me securely upon my high places.

34 He teaches my hands to war, so that my arms can bend a bow of bronze.

35 You have also given me the shield of Your salvation, and Your right hand has held me up; Your gentleness and condescension have made me great.

36 You have given plenty of room for my steps under me, that my feet would not slip.

37 I pursued my enemies and overtook them; neither did I turn again till they were consumed.

38 I smote them so that they were not able to rise; they fell wounded under my feet.

39 For You have girded me with strength for the battle; You have subdued under me and caused to bow down those who rose up against me.

40 You have also made my enemies

turn their backs to me, that I might cut off those who hate me.

41 They cried [for help], but there was none to deliver—even unto the Lord, but He answered them not.

42 Then I beat them small as the dust before the wind; I emptied them out as the dirt *and* mire of the streets.

43 You have delivered me from the strivings of the people; You made me the head of the nations; a people I had not known served me.

44 As soon as they heard of me, they obeyed me; foreigners submitted themselves cringingly *and* yielded feigned obedience to me.

45 Foreigners lost heart and came trembling out of their caves *or* strongholds.

46 The Lord lives! Blessed be my Rock; and let the God of my salvation be exalted,

47 The God Who avenges me and subdues peoples under me,

48 Who delivers me from my enemies; yes, You lift me up above those who rise up against me; You deliver me from the man of violence.

49 Therefore will I give thanks *and* extol You, O Lord, among the nations, and sing praises to Your name. [Rom. 15:9.]

50 Great deliverances *and* triumphs gives He to His king; and He shows mercy *and* steadfast love to His anointed, to David and his offspring forever. [II Sam. 22:2–51.]

PSALM 19
To the Chief Musician. A Psalm of David.

THE HEAVENS declare the glory of God; and the firmament shows *and* proclaims His handiwork. [Rom. 1:20, 21.]

2 Day after day pours forth speech, and night after night shows forth knowledge.

3 There is no speech nor spoken word [from the stars]; their voice is not heard.

4 Yet their voice [in evidence] goes out through all the earth, their sayings to the end of the world. Of the heavens has God made a tent for the sun, [Rom. 10:18.]

5 Which is as a bridegroom coming out of his chamber; and it rejoices as a strong man to run his course.

6 Its going forth is from the end of the heavens, and its circuit to the ends of it; and nothing [yes, no one] is hidden from the heat of it.

7 The law of the Lord is perfect, restoring the [whole] person; the testimony of the Lord is sure, making wise the simple.

8 The precepts of the Lord are right, rejoicing the heart; the commandment of the Lord is pure *and* bright, enlightening the eyes.

9 The [reverent] fear of the Lord is clean, enduring forever; the ordinances of the Lord are true and righteous altogether.

10 More to be desired are they than gold, even than much fine gold; they are sweeter also than honey and drippings from the honeycomb.

11 Moreover, by them is Your servant warned (reminded, illuminated, and instructed); and in keeping them there is great reward.

12 Who can discern his lapses *and* errors? Clear me from hidden [and unconscious] faults.

13 Keep back Your servant also from presumptuous sins; let them not have dominion over me! Then shall I be blameless, and I shall be innocent *and* clear of great transgression.

14 Let the words of my mouth and the meditation of my heart be acceptable in Your sight, O Lord, my [firm, impenetrable] Rock and my Redeemer.

PSALM 20
To the Chief Musician. A Psalm of David.

MAY THE Lord answer you in the day of trouble! May the name of the God of Jacob set you up on high [and defend you];

2 Send you help from the sanctuary and support, refresh, *and* strengthen you from Zion;

3 Remember all your offerings and accept your burnt sacrifice. Selah [pause, and think of that]!

4 May He grant you according to your heart's desire and fulfill all your plans.

5 We will [shout in] triumph at your salvation and victory, and in the name of our God we will set up our banners. May the Lord fulfill all your petitions.

6 Now I know that the Lord saves His anointed; He will answer him from His holy heaven with the saving strength of His right hand.

7 Some trust in *and* boast of chariots and some of horses, but we will trust in *and* boast of the name of the Lord our God.

8 They are bowed down and fallen, but we are risen and stand upright.

9 O Lord, give victory; let the King answer us when we call.

PSALM 21
To the Chief Musician. A Psalm of David.

THE KING [David] shall joy in Your strength, O Lord; and in Your salvation how greatly shall he rejoice!

2 You have given him his heart's desire and have not withheld the request of his lips. Selah [pause, and think of that]!

3 For You send blessings of good things to meet him; You set a crown of *pure gold* on his head.

4 He asked life of You, *and* You gave it to him—long life forever and evermore.

5 His glory is great because of Your aid; splendor and majesty You bestow upon him.

6 For You make him to be blessed *and* a blessing forever; You make him exceedingly glad with the joy of Your presence. [Gen. 12:2.]

7 For the king trusts, relies on, *and* is confident in the Lord, and through the mercy *and* steadfast love of the Most High he will never be moved.

8 Your hand shall find all Your enemies; Your right hand shall find all those who hate You.

9 You will make them as if in a blazing oven in the time of Your anger; the Lord will swallow them up in His wrath, and the fire will utterly consume them.

10 Their offspring You will destroy from the earth, and their sons from among the children of men.

11 For they planned evil against You; they conceived a mischievous plot which they are not able to perform.

12 For You will make them turn their backs; You will aim Your bow [of divine justice] at their faces.

13 Be exalted, Lord, in Your strength; we will sing and praise Your power.

PSALM 22[d]
To the Chief Musician; set to [the tune of] Aijeleth Hashshahar [the hind of the morning dawn]. A Psalm of David.

MY GOD, my God, why have You forsaken me? Why are You so far from helping me, and from the words of my groaning? [Matt. 27:46.]

---

d "This is beyond all others 'The Psalm of the Cross.' It may have been actually repeated by our Lord when hanging on the tree; it would be too bold to say so, but even a casual reader may see that it might have been. It begins with, 'My God, my God, why hast thou forsaken me?' and ends [with the thought], 'It is finished.' For plaintive expressions uprising from unutterable depths of woe, it may say of this psalm, 'There is none like it' " (Charles Haddon Spurgeon, *The Treasury of David*). Quoted in the Gospels (Matt. 27:46; Mark 15:34; and alluded to in Matt. 27:35, 39, 43 and John 19:23-24, 28) as being fulfilled at Christ's crucifixion.

2 O my God, I cry in the daytime, but You answer not; and by night I am not silent or find no rest.

3 But You are holy, O You Who dwell in [the holy place where] the praises of Israel [are offered].

4 Our fathers trusted in You; they trusted (leaned on, relied on You, and were confident) and You delivered them.

5 They cried to You and were delivered; they trusted in, leaned on, and confidently relied on You, and were not ashamed or confounded or disappointed.

6 But I am a worm, and no man; I am the scorn of men, and despised by the people. [Matt. 27:39–44.]

7 All who see me laugh at me and mock me; they shoot out the lip, they shake the head, saying, [Matt. 27:43.]

8 He trusted and rolled himself on the Lord, that He would deliver him. Let Him deliver him, seeing that He delights in him! [Matt. 27:39, 43; Mark 15:29, 30; Luke 23:35.]

9 Yet You are He Who took me out of the womb; You made me hope and trust when I was on my mother's breasts.

10 I was cast upon You from my very birth; from my mother's womb You have been my God.

11 Be not far from me, for trouble is near and there is none to help.

12 Many [foes like] bulls have surrounded me; strong bulls of Bashan have hedged me in. [Ezek. 39:18.]

13 Against me they opened their mouths wide, like a ravening and roaring lion.

14 I am poured out like water, and all my bones are out of joint. My heart is like wax; it is softened [with anguish] and melted down within me.

15 My strength is dried up like a fragment of clay pottery; [with thirst] my tongue cleaves to my jaws; and You have brought me into the dust of death. [John 19:28.]

16 For [like a pack of] dogs they have encompassed me; a company of evildoers has encircled me, they pierced my hands and my feet. [Isa. 53:7; John 19:37.]

17 I can count all my bones; [the evildoers] gaze at me. [Luke 23:27, 35.]

18 They part my clothing among them and cast lots for my raiment [a long, shirtlike garment, a seamless undertunic]. [John 19:23, 24.]

19 But be not far from me, O Lord; O my Help, hasten to aid me!

20 Deliver my life from the sword, my dear life [my only one] from the power of the dog [the agent of execution].

21 Save me from the lion's mouth; for You have answered me [kindly] from the horns of the wild oxen.

22 I will declare Your name to my brethren; in the midst of the congregation will I praise You. [John 20:17; Rom. 8:29; Heb. 2:12.]

23 You who fear (revere and worship) the Lord, praise Him! All you offspring of Jacob, glorify Him. Fear (revere and worship) Him, all you offspring of Israel.

24 For He has not despised or abhorred the affliction of the afflicted; neither has He hidden His face from him, but when he cried to Him, He heard.

25 My praise shall be of You in the great congregation. I will pay to Him my vows [made in the time of trouble] before them who fear (revere and worship) Him.

26 The poor and afflicted shall eat and be satisfied; they shall praise the Lord—they who [diligently] seek for, inquire of and for Him, and require Him [as their greatest need]. May your hearts be quickened now and forever!

27 All the ends of the earth shall remember and turn to the Lord, and all the families of the nations shall bow down and worship before You,

28 For the kingship and the king-

dom are the Lord's, and He is the ruler over the nations.

29 All the mighty ones upon earth shall eat [in thanksgiving] and worship; all they that go down to the dust shall bow before Him, even he who cannot keep himself alive.

30 Posterity shall serve Him; they shall tell of the Lord to the next generation.

31 They shall come and shall declare His righteousness to a people yet to be born—that He has done it [that it is finished]! [John 19:30.]

PSALM 23
A Psalm of David.

THE LORD is my Shepherd [to feed, guide, and shield me], I shall not lack.

2 He makes me lie down in [fresh, tender] green pastures; He leads me beside the still *and* restful waters. [Rev. 7:17.]

3 He refreshes *and* restores my life (my self); He leads me in the paths of righteousness [uprightness and right standing with Him—not for my earning it, but] for His name's sake.

4 Yes, though I walk through the [deep, sunless] valley of the shadow of death, I will fear *or* dread no evil, for You are with me; Your rod [to protect] and Your staff [to guide], they comfort me.

5 You prepare a table before me in the presence of my enemies. You anoint my head with ᵉoil; my [brimming] cup runs over.

6 Surely *or* only goodness, mercy, *and* unfailing *love* shall follow me all the days of my life, and through the length of my days the house of the

Lord [and His presence] shall be my dwelling place.

PSALM 24
A Psalm of David.

THE EARTH is the Lord's, and the fullness of it, the world and they who dwell in it. [I Cor. 10:26.]

2 For He has founded it upon the seas and established it upon the currents *and* the rivers.

3 Who shall go up into the mountain of the Lord? Or who shall stand in His Holy Place?

4 He who has clean hands and a pure heart, who has not lifted himself up to falsehood *or* to what is false, nor sworn deceitfully. [Matt. 5:8.]

5 He shall receive blessing from the Lord and righteousness from the God of his salvation.

6 This is the generation [description] of those who seek Him [who inquire of and for Him and of necessity require Him], who seek Your face, [O God of] Jacob. Selah [pause, and think of that]! [Ps. 42:1.]

7 Lift up your heads, O you gates; and be lifted up, you age-abiding doors, that the King of glory may come in.

8 Who is the King of glory? The Lord strong and mighty, the Lord mighty in battle.

9 Lift up your heads, O you gates; yes, lift them up, you age-abiding doors, that the King of glory may come in.

10 Who is [He then] this King of glory? The Lord of hosts, He is the King of glory. Selah [pause, and think of that]!

---

e It is difficult for those living in a temperate climate to appreciate, but it was customary in hot climates to anoint the body with oil to protect it from excessive perspiration. When mixed with perfume, the oil imparted a delightfully refreshing and invigorating sensation. Athletes anointed their bodies as a matter of course before running a race. As the body, therefore, anointed with oil was refreshed, invigorated, and better fitted for action, so the Lord would anoint His "sheep" with the Holy Spirit, Whom oil symbolizes, to fit them to engage more freely in His service and run in the way He directs—in heavenly fellowship with Him.

PSALM 25

[A Psalm] of David.

U NTO YOU, O Lord, do I bring my life.

2 O my God, I trust, lean on, rely on, *and* am confident in You. Let me not be put to shame *or* [my hope in You] be disappointed; let not my enemies triumph over me.

3 Yes, let none who trust *and* wait hopefully *and* look for You be put to shame *or* be disappointed; let them be ashamed who forsake the right *or* deal treacherously without cause.

4 Show me Your ways, O Lord; teach me Your paths.

5 Guide me in Your truth *and* faithfulness and teach me, for You are the God of my salvation; for You [You only *and* altogether] do I wait [expectantly] all the day long.

6 Remember, O Lord, Your tender mercy *and* loving-kindness; for they have been ever from of old.

7 Remember not the sins (the lapses and frailties) of my youth *or* my transgressions; according to Your mercy *and* steadfast love remember me, for Your goodness' sake, O Lord.

8 Good and upright is the Lord; therefore will He instruct sinners in [His] way.

9 He leads the humble in what is right, and the humble He teaches His way.

10 All the paths of the Lord are mercy *and* steadfast love, even truth *and* faithfulness are they for those who keep His covenant and His testimonies.

11 For Your name's sake, O Lord, pardon my iniquity *and* my guilt, for [they are] great.

12 Who is the man who reverently fears *and* worships the Lord? Him shall He teach in the way that he should choose.

13 He himself shall dwell at ease, and his offspring shall inherit the land.

14 The secret [of the sweet, satisfying companionship] of the Lord have they who fear (revere and worship) Him, and He will show them His covenant *and* reveal to them its [deep, inner] meaning. [John 7:17; 15:15.]

15 My eyes are ever toward the Lord, for He will pluck my feet out of the net.

16 [Lord] turn to me and be gracious to me, for I am lonely and afflicted.

17 The troubles of my heart are multiplied; bring me out of my distresses.

18 Behold my affliction and my pain and forgive all my sins [of thinking and doing].

19 Consider my enemies, for they abound; they hate me with cruel hatred.

20 O keep me, Lord, and deliver me; let me not be ashamed *or* disappointed, for my trust *and* my refuge are in You.

21 Let integrity and uprightness preserve me, for I wait for *and* expect You.

22 Redeem Israel, O God, out of all their troubles.

PSALM 26

[A Psalm] of David.

V INDICATE ME, O Lord, for I have walked in my integrity; I have [expectantly] trusted in, leaned on, *and* relied on the Lord without wavering *and* I shall not slide.

2 Examine me, O Lord, and prove me; test my heart and my mind.

3 For Your loving-kindness is before my eyes, and I have walked in Your truth [faithfully].

4 I do not sit with false persons, nor fellowship with pretenders;

5 I hate the company of evildoers and will not sit with the wicked.

6 I will wash my hands in innocence, and go about Your altar, O Lord,

7 That I may make the voice of

thanksgiving heard and may tell of all Your wondrous works.

8 Lord, I love the habitation of Your house, and the place where Your glory dwells.

9 Gather me not with sinners *and* sweep me not away [with them], nor my life with bloodthirsty men,

10 In whose hands is wickedness, and their right hands are full of bribes.

11 But as for me, I will walk in my integrity; redeem me and be merciful *and* gracious to me.

12 My foot stands on an even place; in the congregations will I bless the Lord.

PSALM 27
[A Psalm] of David.

THE LORD is my Light and my Salvation—whom shall I fear *or* dread? The Lord is the Refuge *and* Stronghold of my life—of whom shall I be afraid?

2 When the wicked, even my enemies and my foes, came upon me to eat up my flesh, they stumbled and fell.

3 Though a host encamp against me, my heart shall not fear; though war arise against me, [even then] in this will I be confident.

4 One thing have I asked of the Lord, that will I seek, inquire for, *and* [insistently] require: that I may dwell in the house of the Lord [in His presence] all the days of my life, to behold *and* gaze upon the beauty [the sweet attractiveness and the delightful loveliness] of the Lord and to meditate, consider, *and* inquire in His temple. [Ps. 16:11; 18:6; 65:4; Luke 2:37.]

5 For *in* the day of trouble He will hide me in His shelter; in the secret place of His tent will He hide me; He will set me high upon a rock.

6 And now shall my head be lifted up above my enemies round about me; in His tent I will offer sacrifices *and* shouting of joy; I will sing, yes, I will sing praises to the Lord.

7 Hear, O Lord, when I cry aloud; have mercy *and* be gracious to me and answer me!

8 You have said, Seek My face [inquire for and require My presence as your vital need]. My heart says to You, Your face (Your presence), Lord, will I seek, inquire for, *and* require [of necessity and on the authority of Your Word].

9 Hide not Your face from me; turn not Your servant away in anger, You Who have been my help! Cast me not off, neither forsake me, O God of my salvation!

10 Although my father and my mother have forsaken me, yet the Lord will take me up [adopt me as His child]. [Ps. 22:10.]

11 Teach me Your way, O Lord, and lead me in a plain *and* even path because of my enemies [those who lie in wait for me].

12 Give me not up to the will of my adversaries, for false witnesses have risen up against me; they breathe out cruelty *and* violence.

13 [What, what would have become of me] had I not believed that I would see the Lord's goodness in the land of the living!

14 Wait *and* hope for *and* expect the Lord; be brave *and* of good courage and let your heart be stout *and* enduring. Yes, wait for *and* hope for *and* expect the Lord.

PSALM 28
[A Psalm] of David.

UNTO YOU do I cry, O Lord my Rock, be not deaf *and* silent to me, lest, if You be silent to me, I become like those going down to the pit [the grave].

2 Hear the voice of my supplication as I cry to You for help, as I lift up my hands toward Your innermost sanctuary (the Holy of Holies).

3 Drag me not away with the wicked, with the workers of iniquity, who

speak peace with their neighbors, but malice *and* mischief are in their hearts.

4 Repay them according to their work and according to the wickedness of their doings; repay them according to the work of their hands; render to them what they deserve. [II Tim. 4:14; Rev. 18:6.]

5 Because they regard not the works of the Lord nor the operations of His hands, He will break them down and not rebuild them.

6 Blessed be the Lord, because He has heard the voice of my supplications.

7 The Lord is my Strength and my [impenetrable] Shield; my heart trusts in, relies on, *and* confidently leans on Him, and I am helped; therefore my heart greatly rejoices, and with my song will I praise Him.

8 The Lord is their [unyielding] Strength, and He is the Stronghold of salvation to [me] His anointed.

9 Save Your people and bless Your heritage; nourish *and* shepherd them and carry them forever.

PSALM 29[f]
A Psalm of David.

ASCRIBE TO the Lord, O sons of the mighty, ascribe to the Lord glory and strength.

2 Give to the Lord the glory due to His name; worship the Lord in the beauty of holiness *or* in holy array.

3 The voice of the Lord is upon the waters; the God of glory thunders; the Lord is upon many (great) waters.

4 The voice of the Lord is powerful; the voice of the Lord is full of majesty.

5 The voice of the Lord breaks the cedars; yes, the Lord breaks in pieces the cedars of Lebanon.

6 He makes them also to skip like a calf; Lebanon and Sirion (Mount Hermon) like a young, wild ox.

7 The voice of the Lord splits *and* flashes forth forked lightning.

8 The voice of the Lord makes the wilderness tremble; the Lord shakes the Wilderness of Kadesh.

9 The voice of the Lord makes the hinds bring forth their young, and His voice strips bare the forests, while in His temple everyone is saying, Glory!

10 The Lord sat as King over the deluge; the Lord [still] sits as King [and] forever!

11 The Lord will give [unyielding and impenetrable] strength to His people; the Lord will bless His people with peace.

PSALM 30
A Psalm; a Song at the Dedication of the Temple. [A Psalm] of David.

I WILL extol You, O Lord, for You have lifted me up and have not let my foes rejoice over me.

2 O Lord my God, I cried to You and You have healed me.

3 O Lord, You have brought my life up from Sheol (the place of the dead); You have kept me alive, that I should not go down to the pit (the grave).

4 Sing to the Lord, O you saints of His, and give thanks at the remembrance of His holy name.

5 For His anger is but for a moment, but His favor is for a lifetime *or* in His favor is life. Weeping may endure for a night, but joy comes in the morning. [II Cor. 4:17.]

6 As for me, in my prosperity I said, I shall never be moved.

7 By Your favor, O Lord, You have established me as a strong mountain; You hid Your face, and I was troubled.

8 I cried to You, O Lord, and to the Lord I made supplication.

9 What profit is there in my blood, when I go down to the pit (the grave)? Will the dust praise You? Will it de-

---

f This psalm has been called "The Song of the Thunderstorm," a glorious psalm of praise sung during an earthshaking tempest which reminds the psalmist of the time of Noah and the deluge (see Ps. 29:10).

clare Your truth *and* faithfulness to men?

10 Hear, O Lord, have mercy *and* be gracious to me! O Lord, be my helper!

11 You have turned my mourning into dancing for me; You have put off my sackcloth and girded me with gladness,

12 To the end that my tongue *and* my heart *and* everything glorious within me may sing praise to You and not be silent. O Lord my God, I will give thanks to You forever.

PSALM 31

To the Chief Musician. A Psalm of David.

IN YOU, O Lord, do I put my trust *and* seek refuge; let me never be put to shame *or* [have my hope in You] disappointed; deliver me in Your righteousness!

2 Bow down Your ear to me, deliver me speedily! Be my Rock of refuge, a strong Fortress to save me!

3 Yes, You are my Rock and my Fortress; therefore for Your name's sake lead me and guide me.

4 Draw me out of the net that they have laid secretly for me, for You are my Strength *and* my Stronghold.

5 Into Your hands I commit my spirit; You have redeemed me, O Lord, the God of truth *and* faithfulness. [Luke 23:46; Acts 7:59.]

6 [You and] I abhor those who pay regard to vain idols; but I trust in, rely on, *and* confidently lean on the Lord.

7 I will be glad and rejoice in Your mercy *and* steadfast love, because *You have seen my* affliction, You have taken note of my life's distresses,

8 And You have not given me into the hand of the enemy; You have set my feet in a broad place.

9 Have mercy *and* be gracious unto me, O Lord, for I am in trouble; with grief my eye is weakened, also my inner self and my body.

10 For my life is spent with sorrow and my years with sighing; my strength has failed because of my iniquity, and even my bones have wasted away.

11 To all my enemies I have become a reproach, but especially to my neighbors, and a dread to my acquaintances, who flee from me on the street.

12 I am forgotten like a dead man, and out of mind; like a broken vessel am I.

13 For I have heard the slander of many; terror is on every side! While they schemed together against me, they plotted to take my life.

14 But I trusted in, relied on, *and* was confident in You, O Lord; I said, You are my God.

15 My times are in Your hands; deliver me from the hands of my foes and those who pursue me *and* persecute me.

16 Let Your face shine on Your servant; save me for Your mercy's sake *and* in Your loving-kindness.

17 Let me not be put to shame, O Lord, *or* disappointed, for I am calling upon You; let the wicked be put to shame, let them be silent in Sheol (the place of the dead).

18 Let the lying lips be silenced, which speak insolently against the [consistently] righteous with pride and contempt.

19 Oh, how great is Your goodness, which You have laid up for those who fear, revere, *and* worship You, goodness which You have wrought for *those* who trust *and* take refuge in You before the sons of men!

20 In the secret place of Your presence You hide them from the plots of men; You keep them secretly in Your pavilion from the strife of tongues.

21 Blessed be the Lord! For He has shown me His marvelous loving favor when I was beset as in a besieged city.

22 As for me, I said in my haste *and* alarm, I am cut off from before Your eyes. But You heard the voice of my supplications when I cried to You for aid.

23 O love the Lord, all you His saints! The Lord preserves the faithful, and plentifully pays back him who deals haughtily.

24 Be strong and let your heart take courage, all you who wait for *and* hope for *and* expect the Lord!

PSALM 32

[A Psalm of David.] A skillful song, *or* a didactic *or* reflective poem.

BLESSED (HAPPY, fortunate, to be envied) is he who has forgiveness of his transgression continually exercised upon him, whose sin is covered.

2 Blessed (happy, fortunate, to be envied) is the man to whom the Lord imputes no iniquity and in whose spirit there is no deceit. [Rom. 4:7, 8.]

3 When I kept silence [before I confessed], my bones wasted away through my groaning all the day long.

4 For day and night Your hand [of displeasure] was heavy upon me; my moisture was turned into the drought of summer. Selah [pause, and calmly think of that]!

5 I acknowledged my sin to You, and my iniquity I did not hide. I said, I will confess my transgressions to the Lord [continually unfolding the past till all is told]—then You [instantly] forgave me the guilt *and* iniquity of my sin. Selah [pause, and calmly think of that]!

6 For this [forgiveness] let everyone who is godly pray—pray to You in a time when You may be found; surely when the great waters [of trial] overflow, they shall not reach [the spirit in] him.

7 You are a hiding place for me; You, Lord, preserve me from trouble,

You surround me with songs *and* shouts of deliverance. Selah [pause, and calmly think of that]!

8 I [the Lord] will instruct you and teach you in the way you should go; I will counsel you with My eye upon you.

9 Be not like the horse or the mule, which lack understanding, which must have their mouths held firm with bit and bridle, or else they will not come with you.

10 Many are the sorrows of the wicked, but he who trusts in, relies on, *and* confidently leans on the Lord shall be compassed about with mercy *and* with loving-kindness.

11 Be glad in the Lord and rejoice, you [uncompromisingly] righteous [you who are upright and in right standing with Him]; shout for joy, all you upright in heart!

PSALM 33

REJOICE IN the Lord, O you [uncompromisingly] righteous [you upright in right standing with God]; for praise is becoming *and* appropriate for those who are upright [in heart].

2 Give thanks to the Lord with the lyre; sing praises to Him with the harp of ten strings.

3 Sing to Him a new song; play skillfully [on the strings] with a loud *and* joyful sound.

4 For the word of the Lord is right; and all His work is done in faithfulness.

5 He loves righteousness and justice; the earth is full of the loving-kindness of the Lord.

6 By the word of the Lord were the heavens made, and all their host by the breath of His mouth. [Heb. 11:3; II Pet. 3:5.]

7 He gathers the waters of the sea as in a bottle; He puts the deeps in storage places.

8 Let all the earth fear the Lord [re-

vere and worship Him]; let all the inhabitants of the world stand in awe of Him.

9 For He spoke, and it was done; He commanded, and it stood fast.

10 The Lord brings the counsel of the nations to nought; He makes the thoughts *and* plans of the peoples of no effect.

11 The counsel of the Lord stands forever, the thoughts of His heart through all generations.

12 Blessed (happy, fortunate, to be envied) is the nation whose God is the Lord, the people He has chosen as His heritage.

13 The Lord looks from heaven, He beholds all the sons of men;

14 From His dwelling place He looks [intently] upon all the inhabitants of the earth—

15 He Who fashions the hearts of them all, Who considers all their doings.

16 No king is saved by the great size *and* power of his army; a mighty man is not delivered by [his] much strength.

17 A horse is devoid of value for victory; neither does he deliver any by his great power.

18 Behold, the Lord's eye is upon those who fear Him [who revere and worship Him with awe], who wait for Him *and* hope in His mercy *and* loving-kindness,

19 To deliver them from death and keep them alive in famine.

20 Our inner selves wait [earnestly] for the Lord; He is our Help and our Shield.

21 For in Him does our heart rejoice, because we have trusted (relied on and been confident) in His holy name.

22 Let Your mercy *and* loving-kindness, O Lord, be upon us, in proportion to our waiting *and* hoping for You.

PSALM 34

[A Psalm] of David; when he pretended to be insane before Abimelech, who drove him out, and he went away.

I WILL bless the Lord at all times; His praise shall continually be in my mouth.

2 My life makes its boast in the Lord; let the humble *and* afflicted hear and be glad.

3 O magnify the Lord with me, and let us exalt His name together.

4 I sought (inquired of) the Lord *and* required Him [of necessity and on the authority of His Word], and He heard me, and delivered me from all my fears. [Ps. 73:25; Matt. 7:7.]

5 They looked to Him and were radiant; their faces shall never blush for shame *or* be confused.

6 This poor man cried, and the Lord heard him, and saved him out of all his troubles.

7 [g]The Angel of the Lord encamps around those who fear Him [who revere and worship Him with awe], and each of them He delivers. [Ps. 18:1; 145:20.]

8 O taste and see that the Lord [our God] is good! Blessed (happy, fortunate, to be envied) is the man who trusts *and* takes refuge in Him. [I Pet. 2:2, 3.]

9 O fear the Lord, you His saints [revere and worship Him]! For there is no want to those who truly revere *and* worship Him *with* godly fear.

10 The young lions lack food and suffer hunger, but they who seek (inquire of and require) the Lord [by right of their need and on the authority of His Word], none of them shall lack any beneficial thing.

11 Come, you children, listen to me; I will teach you to revere *and* worshipfully fear the Lord.

12 What man is he who desires life

g See footnote on Gen. 16:7.

and longs for many days, that he may see good?

13 Keep your tongue from evil and your lips from speaking deceit.

14 Depart from evil and do good; seek, inquire for, *and* crave peace and pursue (go after) it!

15 The eyes of the Lord are toward the [uncompromisingly] righteous and His ears are open to their cry.

16 The face of the Lord is against those who do evil, to cut off the remembrance of them from the earth. [I Pet. 3:10–12.]

17 When the *righteous* cry for help, the Lord hears, and delivers them out of all their distress *and* troubles.

18 The Lord is close to those who are of a broken heart and saves such as are crushed with sorrow for sin *and* are humbly *and* thoroughly penitent.

19 Many evils confront the [consistently] righteous, but the Lord delivers him out of them all.

20 He keeps all his bones; not one of them is broken.

21 Evil shall cause the death of the wicked; and they who hate the just *and* righteous shall be held guilty *and* shall be condemned.

22 The Lord redeems the lives of His servants, and none of those who take refuge *and* trust in Him shall be condemned *or* held guilty.

PSALM 35

[A Psalm] of David.

CONTEND, O Lord, with those who contend with me; fight against those who fight against me!

2 Take hold of shield and buckler, and stand up for my help!

3 Draw out also the spear and javelin *and* close up the way of those who pursue *and* persecute me. Say to me, I am your deliverance!

4 Let them be put to shame and dishonor who seek *and* require my life; let them be turned back and confounded who plan my hurt!

5 Let them be as chaff before the wind, with the [h] Angel of the Lord driving them on!

6 Let their way be through dark and slippery places, with the Angel of the Lord pursuing *and* afflicting them.

7 For without cause they hid for me their net; a pit of destruction without cause they dug for my life.

8 Let destruction befall [my foe] unawares; let the net he hid for me catch him; let him fall into that very destruction.

9 Then I shall be joyful in the Lord; I shall rejoice in His deliverance.

10 All my bones shall say, Lord, who is like You, You Who deliver the poor *and* the afflicted from him who is too strong for him, yes, the poor and the needy from him who snatches away his goods?

11 Malicious *and* unrighteous witnesses rise up; they ask me of things that I know not.

12 They reward me evil for good to my personal bereavement.

13 But as for me, when they were sick, my clothing was sackcloth; I afflicted myself with fasting, and I prayed with head bowed on my breast.

14 I behaved as if grieving for my friend *or* my brother; I bowed down in sorrow, as one who bewails his mother.

15 But in my stumbling *and* limping they rejoiced and gathered together [against me]; the smiters (slanderers and revilers) gathered against me, and I knew them not; they ceased not to slander and revile me.

16 Like profane mockers at feasts [making sport for the price of a cake] they gnashed at me with their teeth.

17 Lord, how long will You look on [without action]? Rescue my life from their destructions, my dear *and* only life from the lions!

h See footnote on Gen. 16:7.

18 I will give You thanks in the great assembly; I will praise You among a mighty throng.

19 Let not those who are wrongfully my foes rejoice over me; neither let them wink with the eye who hate me without cause. [John 15:24, 25.]

20 For they do not speak peace, but they devise deceitful matters against those who are quiet in the land.

21 Yes, they open their mouths wide against me; they say, Aha! Aha! Our eyes have seen it!

22 You have seen this, O Lord; keep not silence! O Lord, be not far from me!

23 Arouse Yourself, awake to the justice due me, even to my cause, my God and my Lord!

24 Judge and vindicate me, O Lord my God, according to Your righteousness (Your rightness and justice); and let [my foes] not rejoice over me!

25 Let them not say in their hearts, Aha, that is what we wanted! Let them not say, We have swallowed him up and utterly destroyed him.

26 Let them be put to shame and confusion together who rejoice at my calamity! Let them be clothed with shame and dishonor who magnify and exalt themselves over me!

27 Let those who favor my righteous cause and have pleasure in my uprightness shout for joy and be glad and say continually, Let the Lord be magnified, Who takes pleasure in the prosperity of His servant.

28 And my tongue shall talk of Your righteousness, rightness, and justice, and of [my reasons for] Your praise all the day long.

PSALM 36

To the Chief Musician. [A Psalm] of David the servant of the Lord.

TRANSGRESSION [like an oracle] speaks to the wicked deep in his heart. There is no fear or dread of God before his eyes. [Rom. 3:18.]

2 For he flatters and deceives himself in his own eyes that his iniquity will not be found out and be hated.

3 The words of his mouth are wrong and deceitful; he has ceased to be wise and to do good.

4 He plans wrongdoing on his bed; he sets himself in a way that is not good; he does not reject or despise evil.

5 Your mercy and loving-kindness, O Lord, extend to the skies, and Your faithfulness to the clouds.

6 Your righteousness is like the mountains of God, Your judgments are like the great deep. O Lord, You preserve man and beast.

7 How precious is Your steadfast love, O God! The children of men take refuge and put their trust under the shadow of Your wings.

8 They relish and feast on the abundance of Your house; and You cause them to drink of the stream of Your pleasures.

9 For with You is the fountain of life; in Your light do we see light. [John 4:10, 14.]

10 O continue Your loving-kindness to those who know You, Your righteousness (salvation) to the upright in heart.

11 Let not the foot of pride overtake me, and let not the hand of the wicked drive me away.

12 There the workers of iniquity fall and lie prostrate; they are thrust down and shall not be able to rise.

PSALM 37

[A Psalm] of David.

FRET NOT yourself because of evil-doers, neither be envious against those who work unrighteousness (that which is not upright or in right standing with God).

2 For they shall soon be cut down like the grass, and wither as the green herb.

3 Trust (lean on, rely on, and be confident) in the Lord and do good; so

shall you dwell in the land and feed surely on His faithfulness, *and* truly you shall be fed.

4 Delight yourself also in the Lord, and He will give you the desires *and* secret petitions of your heart.

5 Commit your way to the Lord [roll and repose each care of your load on Him]; trust (lean on, rely on, and be confident) also in Him and He will bring it to pass.

6 And He will make your uprightness *and* right standing with God go forth as the light, and your justice *and* right as [the shining sun of] the noonday.

7 Be still *and* rest in the Lord; wait for Him *and* patiently lean yourself upon Him; fret not yourself because of him who prospers in his way, because of the man who brings wicked devices to pass.

8 Cease from anger and forsake wrath; fret not yourself—it tends only to evildoing.

9 For evildoers shall be cut off, but those who wait *and* hope and look for the Lord [in the end] shall inherit the earth. [Isa. 57:13c.]

10 For yet a little while, and the evildoers will be no more; though you look with care where they used to be, they will not be found. [Heb. 10:36, 37; Rev. 21:7, 8.]

11 But the meek [in the end] shall inherit the earth and shall delight themselves in the abundance of peace. [Ps. 37:29; Matt. 5:5.]

12 The wicked plot against the [uncompromisingly] righteous (the upright in right standing with God); they gnash at them with their teeth.

13 The Lord laughs at [the wicked], for He sees that their own day [of defeat] is coming.

14 The wicked draw the sword and bend their bows to cast down the poor and needy, to slay those who walk uprightly (blameless in conduct and in conversation).

15 The swords [of the wicked] shall enter their own hearts, and their bows shall be broken.

16 Better is the little that the [uncompromisingly] righteous have than the abundance [of possessions] of many who are wrong *and* wicked. [I Tim. 6:6, 7.]

17 For the arms of the wicked shall be broken, but the Lord upholds the [consistently] righteous.

18 The Lord knows the days of the upright *and* blameless, and their heritage will abide forever.

19 They shall not be put to shame in the time of evil; and in the days of famine they shall be satisfied.

20 But the wicked shall perish, and the enemies of the Lord shall be as the fat of lambs [that is consumed in smoke] *and* as the glory of the pastures. They shall vanish; like smoke shall they consume away.

21 The wicked borrow and pay not again [for they may be unable], but the [uncompromisingly] righteous deal kindly and give [for they are able].

22 For such as are blessed of God shall [in the end] inherit the earth, but they that are cursed of Him shall be cut off. [Isa. 57:13c.]

23 The steps of a [good] man are directed *and* established by the Lord when He delights in his way [and He busies Himself with his every step].

24 Though he falls, he shall not be utterly cast down, for the Lord grasps his hand in support *and* upholds him.

25 I have been young and now am old, yet have I not seen the [uncompromisingly] righteous forsaken or their seed begging bread.

26 All day long they are merciful *and* deal graciously; they lend, and their offspring are blessed.

27 Depart from evil and do good; and you will dwell forever [securely].

28 For the Lord delights in justice and forsakes not His saints; they are preserved forever, but the offspring of the wicked [in time] shall be cut off.

29 [Then] the [consistently] righ-

teous shall inherit the land and dwell upon it forever.

30 The mouth of the [uncompromisingly] righteous utters wisdom, and his tongue speaks with justice.

31 The law of his God is in his heart; none of his steps shall slide.

32 The wicked lie in wait for the [uncompromisingly] righteous and seek to put them to death.

33 The Lord will not leave them in their hands, or [suffer them to] condemn them when they are judged.

34 Wait for *and* expect the Lord and keep *and* heed His way, and He will exalt you to inherit the land; [in the end] when the wicked are cut off, you shall see it.

35 I have seen a wicked man in great power and spreading himself like a green tree in its native soil,

36 Yet he passed away, and behold, he was not; yes, I sought *and* inquired for him, but he could not be found.

37 Mark the blameless man and behold the upright, for there is a happy end for the man of peace.

38 As for transgressors, they shall be destroyed together; in the end the wicked shall be cut off.

39 But the salvation of the [consistently] righteous is of the Lord; He is their Refuge *and* secure Stronghold in the time of trouble.

40 And the Lord helps them and delivers them; He delivers them from the wicked and saves them, because they trust *and* take refuge in Him.

PSALM 38

A Psalm of David; to bring
to remembrance *and make memorial.*

O LORD, rebuke me not in Your wrath, neither chasten me in Your hot displeasure.

2 For Your arrows have sunk into me *and* stick fast, and Your hand has come down upon me *and* pressed me sorely.

3 There is no soundness in my flesh because of Your indignation; neither is there any health *or* rest in my bones because of my sin.

4 For my iniquities have gone over my head [like waves of a flood]; as a heavy burden they weigh too much for me.

5 My wounds are loathsome and corrupt because of my foolishness.

6 I am bent and bowed down greatly; I go about mourning all the day long.

7 For my loins are filled with burning; and there is no soundness in my flesh.

8 I am faint and sorely bruised [deadly cold and quite worn out]; I groan by reason of the disquiet *and* moaning of my heart.

9 Lord, all my desire is before You; and my sighing is not hidden from You.

10 My heart throbs, my strength fails me; as for the light of my eyes, it also is gone from me.

11 My lovers and my friends stand aloof from my plague; and my neighbors *and* my near ones stand afar off. [Luke 23:49.]

12 They also that seek *and* demand my life lay snares for me, and they that seek *and* require my hurt speak crafty *and* mischievous things; they meditate treachery *and* deceit all the day long.

13 But I, like a deaf man, hear not; and I am like a dumb man who opens not his mouth.

14 Yes, I have become like a man who hears not, in whose mouth are no arguments *or* replies.

15 For in You, O Lord, do I hope; You will answer, O Lord my God.

16 For I pray, Let them not rejoice over me, who when my foot slips boast against me.

17 For I am ready to halt *and* fall; my pain *and* sorrow are continually before me.

18 For I do confess my guilt *and* iniquity; I am filled with sorrow for my sin. [II Cor. 7:9, 10.]

19 But my enemies are vigorous

and strong, and those who hate me wrongfully are multiplied.

20 They also that render evil for good are adversaries to me, because I follow the thing that is good.

21 Forsake me not, O Lord; O my God, be not far from me.

22 Make haste to help me, O Lord, my Salvation.

PSALM 39

To the Chief Musician; for Jeduthun [founder of an official musical family]. A Psalm of David.

I SAID, I will take heed *and* guard my ways, that I may sin not with my tongue; I will muzzle my mouth as with a bridle while the wicked are before me.

2 I was dumb with silence, I held my peace without profit and had no comfort away from good, while my distress was renewed.

3 My heart was hot within me. While I was musing, the fire burned; then I spoke with my tongue:

4 Lord, make me to know my end and [to appreciate] the measure of my days—what it is; let me know *and* realize how frail I am [how transient is my stay here].

5 Behold, You have made my days as [short as] handbreadths, and my lifetime is as nothing in Your sight. Truly every man at his best is merely a breath! Selah [pause, and think calmly of that]!

6 Surely every man walks to and fro—like a shadow in a pantomime; surely for futility *and* emptiness he is in turmoil; each one heaps up riches, not knowing who will gather them. [I Cor. 7:31; James 4:14.]

7 And now, Lord, what do I wait for *and* expect? My hope *and* expectation are in You.

8 Deliver me from all my transgressions; make me not the scorn *and* reproach of the [self-confident] fool!

9 I am dumb, I open not my mouth, for it is You Who has done it.

10 Remove Your stroke away from me; I am consumed by the conflict *and* the blow of Your hand.

11 When with rebukes You correct *and* chasten man for sin, You waste his beauty like a moth *and* what is dear to him consumes away; surely every man is a mere breath. Selah [pause, and think calmly of that]!

12 Hear my prayer, O Lord, and give ear to my cry; hold not Your peace at my tears! For I am Your passing guest, a temporary resident, as all my fathers were.

13 O look away from me *and* spare me, that I may recover cheerfulness *and* encouraging strength *and* know gladness before I go and am no more!

PSALM 40

To the Chief Musician. A Psalm of David.

I WAITED patiently *and* expectantly for the Lord; and He inclined to me and heard my cry.

2 He drew me up out of a horrible pit [a pit of tumult *and* of destruction], out of the miry clay (froth and slime), and set my feet upon a rock, steadying my steps *and* establishing my goings.

3 And He has put a new song in my mouth, a song of praise to our God. Many shall see and fear (revere and worship) and put their trust *and* confident reliance in the Lord. [Ps. 5:11.]

4 Blessed (happy, fortunate, to be envied) is the man who makes the Lord his refuge *and* trust, and turns not to the proud or to followers of false gods.

5 Many, O Lord my God, are the wonderful works which You have done, and Your thoughts toward us; no one can compare with You! If I should declare and speak of them, they are too many to be numbered.

6 Sacrifice and offering You do not desire, *nor* have You delight in them; You have given me the capacity to hear *and* obey [Your law, a more valuable service than] burnt offerings and

sin offerings [which] You do not require.

7 Then said I, Behold, I come; in the volume of the book it is written of me;

8 I delight to do Your will, O my God; yes, Your law is within my heart. [Heb. 10:5–9.]

9 I have proclaimed glad tidings of righteousness in the great assembly [tidings of uprightness and right standing with God]. Behold, I have not restrained my lips, as You know, O Lord.

10 I have not concealed Your righteousness within my heart; I have proclaimed Your faithfulness and Your salvation. I have not hid away Your steadfast love and Your truth from the great assembly. [Acts 20:20, 27.]

11 Withhold not Your tender mercy from me, O Lord; let Your lovingkindness and Your truth continually preserve me!

12 For innumerable evils have compassed me about; my iniquities have taken such hold on me that I am not able to look up. They are more than the hairs of my head, and my heart has failed me and forsaken me.

13 Be pleased, O Lord, to deliver me; O Lord, make haste to help me!

14 Let them be put to shame and confounded together who seek and require my life to destroy it; let them be driven backward and brought to dishonor who wish me evil and delight in my hurt!

15 Let them be desolate by reason of their shame who say to me, Aha, aha!

16 Let all those that seek and require You rejoice and be glad in You; let such as love Your salvation say continually, The Lord be magnified!

17 [As for me] I am poor and needy, yet the Lord takes thought and plans for me. You are my Help and my Deliverer. O my God, do not tarry! [Ps. 70:1–5; I Pet. 5:7.]

PSALM 41
To the Chief Musician. A Psalm of David.

BLESSED (HAPPY, fortunate, to be envied) is he who considers the weak and the poor; the Lord will deliver him in the time of evil and trouble.

2 The Lord will protect him and keep him alive; he shall be called blessed in the land; and You will not deliver him to the will of his enemies.

3 The Lord will sustain, refresh, and strengthen him on his bed of languishing; all his bed You [O Lord] will turn, change, and transform in his illness.

4 I said, Lord, be merciful and gracious to me; heal my inner self, for I have sinned against You.

5 My enemies speak evil of me, [saying], When will he die and his name perish?

6 And when one comes to see me, he speaks falsehood and empty words, while his heart gathers mischievous gossip [against me]; when he goes away, he tells it abroad.

7 All who hate me whisper together about me; against me do they devise my hurt [imagining the worst for me].

8 An evil disease, say they, is poured out upon him and cleaves fast to him; and now that he is bedfast, he will not rise up again.

9 Even my own familiar friend, in whom I trusted (relied on and was confident), who ate of my bread, has lifted up his heel against me. [John 13:18.]

10 But You, O Lord, be merciful and gracious to me, and raise me up, that I may requite them.

11 By this I know that You favor and delight in me, because my enemy does not triumph over me.

12 And as for me, You have upheld me in my integrity and set me in Your presence forever.

13 Blessed be the Lord, the God of Israel, from everlasting and to ever-

lasting [from this age to the next, and forever]! Amen and Amen (so be it).

BOOK TWO

PSALM 42

To the Chief Musician. A skillful song, *or* a didactic *or* reflective poem, of the sons of Korah.

AS THE hart pants *and* longs for the water brooks, so I pant *and* long for You, O God.

2 My inner self thirsts for God, for the living God. When shall I come and behold the face of God? [John 7:37; I Thess. 1:9, 10.]

3 My tears have been my food day and night, while men say to me all day long, Where is your God?

4 These things I [earnestly] remember and pour myself out within me: how I went slowly before the throng and led them in procession to the house of God [like a bandmaster before his band, timing the steps to the sound of music and the chant of song], with the voice of shouting and praise, a throng keeping festival.

5 Why are you cast down, O my inner self? And why should you moan over me *and* be disquieted within me? Hope in God *and* wait expectantly for Him, for I shall yet praise Him, my Help and my God.

6 O my God, my life is cast down upon me [and I find the burden more than I can bear]; therefore will I [earnestly] remember You from the land of the Jordan [River] and the [summits of Mount] Hermon, from the little mountain Mizar.

7 [Roaring] deep calls to [roaring] deep at the thunder of Your waterspouts; all Your breakers and Your rolling waves have gone over me.

8 Yet the Lord will command His loving-kindness in the daytime, and in the night His song shall be with me, a prayer to the God of my life.

9 I will say to God my Rock, Why have you forgotten me? Why go I

mourning because of the oppression of the enemy?

10 As with a sword [crushing] in my bones, my enemies taunt *and* reproach me, while they say continually to me, Where is your God?

11 Why are you cast down, O my inner self? And why should you moan over me *and* be disquieted within me? Hope in God *and* wait expectantly for Him, for I shall yet praise Him, Who is the help of my countenance, and my God.

PSALM 43

JUDGE *and* vindicate me, O God; plead and defend my cause against an ungodly nation. O deliver me from the deceitful and unjust man!

2 For You are the God of my strength [my Stronghold—in Whom I take refuge]; why have You cast me off? Why go I mourning because of the oppression of the enemy?

3 O send out Your light and Your truth, let them lead me; let them bring me to Your holy hill and to Your dwelling.

4 Then will I go to the altar of God, to God, my exceeding joy; yes, with the lyre will I praise You, O God, my God!

5 Why are you cast down, O my inner self? And why should you moan over me *and* be disquieted within me? Hope in God *and* wait expectantly for Him, for I shall yet praise Him, Who is the help of my [sad] countenance, and my God.

PSALM 44

To the Chief Musician. [A Psalm] of the sons of Korah. A skillful song, *or* a didactic *or* reflective poem.

WE HAVE heard with our ears, O God; our fathers have told us [what] work You did in their days, in the days of old.

2 You drove out the nations with Your hand *and* it was Your power that gave [Israel] a home by rooting out the

[heathen] peoples, but [Israel] You spread out.

3 For they got not the land [of Canaan] in possession by their own sword, neither did their own arm save them; but Your right hand and Your arm and the light of Your countenance [did it], because You were favorable toward *and* did delight in them.

4 You are my King, O God; command victories *and* deliverance for Jacob (Israel).

5 Through You shall we push down our enemies; through Your name shall we tread them under who rise up against us.

6 For I will not trust in *and* lean on my bow, neither shall my sword save me.

7 But You have saved us from our foes and have put them to shame who hate us.

8 In God we have made our boast all the day long, and we will give thanks to Your name forever. Selah [pause, and calmly think of that]!

9 But now You have cast us off and brought us to dishonor, and You go not out with our armies.

10 You make us to turn back from the enemy, and they who hate us take spoil for themselves.

11 You have made us like sheep intended for mutton and have scattered us in exile among the nations.

12 You sell Your people for nothing, and have not increased Your wealth by their price.

13 You have made us the taunt of our neighbors, a scoffing and a derision to those who are round about us.

14 You make us a byword among the nations, a shaking of the heads among the people.

15 My dishonor is before me all day long, and shame has covered my face

16 At the words of the taunter and reviler, by reason of the enemy and the revengeful.

17 All this is come upon us, yet have we not forgotten You, neither have we been false to Your covenant [which You made with our fathers].

18 Our hearts are not turned back, neither have our steps declined from Your path,

19 Though You have distressingly broken us in the place of jackals and covered us with deep darkness, even with the shadow of death.

20 If we had forgotten the name of our God or stretched out our hands to a strange god,

21 Would not God discover this? For He knows the secrets of the heart.

22 No, but for Your sake we are killed all the day long; we are accounted as sheep for the slaughter. [Rom. 8:35–39.]

23 Awake! Why do You sleep, O Lord? Arouse Yourself, cast us not off forever!

24 Why do You hide Your face *and* forget our affliction and our oppression?

25 For our lives are bowed down to the dust; our bodies cleave to the ground.

26 Rise up! Come to our help, and deliver us for Your mercy's sake *and* because of Your steadfast love!

PSALM 45

To the Chief Musician; [set
to the tune of] "Lilies" [probably
a popular air. A Psalm] of the sons
of Korah. A skillful song,
or a didactic *or* reflective poem.
A song of love.

MY HEART overflows with a goodly theme; I address my

---

i Jesus spoke of what was written of Him "in the Psalms" (see Luke 24:44). This is one such Messianic psalm. However, the capitalization indicating the deity is offered provisionally. The chapter is written against the background of a secular royal wedding. But the New Testament reference to this psalm in Heb. 1:8, 9, where verses 6 and 7 of Psalm 45 are quoted and applied to Christ, makes any other interpretation seem incidental in importance.

psalm to a King. My tongue is like the pen of a ready writer.

2 You are fairer than the children of men; graciousness is poured upon Your lips; therefore God has blessed You forever.

3 Gird Your sword upon Your thigh, O mighty One, in Your glory and Your majesty!

4 And in Your majesty ride on triumphantly for the cause of truth, humility, *and* righteousness (uprightness and right standing with God); and let Your right hand guide You to tremendous things.

5 Your arrows are sharp; the peoples fall under You; Your darts pierce the hearts of the King's enemies.

6 Your throne, O God, is forever and ever; the scepter of righteousness is the scepter of Your kingdom.

7 You love righteousness, uprightness, *and* right standing with God and hate wickedness; therefore God, Your God, has anointed You with the oil of gladness above Your fellows. [Heb. 1:8, 9.]

8 Your garments are all fragrant with myrrh, aloes, *and* cassia; stringed instruments make You glad.

9 Kings' daughters are among Your honorable women; at Your right hand stands the queen in gold of Ophir.

10 Hear, O daughter, consider, submit, *and* consent to my instruction: forget also your own people and your father's house;

11 So will the King desire your beauty; because He is your Lord, be submissive *and* reverence *and* honor Him.

12 And, O daughter of Tyre, the richest of the people shall entreat your favor with a gift.

13 The King's daughter in the inner part [of the palace] is all glorious; her clothing is inwrought with gold. [Rev. 19:7, 8.]

14 She shall be brought to the King in raiment of needlework; with the vir-

gins, her companions that follow her, she shall be brought to You.

15 With gladness and rejoicing will they be brought; they will enter into the King's palace.

16 Instead of Your fathers shall be Your sons, whom You will make princes in all the land.

17 I will make Your name to be remembered in all generations; therefore shall the people praise and give You thanks forever and ever.

PSALM 46

To the Chief Musician. [A Psalm] of the sons of Korah, set to treble voices. A song.

GOD IS our Refuge and Strength [mighty *and* impenetrable to temptation], a very present *and* well-proved help in trouble.

2 Therefore we will not fear, though the earth should change and though the mountains be shaken into the midst of the seas,

3 Though its waters roar and foam, though the mountains tremble at its swelling *and* tumult. Selah [pause, and calmly think of that]!

4 There is a river whose streams shall make glad the city of God, the holy place of the tabernacles of the Most High.

5 God is in the midst of her, she shall not be moved; God will help her right early [at the dawn of the morning].

6 The nations raged, the kingdoms tottered *and* were moved; He uttered His voice, the earth melted.

7 The Lord of hosts is with us; the God of Jacob is our Refuge (our Fortress and High Tower). Selah [pause, and calmly think of that]!

8 Come, behold the works of the Lord, Who has wrought desolations *and* wonders in the earth.

9 He makes wars to cease to the end of the earth; He breaks the bow into pieces and snaps the spear in two; He burns the chariots in the fire.

10 Let be *and* be still, and know (recognize and understand) that I am God. I will be exalted among the nations! I will be exalted in the earth!

11 The Lord of hosts is with us; the God of Jacob is our Refuge (our High Tower and Stronghold). Selah [pause, and calmly think of that]!

PSALM 47

To the Chief Musician. A Psalm of the sons of Korah.

O CLAP your hands, all you peoples! Shout to God with the voice of triumph *and* songs of joy!

2 For the Lord Most High excites terror, awe, *and* dread; He is a great King over all the earth.

3 He subdued peoples under us, and nations under our feet.

4 He chose our inheritance for us, the glory *and* pride of Jacob, whom He loves. Selah [pause, and calmly think of that]! [1 Pet. 1:4, 5.]

5 God has ascended amid shouting, the Lord with the sound of a trumpet.

6 Sing praises to God, sing praises! Sing praises to our King, sing praises!

7 For God is the King of all the earth; sing praises in a skillful psalm *and* with understanding.

8 God reigns over the nations; God sits upon His holy throne.

9 The princes *and* nobles of the peoples are gathered together, a [united] people for the God of Abraham, for the shields of the earth belong to God; He is highly exalted.

PSALM 48

A song; a Psalm of the sons of Korah.

G REAT IS the Lord, and highly to be praised in the city of our God! His holy mountain,

2 Fair *and* beautiful in elevation, is the joy of all the earth—Mount Zion [the City of David], to the northern side [Mount Moriah and the temple], the [whole] city of the Great King! [Matt. 5:35.]

3 God has made Himself known in her palaces as a Refuge (a High Tower and a Stronghold).

4 For, behold, the kings assembled, they came onward *and* they passed away together.

5 They looked, they were amazed; they were stricken with terror *and* took to flight [affrighted and dismayed].

6 Trembling took hold of them there, and pain as of a woman in childbirth.

7 With the east wind You shattered the ships of Tarshish.

8 As we have heard, so have we seen in the city of the Lord of hosts, in the city of our God! God will establish it forever. Selah [pause, and calmly think of that]!

9 We have thought of Your steadfast love, O God, in the midst of Your temple.

10 As is Your name, O God, so is Your praise to the ends of the earth; Your right hand is full of righteousness (rightness and justice).

11 Let Mount Zion be glad! Let the daughters of Judah rejoice because of Your [righteous] judgments!

12 Walk about Zion, and go round about her, number her towers (her lofty and noble deeds of past days),

13 Consider well her ramparts, go through her palaces *and* citadels, that you may tell the next generation [and cease recalling disappointments].

14 For this God is our God forever and ever; He will be our guide [even] until death.

j Psalm 48 is a celebration of the security of Zion. See the beauty of Zion as God's unconquerable fortress.

PSALM 49

To the Chief Musician. A Psalm
of the sons of Korah.

HEAR THIS, all you peoples; give
ear, all you inhabitants of the
world,

2 Both low and high, rich and poor
together:

3 My mouth shall speak wisdom;
and the meditation of my heart shall be
understanding.

4 I will submit *and* consent to a parable *or* proverb; to the music of a lyre
I will unfold my riddle (my problem).

5 Why should I fear in the days of
evil, when the iniquity of those who
would supplant me surrounds me on
every side,

6 Even of those who trust in *and*
lean on their wealth and boast of the
abundance of their riches?

7 None of them can by any means
redeem [either himself or] his brother,
nor give to God a ransom for him—

8 For the ransom of a life is too
costly, and [the price one can pay] can
never suffice—

9 So that he should live on forever
and never see the pit (the grave) *and*
corruption.

10 For he sees that even wise men
die; the [self-confident] fool and the
stupid alike perish and leave their
wealth *to* others.

11 Their inward thought is that
their houses will continue forever, *and*
their dwelling places to all generations; they call their lands their own
[apart from God] *and* after their own
names.

12 But man, with all his honor *and*
pomp, does not remain; he is like the
beasts that perish.

13 This is the fate of those who are
foolishly confident, yet after them men

approve their sayings. Selah [pause,
and calmly think of that]!

14 Like sheep they are appointed
for Sheol (the place of the dead); death
shall be their shepherd. And the upright shall have dominion over them in
the morning; and their form *and* beauty shall be consumed, for Sheol shall
be their dwelling.

15 But God will redeem me from
the power of Sheol (the place of the
dead); for He will receive me. Selah
[pause, and calmly think of that]!

16 Be not afraid when [an ungodly]
one is made rich, when the wealth *and*
glory of his house are increased;

17 For when he dies he will carry
nothing away; his glory will not descend after him.

18 Though while he lives he counts
himself happy *and* prosperous, and
though a man gets praise when he does
well [for himself],

19 He will go to the generation of
his fathers, who will nevermore see the
light.

20 A man who is held in honor *and*
understands not is like the beasts that
perish.

PSALM 50

A Psalm of [k]Asaph

THE MIGHTY One, God, the Lord,
speaks and calls the earth from the
rising of the sun to its setting.

2 Out of Zion, the perfection of
beauty, God shines forth.

3 Our God comes and does not keep
silence; a fire devours before Him, and
round about Him a mighty tempest
rages.

4 He calls to the heavens above and
to the earth, that He may judge His
people:

---

k Asaph was a Levite and one of the leaders of David's choir. He was the head of one of the three
families permanently charged with the temple music. His family formed a guild which bore his name and
is frequently mentioned (II Chron. 20:14; 29:13; 29:30). Twelve psalms (50; 73-83) are attributed in the
titles to the family of Asaph. 128 of Asaph's family members, all singers, came back from Babylon and
took part when the foundations of Zerubbabel's temple were laid (Ezra 2:41; 3:10).

5 Gather together to Me My saints [those who have found grace in My sight], those who have made a covenant with Me by sacrifice.

6 And the heavens declare His righteousness (rightness and justice), for God, He is judge. Selah [pause, and calmly think of that]!

7 Hear, O My people, and I will speak; O Israel, I will testify to you and against you: I am God, your God.

8 I do not reprove you for your sacrifices; your burnt offerings are continually before Me.

9 I will accept no bull from your house nor he-goat out of your folds.

10 For every beast of the forest is Mine, and the cattle upon a thousand hills or upon the mountains where thousands are.

11 I know and am acquainted with all the birds of the mountains, and the wild animals of the field are Mine and are with Me, in My mind.

12 If I were hungry, I would not tell you, for the world and its fullness are Mine. [I Cor. 10:26.]

13 Shall I eat the flesh of bulls or drink the blood of goats?

14 Offer to God the sacrifice of thanksgiving, and pay your vows to the Most High,

15 And call on Me in the day of trouble; I will deliver you, and you shall honor and glorify Me.

16 But to the wicked, God says: What right have you to recite My statutes or take My covenant or pledge on your lips,

17 Seeing that you hate instruction and correction and cast My words behind you [discarding them]?

18 When you see a thief, you associate with him, and you have taken part with adulterers.

19 You give your mouth to evil, and your tongue frames deceit.

20 You sit and speak against your brother; you slander your own mother's son.

21 These things you have done and I kept silent; you thought I was once entirely like you. But [now] I will reprove you and put [the charge] in order before your eyes.

22 Now consider this, you who forget God, lest I tear you in pieces, and there be none to deliver.

23 He who brings an offering of praise and thanksgiving honors and glorifies Me; and he who orders his way aright [who prepares the way that I may show him], to him I will demonstrate the salvation of God.

PSALM 51

To the Chief Musician. A Psalm of David; when Nathan the prophet came to him after he had sinned with Bathsheba.

HAVE MERCY upon me, O God, according to Your steadfast love; according to the multitude of Your tender mercy and loving-kindness blot out my transgressions.

2 Wash me thoroughly [and repeatedly] from my iniquity and guilt and cleanse me and make me wholly pure from my sin!

3 For I am conscious of my transgressions and I acknowledge them; my sin is ever before me.

4 Against You, You only, have I sinned and done that which is evil in Your sight, so that You are justified in Your sentence and faultless in Your judgment. [Rom. 3:4.]

5 Behold, I was brought forth in [a state of] iniquity; my mother was sinful who conceived me [and I too am sinful]. [John 3:6; Rom. 5:12; Eph. 2:3.]

6 Behold, You desire truth in the inner being; make me therefore to know wisdom in my inmost heart.

7 Purify me with hyssop, and I shall be clean [ceremonially]; wash me, and I shall [in reality] be whiter than snow.

8 Make me to hear joy and gladness

and be satisfied; let the bones which You have broken rejoice.

9 Hide Your face from my sins and blot out all my guilt *and* iniquities.

10 Create in me a clean heart, O God, and renew a right, persevering, *and* steadfast spirit within me.

11 Cast me not away from Your presence and take not Your Holy Spirit from me.

12 Restore to me the joy of Your salvation and uphold me with a willing spirit.

13 Then will I teach transgressors Your ways, and sinners shall be converted *and* return to You.

14 Deliver me from bloodguiltiness *and* death, O God, the God of my salvation, *and* my tongue shall sing aloud of Your righteousness (Your rightness and Your justice).

15 O Lord, open my lips, and my mouth shall show forth Your praise.

16 For You delight not in sacrifice, or else would I give it; You find no pleasure in burnt offering. [I Sam. 15:22.]

17 My sacrifice [the sacrifice acceptable] to God is a broken spirit; a broken and a contrite heart [broken down with sorrow for sin and humbly and thoroughly penitent], such, O God, You will not despise.

18 Do good in Your good pleasure to Zion; rebuild the walls of Jerusalem.

19 Then will You delight in the sacrifices of righteousness, justice, *and* right, with burnt offering and whole burnt offering; then bullocks will be offered upon Your altar.

PSALM 52

To the Chief Musician. A skillful
song, *or* a didactic *or* reflective poem.
[A Psalm] of David, when Doeg
the Edomite came and told Saul,
David has come to the house
of Ahimelech.

WHY BOAST you of mischief done against the loving-kind-ness of God [and the godly], O mighty [sinful] man, day after day?

2 Your tongue devises wickedness; it is like a sharp razor, working deceitfully.

3 You love evil more than good, and lying rather than to speak righteousness, justice, *and* right. Selah [pause, and calmly think of that]!

4 You love all destroying *and* devouring words, O deceitful tongue.

5 God will likewise break you down *and* destroy you forever; He will lay hold of you and pluck you out of your tent and uproot you from the land of the living. Selah [pause, and calmly think of that]!

6 The [uncompromisingly] righteous also shall see [it] and be in reverent fear *and* awe, but about you they will [scoffingly] laugh, saying,

7 See, this is the man who made not God his strength (his stronghold and high tower) but trusted in *and* confidently relied on the abundance of his riches, seeking refuge *and* security for himself through his wickedness.

8 But I am like a green olive tree in the house of God; I trust in *and* confidently rely on the loving-kindness *and* the mercy of God forever and ever.

9 I will thank You *and* confide in You forever, because You have done it [delivered me and kept me safe]. I will wait on, hope in *and* expect in Your name, for it is good, in the presence of Your saints (Your kind and pious ones).

PSALM 53

To the Chief Musician; in a mournful
strain. A skillful song, *or* didactic
or reflective poem of David.

THE [empty-headed] fool has said in his heart, There is no God. Corrupt *and* evil are they, and doing abominable iniquity; there is none who does good.

2 God looked down from heaven upon the children of men to see if there were any who understood, who sought

(inquired after and desperately required] God.

3 Every one of them has gone back [backslidden and fallen away]; they have altogether become filthy *and* corrupt; there is none who does good, no, not one. [Rom. 3:10–12.]

4 Have those who work evil no knowledge (no understanding)? They eat up My people as they eat bread; they do not call upon God.

5 There they are, in terror *and* dread, where there was [and had been] no terror *and* dread! For God has scattered the bones of him who encamps against you; you have put them to shame, because God has rejected them.

6 Oh, that the salvation *and* deliverance of Israel would come out of Zion! When God restores the fortunes of His people, then will Jacob rejoice and Israel be glad.

PSALM 54

To the Chief Musician; with stringed instruments. A skillful song, or a didactic *or* reflective poem, of David, when the Ziphites went and told Saul, David is hiding among us.

SAVE ME, O God, by Your name; judge *and* vindicate me by Your mighty strength *and* power.

2 Hear my pleading *and* my prayer, O God; give ear to the words of my mouth.

3 For strangers *and* insolent men are rising up against me, and violent men *and* ruthless ones seek *and* demand my life; they do not set God before them. Selah [pause, and calmly think of that]!

4 Behold, God is my helper *and* ally; the Lord is my upholder *and* is with them who uphold my life.

5 He will pay back evil to my enemies; in Your faithfulness [Lord] put an end to them.

6 With a freewill offering I will sacrifice to You; I will give thanks *and* praise Your name, O Lord, for it is good.

7 For He has delivered me out of every trouble, and my eye has looked [in triumph] on my enemies.

PSALM 55

To the Chief Musician; with stringed instruments. A skillful song, or a didactic *or* reflective poem, of David.

LISTEN TO my prayer, O God, and hide not Yourself from my supplication!

2 Attend to me and answer me; I am restless *and* distraught in my complaint and must moan

3 [And I am distracted] at the noise of the enemy, because of the oppression *and* threats of the wicked; for they would cast trouble upon me, and in wrath they persecute me.

4 My heart is grievously pained within me, and the terrors of death have fallen upon me.

5 Fear and trembling have come upon me; horror *and* fright have overwhelmed me.

6 And I say, Oh, that I had wings like a dove! I would fly away and be at rest.

7 Yes, I would wander far away, I would lodge in the wilderness. Selah [pause, and calmly think of that]!

8 I would hasten to escape *and* to find a shelter from the stormy wind and tempest.

9 Destroy [their schemes], O Lord, confuse their tongues, for I have seen violence and strife in the city.

10 Day and night they go about on its walls; iniquity and mischief are in its midst.

11 Violence *and* ruin are within it; fraud and guile do not depart from its streets *and* marketplaces.

12 For it is not an enemy who reproaches *and* taunts me—then I might

bear it; nor is it one who has hated me who insolently vaunts *himself* against me—then I might hide from him.

13 But it was you, a man my equal, my companion and my familiar friend.

14 We had sweet fellowship together and used to walk to the house of God in company.

15 Let desolations *and* death come suddenly upon them; let them go down alive to Sheol (the place of the dead), for evils are in (their habitations, in their hearts, *and* their inmost part.

16 As for me, I will call upon God, and the Lord will save me.

17 Evening and morning and at noon will I utter my complaint and moan *and* sigh, and He will hear my voice.

18 He has redeemed my life in peace from the battle that was against me [so that none came near me], for they were many who strove with me.

19 God will hear and humble them, even He Who abides of old—Selah [pause, and calmly think of that]!—because in them there has been no change [of heart], and they do not fear, revere, *and* worship God.

20 [My companion] has put forth his hands against those who were at peace with him; he has broken *and* profaned his agreement [of friendship and loyalty].

21 The words of his mouth were smoother than cream *or* butter, but war was in his heart; his words were softer than oil, yet they were drawn swords.

22 Cast your burden on the Lord [releasing the weight of it] and He will sustain you; He will never allow the [consistently] righteous to be moved (made to slip, fall, or fail). [I Pet. 5:7.]

23 But You, O God, will bring down the wicked into the pit of destruction; men of blood and treachery shall not live out half their days. But I will trust in, lean on, *and* confidently rely on You.

PSALM 56

To the Chief Musician; [set to the tune of] "Silent Dove Among Those Far Away." Of David. A record of memorable thoughts when the Philistines seized him in Gath.

BE MERCIFUL *and* gracious to me, O God, for man would trample me *or* devour me; all the day long the adversary oppresses me.

2 They that lie in wait for me would swallow me up *or* trample me all day long, for they are many who fight against me, O Most High!

3 What time I am afraid, I will have confidence in *and* put my trust *and* reliance in You.

4 By [the help of] God I will praise His word; on God I lean, rely, *and* confidently put my trust; I will not fear. What can man, who is flesh, do to me?

5 All day long they twist my words *and* trouble my affairs; all their thoughts are against me for evil and my hurt.

6 They gather themselves together, they hide themselves, they watch my steps, even as they have [expectantly] waited for my life.

7 They think to escape with iniquity, *and* shall they? In Your indignation bring down the peoples, O God.

8 You number *and* record my wanderings; put my tears into Your bottle—are they not in Your book?

9 Then shall my enemies turn back in the day that I cry out; this I know, for God is for me. [Rom. 8:31.]

10 In God, Whose word I praise, in the Lord, Whose word I praise,

11 In God have I put my trust *and* confident reliance; I will not be afraid. What can man do to me?

12 Your vows are upon me, O God; I will render praise to You *and* give You thank offerings.

13 For You have delivered my life from death, yes, and my feet from falling, that I may walk before God in the light of life *and* of the living.

PSALM 57

To the Chief Musician;
[set to the tune of] "Do Not Destroy."
A record of memorable thoughts
of David when he fled from Saul
in the cave.

BE MERCIFUL *and* gracious to
me, O God, be merciful *and* gracious to me, for my soul takes refuge
and finds shelter *and* confidence in
You; yes, in the shadow of Your wings
will I take refuge *and* be confident until calamities *and* destructive storms
are passed.

2 I will cry to God Most High, Who
performs on my behalf *and* rewards
me [Who brings to pass His purposes
for me and surely completes them]!

3 He will send from heaven and
save me from the slanders *and* reproaches of him who would trample
me down *or* swallow me up, *and* He
will put him to shame. Selah [pause,
and calmly think of that]! God will
send forth His mercy *and* loving-kindness *and* His truth *and* faithfulness.

4 My life is among lions; I must lie
among those who are aflame—the
sons of men whose teeth are spears and
arrows, their tongues sharp swords.

5 Be exalted, O God, above the
heavens! Let Your glory be over all the
earth!

6 They set a net for my steps; my
very life was bowed down. They dug
a pit in my way; into the midst of it
they themselves have fallen. Selah
[pause, and calmly think of that]!

7 My heart is fixed, O God, my
heart is steadfast *and* confident! I will
sing and make melody.

8 Awake, my glory (*my inner self*);
awake, harp and lyre! I will awake
right early [I will awaken the dawn]!

9 I will praise *and* give thanks to
You, O Lord, among the peoples; I
will sing praises to You among the
nations.

10 For Your mercy *and* loving-
kindness are great, reaching to the
heavens, and Your truth *and* faithfulness to the clouds.

11 Be exalted, O God, above the
heavens; let Your glory be over all the
earth.

PSALM 58

To the Chief Musician;
[set to the tune of] "Do Not Destroy."
A record of memorable thoughts
of David.

DO YOU indeed in silence speak
righteousness, O you mighty
ones? [Or is the righteousness, rightness, and justice you should speak
quite dumb?] Do you judge fairly *and*
uprightly, O you sons of men?

2 No, in your heart you devise
wickedness; you deal out in the land
the violence of your hands.

3 The ungodly are perverse *and* es-
tranged from the womb; they go astray
as soon as they are born, speaking lies.

4 Their poison is like the venom of
a serpent; they are like the deaf adder
or asp that stops its ear,

5 Which listens not to the voice of
charmers *or* of the enchanter never
casting spells so cunningly.

6 Break their teeth, O God, in their
mouths; break out the fangs of the
young lions, O Lord.

7 Let them melt away as water
which runs on apace; when he aims his
arrows, let them be as if they were
headless *or* split apart.

8 Let them be as a snail dissolving
slime as it passes on *or* as a festering
sore which wastes away, like [the child
to which] a woman gives untimely
birth that has not seen the sun.

9 Before your pots can feel the
thorns [that are placed under them for
fuel], He will take them away as with
a whirlwind, the green and the burning
ones alike.

10 The [unyieldingly] righteous
shall rejoice when he sees the vengeance; he will bathe his feet in the
blood of the wicked.

11 Men will say, Surely there is a

reward for the [uncompromisingly] righteous; surely there is a God Who judges on the earth.

PSALM 59

To the Chief Musician;
[set to the tune of] "Do Not Destroy."
Of David, a record of memorable
thoughts when Saul sent men to watch
his house in order to kill him.

DELIVER ME from my enemies, O my God; defend *and* protect me from those who rise up against me.

2 Deliver me from *and* lift me above those who work evil and save me from bloodthirsty men.

3 For, behold, they lie in wait for my life; fierce *and* mighty men are banding together against me, not for my transgression nor for any sin of mine, O Lord.

4 They run and prepare themselves, though there is no fault in me; rouse Yourself [O Lord] to meet *and* help me, and see!

5 You, O Lord God of hosts, the God of Israel, arise to visit all the nations; spare none *and* be not merciful to any who treacherously plot evil. Selah [pause, and calmly think of that]!

6 They return at evening, they howl *and* snarl like dogs, and go [prowling] about the city.

7 Behold, they belch out [insults] with their mouths; swords [of sarcasm, ridicule, slander, and lies] are in their lips, for who, they think, hears us?

8 But You, O Lord, will laugh at them [in scorn]; You will hold all the nations in derision.

9 O my Strength, I will watch *and* give heed to You *and* sing praises; for God is my Defense (my Protector and High Tower).

10 My God in His mercy *and* steadfast love will meet me; God will let me look [triumphantly] on my enemies (those who lie in wait for me).

11 Slay them not, lest my people forget; scatter them by Your power *and* make them wander to and fro, and bring them down, O Lord our Shield!

12 For the sin of their mouths and the words of their lips, let them even be trapped *and* taken in their pride, and for the cursing and lying which they utter.

13 Consume them in wrath, consume them so that they shall be no more; and let them know unto the ends of the earth that God rules over Jacob (Israel). Selah [pause, and calmly think of that]!

14 And at evening let them return; let them howl *and* snarl like dogs, and go prowling about the city.

15 Let them wander up and down for food and tarry all night if they are not satisfied (not getting their fill).

16 But I will sing of Your mighty strength *and* power; yes, I will sing aloud of Your mercy *and* loving-kindness in the morning; for You have been to me a defense (a fortress and a high tower) and a refuge in the day of my distress.

17 Unto You, O my Strength, I will sing praises; for God is my Defense, my Fortress, *and* High Tower, the God Who shows me mercy *and* steadfast love.

PSALM 60

To the Chief Musician;
[set to the tune of] "The Lily
of the Testimony." A poem of David
intended to record memorable
thoughts and to teach; when he had
striven with the Arameans
of Mesopotamia and the Arameans
of Zobah, and when Joab returned
and smote twelve thousand Edomites
in the Valley of Salt.

O GOD, You have rejected us *and* cast us off, broken down [our defenses], *and* scattered us; You have been angry—O restore us *and* turn Yourself to us again!

2 You have made the land to quake *and* tremble, You have rent it [open]; repair its breaches, for it shakes *and* totters.

3 You have made Your people suffer hard things; You have given us to drink wine that makes us reel *and* be dazed.

4 [But now] You have set up a banner for those who fear *and* worshipfully revere You [to which they may flee from the bow], a standard displayed because of the truth. Selah [pause, and calmly think of that]!

5 That Your beloved ones may be delivered, save with Your right hand and answer us [or me].

6 God has spoken in His holiness [in His promises]: I will rejoice, I will divide and portion out [the land] Shechem and the Valley of Succoth [west to east].

7 Gilead is Mine, and Manasseh is Mine; Ephraim also is My helmet (the defense of My head); Judah is My scepter *and* My lawgiver.

8 Moab is My washpot [reduced to vilest servitude]; upon Edom I cast My shoe in triumph; over Philistia I raise the shout of victory.

9 Who will bring me [David] into the strong city [of Petra]? Who will lead me into Edom?

10 Have You not rejected us, O God? And will You not go forth, O God, with our armies?

11 O give us help against the adversary, for vain (ineffectual and to no purpose) is the help or salvation of man.

12 Through God we shall do valiantly, for He it is Who shall tread down our adversaries.

PSALM 61

To the Chief Musician; on stringed instruments. [A Psalm] of David.

HEAR MY cry, O God; listen to my prayer.

2 From the end of the earth will I cry to You, when my heart is overwhelmed *and* fainting; lead me to the rock that is higher than I [yes, a rock that is too high for me].

3 For You have been a shelter *and* a refuge for me, a strong tower against the adversary.

4 I will dwell in Your tabernacle forever; let me find refuge *and* trust in the shelter of Your wings. Selah [pause, and calmly think of that]!

5 For You, O God, have heard my vows; You have given me the heritage of those who fear, revere, *and* honor Your name.

6 May You prolong the [true] [1]King's life [adding days upon days], and may His years be to the last generation [of this world and the generations of the world to come].

7 May He sit enthroned forever before [the face of] God; O ordain that loving-kindness and faithfulness may watch over Him!

8 So will I sing praise to Your name forever, paying my vows day by day.

PSALM 62

To the Chief Musician; according to Jeduthun [Ethan, the noted musician, founder of an official musical family]. A Psalm of David.

FOR GOD alone my soul waits in silence; from Him comes my salvation.

2 He only is my Rock and my Salvation, my Defense *and* my Fortress, I shall not be greatly moved.

3 How long will you set upon a man that you may slay him, all of you, like a leaning wall, like a tottering fence?

4 They only consult to cast him down from his height [to dishonor him]; they delight in lies. They bless *with* their mouths, but they curse inwardly. Selah [pause, and calmly think of that]!

5 My soul, wait only upon God *and* silently submit to Him; for my hope *and* expectation are from Him.

6 He only is my Rock and my Sal-

1 The thoughts of these verses (6-7) are fulfilled in Christ, David's great Son.

vation; He is my Defense *and* my Fortress, I shall not be moved.

7 With God rests my salvation and my glory; He is my Rock of unyielding strength *and* impenetrable hardness, and my refuge is in God!

8 Trust in, lean on, rely on, *and* have confidence in Him at all times, you people; pour out your hearts before Him. God is a refuge for us (a fortress and a high tower). Selah [pause, and calmly think of that]!

9 Men of low degree [in the social scale] are emptiness (futility, a breath) *and* men of high degree [in the same scale] are a lie *and* a delusion. In the balances they go up; they are together lighter than a breath.

10 Trust not in *and* rely confidently not on extortion *and* oppression, and do not vainly hope in robbery; if riches increase, set not your heart on them.

11 God has spoken once, twice have I heard this: that power belongs to God.

12 Also to You, O Lord, belong mercy *and* loving-kindness, for You render to every man according to his work. [Jer. 17:10; Rev. 22:12.]

PSALM 63

A Psalm of David; when he was
in the Wilderness of Judah.

O GOD, you are my God, earnestly will I seek You; my inner self thirsts for You, my flesh longs *and* is faint for You, in a dry and weary land where no water is.

2 So I have looked upon You in the sanctuary to see Your power and Your glory.

3 Because Your loving-kindness is better than life, my lips shall praise You.

4 So will I bless You while I live; I will lift up my hands in Your name.

5 My whole being shall be satisfied as with marrow and fatness; and my mouth shall praise You with joyful lips

6 When I remember You upon my

bed and meditate on You in the night watches.

7 For You have been my help, and in the shadow of Your wings will I rejoice.

8 My whole being follows hard after You *and* clings closely to You; Your right hand upholds me.

9 But those who seek *and* demand my life to ruin and destroy it shall [themselves be destroyed and] go into the lower parts of the earth [into the underworld of the dead].

10 They shall be given over to the power of the sword; they shall be a prey for foxes *and* jackals.

11 But the king shall rejoice in God; everyone who swears by Him [that is, who binds himself by God's authority, acknowledging His supremacy, and devoting himself to His glory and service alone; every such one] shall glory, for the mouths of those who speak lies shall be stopped.

PSALM 64

To the Chief Musician. A Psalm
of David.

H EAR MY voice, O God, in my complaint; guard *and* preserve my life from the terror of the enemy.

2 Hide me from the secret counsel *and* conspiracy of the ungodly, from the scheming of evildoers,

3 Who whet their tongues like a sword, who aim venomous words like arrows,

4 Who shoot from ambush at the blameless man; suddenly do they shoot at him, without self-reproach *or* fear.

5 They encourage themselves in an evil purpose, they talk of laying snares secretly; they say, Who will discover *us*?

6 They think out acts of injustice and say, We have accomplished a well-devised thing! For the inward thought of each one [is unsearchable] and his heart is deep.

7 But God will shoot an unexpected

arrow at them; and suddenly shall they be wounded.

8 And they will be made to stumble, their own tongues turning against them; all who gaze upon them will shake their heads and flee away.

9 And all men shall [reverently] fear and be in awe; and they will declare the work of God, for they will wisely consider and acknowledge that it is His doing.

10 The [uncompromisingly] righteous shall be glad in the Lord and shall trust and take refuge in Him; and all the upright in heart shall glory and offer praise.

PSALM 65
To the Chief Musician. A Psalm of David. A song.

TO YOU belongs silence (the submissive wonder of reverence which bursts forth into praise) and praise is due and fitting to You, O God, in Zion; and to You shall the vow be performed.

2 O You Who hear prayer, to You shall all flesh come.

3 Iniquities and much varied guilt prevail against me; [yet] as for our transgressions, You forgive and purge them away [make atonement for them and cover them out of Your sight]!

4 Blessed (happy, fortunate, to be envied) is the man whom You choose and cause to come near, that he may dwell in Your courts! We shall be satisfied with the goodness of Your house, Your holy temple.

5 By fearful and glorious things [that terrify the wicked but make the godly sing praises] do You answer us in righteousness (rightness and justice), O God of our salvation, You Who are the confidence and hope of all the ends of the earth and of those far off on the seas;

6 Who by [Your] might have founded the mountains, being girded with power,

7 Who still the roaring of the seas, the roaring of their waves, and the tumult of the peoples,

8 So that those who dwell in earth's farthest parts are afraid of [nature's] signs of Your presence. You make the places where morning and evening have birth to shout for joy.

9 You visit the earth and saturate it with water; You greatly enrich it; the river of God is full of water; You provide them with grain when You have so prepared the earth.

10 You water the field's furrows abundantly, You settle the ridges of it; You make the soil soft with showers, blessing the sprouting of its vegetation.

11 You crown the year with Your bounty and goodness, and the tracks of Your [chariot wheels] drip with fatness.

12 The [luxuriant] pastures in the uncultivated country drip [with moisture], and the hills gird themselves with joy.

13 The meadows are clothed with flocks, the valleys also are covered with grain; they shout for joy and sing together.

PSALM 66
To the Chief Musician. A song. A Psalm.

MAKE A joyful noise unto God, all the earth;

2 Sing forth the honor and glory of His name; make His praise glorious!

3 Say to God, How awesome and fearfully glorious are Your works! Through the greatness of Your power shall Your enemies submit themselves to You [with feigned and reluctant obedience].

4 All the earth shall bow down to You and sing [praises] to You; they shall praise Your name in song. Selah [pause, and calmly think of that]!

5 Come and see the works of God; see how [to save His people He smites their foes; He is] terrible in His doings toward the children of men.

6 He turned the sea into dry land, they crossed through the river on foot; there did we rejoice in Him.

7 He rules by His might forever, His eyes observe *and* keep watch *over* the nations; let not the rebellious exalt themselves. Selah [pause, and calmly think of that]!

8 Bless our God, O peoples, give Him grateful thanks *and* make the voice of His praise be heard,

9 Who put *and* kept us among the living, and has not allowed our feet to slip.

10 For You, O God, have proved us; You have tried us as silver is tried, refined, *and* purified.

11 You brought us into the net (the prison fortress, the dungeon); You laid a heavy burden upon our loins.

12 You caused men to ride over our heads [when we were prostrate]; we went through fire and through water, but You brought us out into a broad, moist place [to abundance and refreshment and the open air].

13 I will come into Your house with burnt offerings [of entire consecration]; I will pay You my vows,

14 Which my lips uttered and my mouth promised when I was in distress.

15 I will offer to You burnt offerings of fat lambs, with rams consumed in sweet-smelling smoke; I will offer *bullocks* and he-goats. Selah [pause, and calmly think of that]!

16 Come and hear, all you who reverently *and* worshipfully fear God, and I will declare what He has done for me!

17 I cried aloud to Him; He was extolled *and* high praise was under my tongue.

18 If I regard iniquity in my heart, the Lord will not hear me; [Prov. 15:29; 28:9; Isa. 1:15; John 9:31; James 4:3.]

19 But certainly God has heard me; He has given heed to the voice of my prayer.

20 Blessed be God, Who has not rejected my prayer nor removed His mercy *and* loving-kindness from being [as it always is] with me.

PSALM 67

To the Chief Musician; on stringed instruments. A Psalm. A song.

GOD BE merciful *and* gracious to us and bless us and cause His face to shine upon us *and* among us—Selah [pause, and calmly think of that]!—

2 That Your way may be known upon earth, Your saving power (Your deliverances and Your salvation) among all nations.

3 Let the peoples praise You [turn away from their idols] *and* give thanks to You, O God; let all the peoples praise *and* give thanks to You.

4 O let the nations be glad and sing for joy, for You will judge the peoples fairly and guide, lead, *or* drive the nations upon earth. Selah [pause, and calmly think of that]!

5 Let the peoples praise You [turn away from their idols] *and* give thanks to You, O God; let all the peoples praise *and* give thanks to You!

6 The earth has yielded its harvest [in evidence of God's approval]; God, even our own God, will bless us.

7 God will bless us, and all the ends of the earth shall reverently fear Him.

PSALM 68

To the Chief Musician. A Psalm of David. A song.

GOD IS [already] beginning to arise, and His enemies to scatter; let them also who hate Him flee before Him!

2 As smoke is driven away, so drive them away; as wax melts before the fire, so let the wicked perish before the presence of God.

3 But let the [uncompromisingly] righteous be glad; let them be in high spirits *and* glory before God, yes, let them [jubilantly] rejoice!

4 Sing to God, sing praises to His

name, cast up a highway for Him Who rides through the deserts—His name is the Lord—be in high spirits *and* glory before Him!

5 A father of the fatherless and a judge *and* protector of the widows *is* God in His holy habitation.

6 God places the solitary in families *and* gives the desolate a home in which to dwell; He leads the prisoners out to prosperity; but the rebellious dwell in a parched land.

7 O God, when You went forth before Your people, when You marched through the wilderness—Selah [pause, and calmly think of that]!—

8 The earth trembled, the heavens also poured down [rain] at the presence of God; yonder Sinai quaked at the presence of God, the God of Israel.

9 You, O God, did send a plentiful rain; You did restore *and* confirm Your heritage when it languished *and* was weary.

10 Your flock found a dwelling place in it; You, O God, in Your goodness did provide for the poor *and* needy.

11 The Lord gives the word [of power]; the women who bear *and* publish [the news] are a great host.

12 The kings of the enemies' armies, they flee, they flee! She who tarries at home divides the spoil [left behind].

13 Though you [the slackers] may lie among the sheepfolds [in slothful ease, yet for Israel] the wings of a dove are covered with silver, its pinions excessively green with gold [are trophies taken from the enemy].

14 When the Almighty scattered kings in [the land], it was as when it snows on Zalmon [a wooded hill near Shechem].

15 Is Mount Bashan the high mountain of summits, Mount Bashan [east of the Jordan] the mount of God?

16 Why do you look with grudging *and* envy, you many-peaked mountains, at the mountain [of the city called Zion] which God has desired for His dwelling place? Yes, the Lord will dwell in it forever.

17 The chariots of God are twenty thousand, even thousands upon thousands. The Lord is among them as He was in Sinai, [so also] in the Holy Place (the sanctuary in Jerusalem).

18 [m] You have ascended on high. You have led away captive a train of vanquished foes; You have received gifts of men, yes, of the rebellious also, that the Lord God might dwell there with them. [Eph. 4:8.]

19 Blessed be the Lord, Who bears our burdens *and* carries us day by day, even the God Who is our salvation! Selah [pause, and calmly think of that]!

20 God is to us a God of deliverances *and* salvation; and to God the Lord belongs escape from death [setting us free].

21 But God will shatter the heads of His enemies, the hairy scalp of such a one as goes on still in his trespasses *and* guilty ways.

22 The Lord said, I will bring back [your enemies] from Bashan; I will bring them back from the depths of the [Red] Sea,

23 That you may crush them, dipping your foot in blood, that the tongues of your dogs may have their *share* from the foe.

---

m David sang of the ark of the covenant, which after a great victory was transferred or brought back to Zion. In this fact he sees the principle of the history of the kingdom of God appearing in ever-widening circles and nobler manner. The earthly celebration of victory in battle, with the processional bearing of the ark into the temple, is to him a type of the method and course of the Messiah's kingdom, i.e., the certain triumph of God's kingdom and Christ's ascension to His place of enthronement. So the apostle Paul in Eph. 4:8) is perfectly justified in finding the psalmist's eye directed toward Christ and so interpreting it. The "on high" in the psalm is first of all Mount Zion, but this is a type of heaven, as Paul makes clear (J.P. Lange, *A Commentary*).

24 They see Your goings, O God, even the [solemn processions] of my God, my King, into the sanctuary [in holiness].

25 The singers go in front, the players on instruments last; between them the maidens are playing on tambourines.

26 Bless, give thanks, *and* gratefully praise God in full congregations, even the Lord, O you who are from [Jacob] the fountain of Israel.

27 There is little Benjamin in the lead [in the procession], the princes of Judah and their company, the princes of Zebulun, and the princes of Naphtali.

28 Your God has commanded your strength [your might in His service and impenetrable hardness to temptation]; O God, display Your might *and* strengthen what You have wrought for us!

29 [Out of respect] for Your temple at Jerusalem kings shall bring gifts to You.

30 Rebuke the wild beasts dwelling among the reeds [in Egypt], the herd of bulls (the leaders) with the calves of the peoples; trample underfoot those who lust for tribute money; scatter the peoples who delight in war.

31 Princes shall come out of Egypt; Ethiopia shall hasten to stretch out her hands [with the offerings of submission] to God.

32 Sing to God, O kingdoms of the earth, sing praises to the Lord! Selah [pause, and calmly think of that]!

33 [Sing praises] to Him Who rides upon the heavens, the ancient heavens; behold, He sends forth His voice, His mighty voice.

34 Ascribe power *and* strength to God; His majesty is over Israel, and His strength *and* might are in the skies.

35 O God, awe-inspiring, profoundly impressive, *and* terrible are You out of Your holy places; the God of Israel Himself gives strength and fullness of might to His people. Blessed be God!

PSALM 69

To the Chief Musician; [set to the tune of] "Lilies." [A Psalm] of David.

SAVE ME, O God, for the waters have come up to my neck [they threaten my life].

2 I sink in deep mire, where there is no foothold; I have come into deep waters, where the floods overwhelm me.

3 I am weary with my crying; my throat is parched; my eyes fail with waiting [hopefully] for my God.

4 Those who hate me without cause are more than the hairs of my head; those who would cut me off *and* destroy me, being my enemies wrongfully, are many *and* mighty. I am [forced] to restore what I did not steal. [John 15:25.]

5 O God, You know my folly *and* blundering; my sins *and* my guilt are not hidden from You.

6 Let not those who wait *and* hope *and* look for You, O Lord of hosts, be put to shame through me; let not those who seek *and* inquire for *and* require You [as their vital necessity] be brought to confusion *and* dishonor through me, O God of Israel.

7 Because for Your sake I have borne taunt *and* reproach; confusion *and* shame have covered my face.

8 I have become a stranger to my brethren, and an alien to my mother's children. [John 7:3–5.]

9 For zeal for Your house has eaten me up, and the reproaches *and* insults of those who reproach *and* insult You have fallen upon me. [John 2:17; Rom. 15:3.]

10 When I wept *and* humbled myself with fasting, I was jeered at *and* humiliated;

11 When I made sackcloth my clothing, I became a byword (an object of scorn) to them.

12 They who sit in [the city's] gate talk about me, and I am the song of the drunkards.

13 But as for me, my prayer is to You, O Lord. At an acceptable *and* opportune time, O God, in the multitude of Your mercy *and* the abundance of Your loving-kindness hear me, *and* in the truth *and* faithfulness of Your salvation answer me.

14 Rescue me out of the mire, and let me not sink; let me be delivered from those who hate me and from out of the deep waters.

15 Let not the floodwaters overflow *and* overwhelm me, neither let the deep swallow me up nor the [dug] pit [with water perhaps in the bottom] close its mouth over me.

16 Hear *and* answer me, O Lord, for Your loving-kindness is sweet *and* comforting; according to Your plenteous tender mercy *and* steadfast love turn to me.

17 Hide not Your face from Your servant, for I am in distress; O answer me speedily!

18 Draw close to me and redeem me; ransom *and* set me free because of my enemies [lest they glory in my prolonged distress]!

19 You know my reproach and my shame and my dishonor; my adversaries are all before You [fully known to You].

20 Insults *and* reproach have broken my heart; I am full of heaviness *and* I am distressingly sick. I looked for pity, but there was none, and for comforters, but I found none.

21 They gave me also gall [poisonous and bitter] for my food, and in my thirst they gave me vinegar (a soured wine) to drink. [Matt. 27:34, 48.]

22 Let their own table [with all its abundance and luxury] become a snare to them; and when they are secure in peace [or at their sacrificial feasts, let it become] a trap to them.

23 Let their eyes be darkened so that they cannot see, and make their loins tremble continually [from terror, dismay, and feebleness].

24 Pour out Your indignation upon them, and let the fierceness of Your burning anger catch up with them.

25 Let their habitation *and* their encampment be a desolation; let no one dwell in their tents. [Matt. 23:38; Acts 1:20.]

26 For they pursue *and* persecute him whom You have smitten, and they gossip about those whom You have wounded, [adding] to their grief *and* pain.

27 Let one [unforgiven] perverseness *and* iniquity accumulate upon another for them [in Your book], and let them not come into Your righteousness *or* be justified and acquitted by You.

28 Let them be blotted out of the book of the living *and* the book of life and not be enrolled among the [uncompromisingly] righteous (those upright and in right standing with God). [Rev. 3:4, 5; 20:12, 15; 21:27.]

29 But I am poor, sorrowful, and in pain; let Your salvation, O God, set me up on high.

30 I will praise the name of God with a song and will magnify Him with thanksgiving,

31 And it will please the Lord better than an ox or a bullock that has horns and hoofs.

32 The humble shall see it and be glad; you who seek God, inquiring for *and* requiring Him [as your first need], let your hearts revive *and* live! [Ps. 22:26; 42:1.]

33 For the Lord hears the poor *and* needy and despises not His prisoners (*His miserable and* wounded ones).

34 Let heaven and earth praise Him, the seas and everything that moves in them.

35 For God will save Zion and rebuild the cities of Judah; and [His servants] shall remain *and* dwell there and have it in their possession;

36 The children of His servants

shall inherit it, and those who love His name shall dwell in it.

PSALM 70

To the Chief Musician. [A Psalm] of David, to bring to remembrance *or* make memorial.

MAKE HASTE, O God, to deliver me; make haste to help me, O Lord!

2 Let them be put to shame *and* confounded that seek *and* demand my life; let them be turned backward and brought to confusion *and* dishonor who desire *and* delight in my hurt.

3 Let them be turned back *and* appalled because of their shame *and* disgrace who say, Aha, aha!

4 May all those who seek, inquire of *and* for You, *and* require You [as their vital need] rejoice and be glad in You; and may those who love Your salvation say continually, Let God be magnified!

5 But I am poor and needy; hasten to me, O God! You are my Help and my Deliverer; O Lord, do not tarry!

PSALM 71

IN YOU, O Lord, do I put my trust *and* confidently take refuge; let me never be put to shame *or* confusion!

2 Deliver me in Your righteousness and cause me to escape; bow down Your ear to me and save me!

3 Be to me a rock of refuge in which to dwell, *and* a sheltering stronghold to which I may continually resort, which You have appointed to save me, for You are my Rock and my Fortress.

4 Rescue me, O my God, out of the hand of the wicked, out of the grasp of the unrighteous and ruthless man.

5 For You are my hope; O Lord God, You are my trust from my youth *and* the source of my confidence.

6 Upon You have I leaned *and* relied from birth; You are He Who took me from my mother's womb *and* You have been my benefactor from that day. My praise is continually of You.

7 I am as a wonder *and* surprise to many, but You are my strong refuge.

8 My mouth shall be filled with Your praise and with Your honor all the day.

9 Cast me not off *nor* send me away in the time of old age; forsake me not when my strength is spent *and* my powers fail.

10 For my enemies talk against me; those who watch for my life consult together,

11 Saying, God has forsaken him; pursue *and* persecute and take him, for there is none to deliver him.

12 O God, be not far from me! O my God, make haste to help me!

13 Let them be put to shame and consumed who are adversaries to my life; let them be covered with reproach, scorn, *and* dishonor who seek *and* require my hurt.

14 But I will hope continually, and will praise You yet more and more.

15 My mouth shall tell of Your righteous acts *and* of Your deeds of salvation all the day, for their number is more than I know.

16 I will come in the strength *and* with the mighty acts of the Lord God; I will mention *and* praise Your righteousness, even Yours alone.

17 O God, You have taught me from my youth, and hitherto have I declared Your wondrous works.

18 Yes, even when I am old and gray-headed, O God, forsake me not, [but keep me alive] until I have declared Your mighty strength to [this] generation, and Your might *and* power to all that are to come.

19 Your righteousness also, O God, is very high [reaching to the heavens]; You Who have done great things; O God, who is like You, *or* who is Your equal?

20 You Who have shown us [all] troubles great and sore will quicken us again and will bring us up again from the depths of the earth.

21 Increase my greatness (my honor) and turn and comfort me.

22 I will also praise You with the harp, even Your truth and faithfulness, O my God; unto You will I sing praises with the lyre, O Holy One of Israel.

23 My lips shall shout for joy when I sing praises to You, and my inner being, which You have redeemed.

24 My tongue also shall talk of Your righteousness all the day long; for they are put to shame, for they are confounded, who seek and demand my hurt.

PSALM 72[n]

[A Psalm] for Solomon.

GIVE THE king [knowledge of] Your [way of] judging, O God, and [the spirit of] Your righteousness to the king's son [to control all his actions].

2 Let him judge and govern Your people with righteousness, and Your poor and afflicted ones with judgment and justice.

3 The mountains shall bring peace to the people, and the hills, through [the general establishment of] righteousness.

4 May he judge and defend the poor of the people, deliver the children of the needy, and crush the oppressor,

5 So that they may revere and fear You while the sun and moon endure, throughout all generations.

6 May he [Solomon as a type of King David's greater Son] be like rain that comes down upon the mown grass, like showers that water the earth.

7 In [o]His [Christ's] days shall the [uncompromisingly] righteous flourish and peace abound till there is a moon no longer. [Isa. 11:3–9.]

8 He [Christ] shall have dominion also from sea to sea and from the River [Euphrates] to the ends of the earth. [Zech. 14:9.]

9 Those who dwell in the wilderness shall bow before Him and His enemies shall lick the dust.

10 The kings of Tarshish and of the coasts shall bring offerings; the kings of Sheba and Seba shall offer gifts.

11 Yes, all kings shall fall down before Him, all nations shall serve Him. [Ps. 138:4.]

12 For He delivers the needy when he calls out, the poor also and him who has no helper.

13 He will have pity on the poor and weak and needy and will save the lives of the needy.

14 He will redeem their lives from oppression and fraud and violence, and precious and costly shall their blood be in His sight.

15 And He shall live; and to Him shall be given gold of Sheba; prayer also shall be made for Him and through Him continually, and they shall bless and praise Him all the day long.

16 There shall be abundance of grain in the soil upon the top of the mountains [the least fruitful places in the land]; the fruit of it shall wave like [the forests of] Lebanon [like the inhabitants of] the city shall flourish like grass of the earth.

17 His name shall endure forever; His name shall continue as long as the

n "This psalm, in highly wrought figurative style, describes the reign of a king as 'righteous, universal, beneficent, and perpetual.' By the older Jewish and most of the modern Christian interpreters it has been applied to Christ, Whose reign present and prospective alone corresponds with its statements. As the imagery of the Second Psalm was drawn from the martial character of David's reign, that of this is from the peaceful and prosperous state of Solomon's" (Robert Jamieson, A.R. Fausset and David Brown, A Commentary). "Jesus is here, beyond all doubt, in the glory of His reign, both as He now is and as He shall be revealed in the latter-day glory" (Charles Haddon Spurgeon, The Treasury of David).   o See footnote on Ps. 72:1. The ideal concept of the king and the glorious effects of his reign are described, the fulfillment of which is experienced in Christ.

sun [indeed, His name continues before the sun]. And men shall be blessed *and* bless themselves by Him; all nations shall call Him blessed!

18 Blessed be the Lord God, the God of Israel, Who alone does wondrous things!

19 Blessed be His glorious name forever; let the whole earth be filled with His glory! Amen and Amen!

20 The prayers of David son of Jesse are ended.

BOOK THREE

PSALM 73

A Psalm of Asaph.

TRULY GOD is [only] good to Israel, even to those who are upright *and* pure in heart.

2 But as for me, my feet were almost gone, my steps had well-nigh slipped.

3 For I was envious of the foolish *and* arrogant when I saw the prosperity of the wicked.

4 For they suffer no violent pangs in their death, but their strength is firm.

5 They are not in trouble as other men; neither are they smitten *and* plagued like other men.

6 Therefore pride is about their necks like a chain; violence covers *them* like a garment [like a long, luxurious robe].

7 Their eyes stand out with fatness, they have more than heart could wish; *and* the imaginations of their minds overflow [with follies].

8 They scoff, and wickedly utter oppression; they speak loftily [from on high, maliciously and blasphemously].

9 They set their mouths against *and* speak down from heaven, and their tongues swagger through the earth [invading even heaven with blasphemy and smearing earth with slanders]. [Rev. 13:6.]

10 Therefore His people return here, and waters of a full cup [offered by the wicked] are [blindly] drained by them.

11 And they say, How does God know? Is there knowledge in the Most High?

12 Behold, these are the ungodly, who always prosper *and* are at ease in the world; they increase in riches.

13 Surely then in vain have I cleansed my heart and washed my hands in innocency.

14 For all the day long have I been smitten *and* plagued, and chastened every morning.

15 Had I spoken thus [and given expression to my feelings], I would have been untrue *and* have dealt treacherously against the generation of Your children.

16 But when I considered how to understand this, it was too great an effort for me *and* too painful

17 Until I went into the sanctuary of God; then I understood [for I considered] their end.

18 [After all] You do set the [wicked] in slippery places; You cast them down to ruin *and* destruction.

19 How they become a desolation in a moment! They are utterly consumed with terrors!

20 As a dream [which seems real] until one awakens, so, O Lord, when You arouse Yourself [to take note of the wicked], You will despise their outward show.

21 For my heart was grieved, embittered, *and* in a state of ferment, and I was pricked in my heart [as with the sharp fang of an adder].

22 So foolish, stupid, *and* brutish was I, and ignorant; I was like a beast before You.

23 Nevertheless I am continually with You; You do hold my right hand.

24 You will guide me with Your counsel, and afterward receive me to honor *and* glory.

25 Whom have I in heaven but You? And I have no delight *or* desire on earth besides You.

26 My flesh and my heart may fail, but God is the Rock *and* firm Strength of my heart and my Portion forever.

27 For behold, those who are far from You shall perish; You will destroy all who are false to You *and* like [spiritual] harlots depart from You.

28 But it is good for me to draw near to God; I have put my trust in the Lord God *and* made Him my refuge, that I may tell of all Your works.

PSALM 74

A skillful song, or a didactic or reflective poem, of Asaph.

O GOD, why do You cast us off forever? Why does Your anger burn *and* smoke against the sheep of Your pasture?

2 [Earnestly] remember Your congregation which You have acquired of old, which You have redeemed to be the tribe of Your heritage; remember Mount Zion, where You have dwelt.

3 Direct Your feet [quickly] to the perpetual ruins *and* desolations: the foe has devastated *and* desecrated everything in the sanctuary.

4 In the midst of Your Holy Place Your enemies have roared [with their battle cry]; they set up their own [idol] emblems for signs [of victory].

5 They seemed like men who lifted up axes upon a thicket of trees to make themselves a record.

6 And then all the carved wood of the Holy Place they broke down with hatchets and hammers.

7 They have set Your sanctuary on fire; they have profaned the dwelling place of Your *ᵖ*Name by casting it to the ground.

8 They said in their hearts, Let us make havoc [of such places] altogether. They have burned up all God's meetinghouses in the land.

9 We do not see our symbols; there is no longer any prophet, neither does any among us know for how long.

10 O God, how long is the adversary to scoff *and* reproach? Is the enemy to blaspheme *and* revile Your name forever?

11 Why do You hold back Your hand, even Your right hand? Draw it out of Your bosom *and* consume them [make an end of them]!

12 Yet God is my King of old, working salvation in the midst of the earth.

13 You did divide the [Red] Sea by Your might; You broke the heads of the [Egyptian] dragons in the waters. [Exod. 14:21.]

14 You crushed the heads of Leviathan (Egypt); You did give him as food for the creatures inhabiting the wilderness.

15 You did cleave open [the rock bringing forth] fountains and streams; You dried up mighty, ever-flowing rivers (the Jordan). [Exod. 17:6; Num. 20:11; Josh. 3:13.]

16 The day is Yours, the night also is Yours; You have established the [starry] light and the sun.

17 You have fixed all the borders of the earth [the divisions of land and sea and of the nations]; You have made summer and winter. [Acts 17:26.]

18 [Earnestly] remember how the enemy has scoffed, O Lord, *and* reproached You, and how a foolish *and* impious people has blasphemed Your name.

19 Oh, do not deliver the life of your turtledove to the wild beast (to the greedy multitude); forget not the life [of the multitude] of Your poor forever.

20 Have regard for the covenant [You made with Abraham], for the dark places of the land are full of the habitations of violence.

21 Oh, let not the downtrodden return in shame; let the oppressed and needy praise Your name.

22 Arise, O God, plead Your own

ᵖ See footnote on Deut. 12:5.

cause; remember [earnestly] how the foolish *and* impious man scoffs *and* reproaches You day after day *and* all day long.

23 Do not forget the [clamoring] voices of Your adversaries, the tumult of those who rise up against You, which ascends continually.

PSALM 75

To the Chief Musician; [set
to the tune of] "Do Not Destroy."
A Psalm of Asaph. A song.

W E GIVE praise *and* thanks to You, O God, we praise *and* give thanks; Your wondrous works declare that Your *q*Name is near *and* they who invoke Your Name rehearse Your wonders.

2 When the proper time has come [for executing My judgments], I will judge uprightly [says the Lord].

3 When the earth totters, and all the inhabitants of it, it is I Who will poise *and* keep steady its pillars. Selah [pause, and calmly think of that]!

4 I said to the arrogant *and* boastful, Deal not arrogantly [do not boast]; and to the wicked, Lift up not the horn [of personal aggrandizement].

5 Lift not up your [aggressive] horn on high, speak not with a stiff neck *and* insolent arrogance.

6 For not from the east nor from the west nor from the south come promotion *and* lifting up. [Isa. 14:13.]

7 But God is the Judge! He puts down one and lifts up another.

8 For in the hand of the Lord there is a cup [of His wrath], and the wine foams *and* is red, well mixed; and He pours out from it, and all the wicked of the earth must drain it and drink its dregs. [Ps. 60:3; Jer. 25:15; Rev. 14:9, 10; 16:19.]

9 But I will declare *and* rejoice forever; I will sing praises to the God of Jacob.

10 All the horns of the ungodly also

will I cut off [says the Lord], but the horns of the [uncompromisingly] righteous shall be exalted.

PSALM 76

To the Chief Musician; on stringed
instruments. A Psalm of Asaph.
A song.

I N JUDAH God is known *and* renowned; His name is highly praised *and* is great in Israel.

2 In [Jeru]Salem also is His tabernacle, and His dwelling place is in Zion.

3 There He broke the bow's flashing arrows, the shield, the sword, and the weapons of war. Selah [pause, and calmly think of that]!

4 Glorious *and* excellent are You from the mountains of prey [splendid and majestic, more than the everlasting mountains].

5 The stouthearted are stripped of their spoil, they have slept the sleep [of death]; and none of the men of might could raise their hands.

6 At Your rebuke, O God of Jacob, both chariot [rider] and horse are cast into a dead sleep [of death]. [Exod. 15:1, 21; Nah. 2:13; Zech. 12:4.]

7 You, even You, are to be feared [with awe and reverence]! Who may stand in Your presence when once Your anger is roused?

8 You caused sentence to be heard from heaven; the earth feared and was still—

9 When God arose to [establish] judgment, to save all the meek *and* oppressed of the earth. Selah [pause, and calmly think of that]!

10 Surely the wrath of man shall praise You; the remainder of wrath shall You restrain *and* gird *and* arm Yourself with it.

11 Vow and pay to the Lord your God; let all who are round about Him bring presents to Him Who ought to be [reverently] feared.

q See footnote on Deut. 12:5.

12 He will cut off the spirit [of pride and fury] of princes; He is terrible to the [ungodly] kings of the earth.

PSALM 77

To the Chief Musician; after the
manner of Jeduthun [one of David's
three chief musicians, founder
of an official musical family].
A Psalm of Asaph.

I WILL cry to God with my voice, even to God with my voice, and He will give ear *and* hearken to me.

2 In the day of my trouble I seek (inquire of and desperately require) the Lord; in the night my hand is stretched out [in prayer] without slacking up; I refuse to be comforted.

3 I [earnestly] remember God; I am disquieted *and* I groan; I muse in prayer, and my spirit faints [overwhelmed]. Selah [pause, and calmly think of that]!

4 You hold my eyes from closing; I am so troubled that I cannot speak.

5 I consider the days of old, the years of bygone times [of prosperity].

6 I call to remembrance my song in the night; with my heart I meditate and my spirit searches diligently:

7 Will the Lord cast off forever? And will He be favorable no more?

8 Have His mercy *and* loving-kindness ceased forever? Have His promises ended for all time?

9 Has God [deliberately] abandoned *or* forgotten His graciousness? Has He in anger shut up His compassion? Selah [pause, and calmly think of that]!

10 And I say, This [apparent desertion of Israel by God] is my appointed lot *and* trial, but I will recall the years of the right hand of the Most High [in loving-kindness extended toward us], for this is my grief, that the right hand of the Most High changes.

11 I will [earnestly] recall the deeds of the Lord; yes, I will [earnestly] remember the wonders [You performed for our fathers] of old.

12 I will meditate also upon all Your works and consider all Your [mighty] deeds.

13 Your way, O God, is in the sanctuary [in holiness, away from sin and guilt]. Who is a great God like our God?

14 You are the God Who does wonders; You have demonstrated Your power among the peoples.

15 You have with Your [mighty] arm redeemed Your people, the sons of Jacob and Joseph. Selah [pause, and calmly think of that]!

16 When the waters [at the Red Sea and the Jordan] saw You, O God, they were afraid; the deep shuddered also, for [all] the waters saw You.

17 The clouds poured down water, the skies sent out a sound [of rumbling thunder]; Your arrows went forth [in forked lightning].

18 The voice of Your thunder was in the whirlwind, the lightnings illumined the world; the earth trembled and shook.

19 Your way [in delivering Your people] was through the sea, and Your paths through the great waters, yet Your footsteps were not traceable, *but* were obliterated.

20 You led Your people like a flock by the hand of Moses and Aaron.

PSALM 78

A skillful song, *or* a didactic
or reflective poem, of Asaph.

G IVE EAR, O my people, to my teaching; incline your ears to the words of my mouth.

2 I will open my mouth in a parable (in instruction by numerous examples); I will utter dark sayings of old [that hide important truth]—[Matt. 13:34, 35.]

3 Which we have heard and known, and our fathers have told us.

4 We will not hide them from their children, but we will tell to the generation to come the praiseworthy deeds of

the Lord, and His might, and the wonderful works that He has performed.

5 For He established a testimony (an express precept) in Jacob and appointed a law in Israel, commanding our fathers that they should make [the great facts of God's dealings with Israel] known to their children,

6 That the generation to come might know them, that the children still to be born might arise and recount them to their children,

7 That they might set their hope in God and not forget the works of God, but might keep His commandments

8 And might not be as their fathers—a stubborn and rebellious generation, a generation that set not their hearts aright *nor* prepared their hearts to know God, and whose spirits were not steadfast and faithful to God.

9 The children of Ephraim were armed and carrying bows, yet they turned back in the day of battle.

10 They kept not the covenant of God and refused to walk according to His law

11 And forgot His works and His wonders that He had shown them.

12 Marvelous things did He in the sight of their fathers in the land of Egypt, in the field of Zoan [where Pharaoh resided].

13 He divided the [Red] Sea and caused them to pass through it, and He made the waters stand like a heap. [Exod. 14:22.]

14 In the daytime also He led them with a [pillar of] cloud and all the night with a light of fire. [Exod. 13:21; 14:24.]

15 He split rocks in the wilderness and gave them drink abundantly as out of the deep.

16 He brought streams also out of the rock [at Rephidim and Kadesh] and caused waters to run down like rivers. [Exod. 17:6; Num. 20:11.]

17 Yet they still went on to sin against Him by provoking *and* rebelling against the Most High in the wilderness (in the land of drought).

18 And they tempted God in their hearts by asking for food according to their [selfish] desire *and* appetite.

19 Yes, they spoke against God; they said, Can God furnish [the food for] a table in the wilderness?

20 Behold, He did smite the rock so that waters gushed out and the streams overflowed; but can He give bread also? Can He provide flesh for His people?

21 Therefore, when the Lord heard, He was [full of] wrath; a fire was kindled against Jacob, His anger mounted up against Israel,

22 Because in God they believed not [they relied not on Him, they adhered not to Him], and they trusted not in His salvation (His power to save).

23 Yet He commanded the clouds above and opened the doors of heaven;

24 And He rained down upon them manna to eat and gave them heaven's grain. [Exod. 16:14; John 6:31.]

25 Everyone ate the bread of the mighty [man ate angels' food]; God sent them meat in abundance.

26 He let forth the east wind to blow in the heavens, and by His power He guided the south wind.

27 He rained flesh also upon them like the dust, and winged birds [quails] like the sand of the seas. [Num. 11:31.]

28 And He let [the birds] fall in the midst of their camp, round about their tents.

29 So they ate and were well filled; He gave them what they craved *and* lusted after.

30 But scarce had they stilled their craving, and while their meat was yet in their mouths, [Num. 11:33.]

31 The wrath of God came upon them and slew the strongest *and* sturdiest of them and smote down Israel's chosen youth.

32 In spite of all this, they sinned still more, for they believed not in (re-

lied not on and adhered not to Him for) His wondrous works.

33 Therefore their days He consumed like a breath [in emptiness, falsity, and futility] and their years in terror and sudden haste.

34 When He slew [some of] them, [the remainder] inquired after Him diligently, and they repented and sincerely sought God [for a time].

35 And they [earnestly] remembered that God was their Rock, and the Most High God their Redeemer.

36 Nevertheless they flattered Him with their mouths and lied to Him with their tongues.

37 For their hearts were not right or sincere with Him, neither were they faithful and steadfast to His covenant. [Acts 8:21.]

38 But He, full of [merciful] compassion, forgave their iniquity and destroyed them not; yes, many a time He turned His anger away and did not stir up all His wrath and indignation.

39 For He [earnestly] remembered that they were but flesh, a wind that goes and does not return.

40 How often they defied and rebelled against Him in the wilderness and grieved Him in the desert!

41 And time and again they turned back and tempted God, provoking and incensing the Holy One of Israel.

42 They remembered not [seriously the miracles of the working of] His hand, nor the day when He delivered them from the enemy,

43 How He wrought His miracles in Egypt and His wonders in the field of Zoan [where Pharaoh resided]

44 And turned their rivers into blood, and their streams, so that they could not drink from them.

45 He sent swarms of [venomous] flies among them which devoured them, and frogs which destroyed them.

46 He gave also their crops to the caterpillar and [the fruit of] their labor to the locust.

47 He destroyed their vines with hail and their sycamore trees with frost and [great chunks of] ice.

48 He [caused them to shut up their cattle or] gave them up also to the hail and their flocks to hot thunderbolts. [Exod. 9:18-21.]

49 He let loose upon them the fierceness of His anger, His wrath and indignation and distress, by sending [a mission of] angels of calamity and woe among them.

50 He leveled and made a straight path for His anger [to give it free course]; He did not spare [the Egyptian families] from death but gave their beasts over to the pestilence and the life [of their eldest] over to the plague.

51 He smote all the firstborn in Egypt, the chief of their strength in the tents [of the land of the sons] of Ham.

52 But [God] led His own people forth like sheep and guided them [with a shepherd's care] like a flock in the wilderness.

53 And He led them on safely and in confident trust, so that they feared not; but the sea overwhelmed their enemies. [Exod. 14:27, 28.]

54 And He brought them to His holy border, the border of [Canaan] His sanctuary, even to this mountain [Zion] which His right hand had acquired.

55 He drove out the nations also before [Israel] and allotted their land as a heritage, measured out and partitioned; and He made the tribes of Israel to dwell in the tents of those dispossessed.

56 Yet they tempted and provoked and rebelled against the Most High God and kept not His testimonies.

57 But they turned back and dealt unfaithfully and treacherously like their fathers; they were twisted like a warped and deceitful bow [that will not respond to the archer's aim].

58 For they provoked Him to [righteous] anger with their high places [for

idol worship] and moved Him to jealousy with their graven images.

59 When God heard this, He was full of [holy] wrath; and He utterly rejected Israel, greatly abhorring *and* loathing [her ways].

60 So that He forsook the tabernacle at Shiloh, the tent in which He had dwelt among men [and never returned to it again],

61 And delivered His strength *and* power (the ark of the covenant) into captivity, and His glory into the hands of the foe (the Philistines). [I Sam. 4:21.]

62 He gave His people over also to the sword and was wroth with His heritage [Israel]. [I Sam. 4:10.]

63 The fire [of war] devoured their young men, and their bereaved virgins were not praised in a wedding song.

64 Their priests [Hophni and Phinehas] fell by the sword, and their widows made no lamentation [for the bodies came not back from the scene of battle, and the widow of Phinehas also died that day]. [I Sam. 4:11, 19, 20.]

65 Then the Lord awakened as from sleep, as a strong man whose consciousness of power is heightened by wine.

66 And He smote His adversaries in the back [as they fled]; He put them to lasting shame and reproach.

67 Moreover, He rejected the tent of Joseph and chose not the tribe of Ephraim [in which the tabernacle had been accustomed to stand].

68 But He chose the tribe of Judah [as Israel's leader], Mount Zion, which He loved [to replace Shiloh as His capital].

69 And He built His sanctuary [exalted] like the heights [of the heavens] and like the earth which He established forever.

70 He chose David His servant and took him from the sheepfolds; [I Sam. 16:11, 12.]

71 From tending the ewes that had

their young He brought him to be the shepherd of Jacob His people, of Israel His inheritance. [II Sam. 7:7, 8.]

72 So [David] was their shepherd with an upright heart; he guided them by the discernment *and* skillfulness [which controlled] his hands.

PSALM 79

A Psalm of Asaph.

O GOD, the nations have come into [the land of Your people] Your inheritance; Your sacred temple have they defiled; they have made Jerusalem heaps of ruins.

2 The dead bodies of Your servants they have given as food to the birds of the heavens, the flesh of Your saints to the beasts of the earth.

3 Their blood they have poured out like water round about Jerusalem, and there was none to bury them.

4 [Because of such humiliation] we have become a taunt *and* reproach to our neighbors, a mocking and derision to those who are round about us.

5 How long, O Lord? Will You be angry forever? Shall Your jealousy [which cannot endure a divided allegiance] burn like fire?

6 Pour out Your wrath on the Gentile nations who do not acknowledge You, and upon the kingdoms that do not call on Your name. [II Thess. 1:8.]

7 For they have devoured Jacob and laid waste his dwelling *and* his pasture.

8 O do not [earnestly] remember against us the iniquities *and* guilt of our forefathers! Let Your compassion *and* tender mercy speedily come to meet us, for we are brought very low.

9 Help us, O God of our salvation, for the glory of Your name! Deliver us, forgive us, *and* purge away our sins for Your name's sake.

10 Why should the Gentile nations say, Where is their God? Let vengeance for the blood of Your servants

which is poured out be known among the nations in our sight [not delaying until some future generation]!

11 Let the groaning *and* sighing of the prisoner come before You; according to the greatness of Your power *and* Your arm spare those who are appointed to die!

12 And return into the bosom of our neighbors sevenfold the taunts with which they have taunted *and* scoffed at You, O Lord!

13 Then we Your people, the sheep of Your pasture, will give You thanks forever; we will show forth *and* publish Your praise from generation to generation.

PSALM 80

To the Chief Musician; [set to the tune of "Lilies, a Testimony." A Psalm of Asaph.

GIVE EAR, O Shepherd of Israel, You Who lead Joseph like a flock; You Who sit enthroned upon the cherubim [of the ark of the covenant], shine forth

2 Before 'Ephraim and Benjamin and Manasseh! Stir up Your might, and come to save us!

3 Restore us again, O God; and cause Your face to shine [in pleasure and approval on us], and we shall be saved!

4 O Lord God of hosts, how long will You be angry with Your people's prayers?

5 You have fed them with the bread of tears, and You have given them tears to drink in large measure.

6 *You* make us a strife *and* scorn to our neighbors, and our enemies laugh among themselves.

7 Restore us again, O God of hosts;

and cause Your face to shine [upon us with favor as of old], and we shall be saved!

8 You brought a vine [Israel] out of Egypt; You drove out the [heathen] nations and planted it [in Canaan].

9 You prepared room before it, and it took deep root and it filled the land.

10 The mountains were covered with the shadow of it, and the boughs of it were like the great cedars [cedars of God].

11 [Israel] sent out its boughs to the [Mediterranean] Sea and its branches to the [Euphrates] River. [I Kings 4:21.]

12 Why have You broken down its hedges *and* walls so that all who pass by pluck from its fruit?

13 The boar out of the wood wastes it and the wild beast of the field feeds on it.

14 Turn again, we beseech You, O God of hosts! Look down from heaven and see, visit, *and* have regard for this vine!

15 [Protect and maintain] the stock which Your right hand planted, and the branch (the son) that You have reared *and* made strong for Yourself.

16 They have burned it with fire, it is cut down; may they perish at the rebuke of Your countenance.

17 Let Your hand be upon the man of Your right hand, upon the son of man whom You have made strong for Yourself.

18 Then will we not depart from You; revive us (give us life) and we will call upon Your name.

19 Restore us, O Lord God of hosts; cause Your face to shine [in pleasure, approval, and favor on us], and we shall be saved!

r It is supposed that these three tribes represented the whole twelve tribes of Israel, Benjamin being incorporated with Judah, Manasseh embracing the country beyond the Jordan, and Ephraim the remainder. It was natural for the Israelites to think of the three in one group, for they had camped together on the west side of the tabernacle during the years in the wilderness, and also they were the only descendants of Jacob's wife Rachel.

PSALM 81

To the Chief Musician; set
to Philistine lute, or [possibly]
a particular Gittite tune. [A Psalm]
of Asaph.

SING ALOUD to God our Strength!
Shout for joy to the God of Jacob!

2 Raise a song, sound the timbrel,
the sweet lyre with the harp.

3 Blow the trumpet at the New
Moon, at the full moon, on our feast
day.

4 For this is a statute for Israel, an
ordinance of the God of Jacob.

5 This He ordained in Joseph [the
ˢ savior] for a testimony when He
went out over the land of Egypt. The
speech of One Whom I knew not did
I hear [saying],

6 I removed his shoulder from the
burden; his hands were freed from the
basket.

7 You called in distress and I delivered you; I answered you in the secret
place of thunder; I tested you at the
waters of Meribah. Selah [pause, and
calmly think of that]! [Num. 20:3,
13, 24.]

8 Hear, O My people, and I will ad-
monish you—O Israel, if you would
listen to Me!

9 There shall no strange god be
among you, neither shall you worship
any alien god.

10 I am the Lord your God, Who
brought you up out of the land of
Egypt. Open your mouth wide and I
will fill it.

11 But My people would not
hearken to My voice, and Israel would
have none of Me.

12 So I gave them up to their own
hearts' lust *and* let them go after their
own stubborn will, that they might follow their own counsels. [Acts 7:42,
43; 14:16; Rom. 1:24, 26.]

13 Oh, that My people would listen
to Me, that Israel would walk in My
ways!

14 Speedily then I would subdue
their enemies and turn My hand
against their adversaries.

15 [Had Israel listened to Me in
Egypt, then] those who hated the Lord
would have come cringing before
Him, and their defeat would have last-
ed forever.

16 [God] would feed [Israel now]
also with the finest of the wheat; and
with honey out of the rock would I
satisfy them.

PSALM 82

A Psalm of Asaph.

GOD STANDS in the assembly [of
the representatives] of God; in
the midst of the magistrates *or* judges
He gives judgment [as] among the
gods.

2 How long will you [magistrates
or judges] judge unjustly and show
partiality to the wicked? Selah [pause,
and calmly think of that]!

3 Do justice to the weak (poor) and
fatherless; maintain the rights of the
afflicted and needy.

4 Deliver the poor and needy; rescue them out of the hand of the
wicked.

5 [The magistrates and judges]
know not, neither will they understand; they walk on in the darkness [of
complacent satisfaction]; all the foundations of the earth [the fundamental
principles upon which rests the admin-
istration of justice] are shaking.

6 I said, You are gods [since you
judge on My behalf, as My representa-

ˢ Joseph had once gone out over Egypt with the title "Zaphenath-paneah," meaning, according to some,
"Savior of the Age," to bring deliverance from famine to the Egyptians (Gen. 41:45). Later they forgot
their benefactor and severely oppressed his family and their descendants. "Then Joseph's God arose and
went forth over the land [of Egypt] in righteous judgment, yet still as Savior of that people [Israel], in
whom dwelt the germ of blessing for all nations." (David M. Kay, cited by James C. Gray and George M.
Adams, *Bible Commentary*).

tives]; indeed, all of you are children of the Most High. [John 10:34–36; Rom. 13:1, 2.]

7 But you shall die as men and fall as one of the princes.

8 Arise, O God, judge the earth! For to You belong all the nations. [Rev. 11:15.]

PSALM 83

A song. A Psalm of Asaph.

KEEP NOT silence, O God; hold not Your peace or be still, O God.

2 For, behold, Your enemies are in tumult, and those who hate You have raised their heads. [Acts 4:25, 26.]

3 They lay crafty schemes against Your people and consult together against Your hidden *and* precious ones.

4 They have said, Come, and let us wipe them out as a nation; let the name of Israel be in remembrance no more.

5 For they have consulted together with one accord *and* one heart; against You they make a covenant—

6 The tents of Edom and the Ishmaelites, of Moab and the Hagrites,

7 Gebal and Ammon and Amalek, the Philistines, with the inhabitants of Tyre.

8 Assyria also has joined with them; they have helped the children of Lot [the Ammonites and the Moabites] *and* have been an arm to them. Selah [pause, and calmly think of that!]

9 Do to them as [You did to] the Midianites, as to Sisera and Jabin at the brook of Kishon, [Judg. 4:12–24.]

10 Who perished at Endor, who became like manure for the earth.

11 Make their nobles like Oreb and Zeeb, yes, all their princes as Zebah and Zalmunna, [Judg. 7:23–25; 8:10–21.]

12 Who say, Let us take possession for ourselves of the pastures of God.

13 O my God, make them like whirling dust, like stubble *or* chaff before the wind!

14 As fire consumes the forest, and as the flame sets the mountains ablaze,

15 So pursue *and* afflict them with Your tempest and terrify them with Your tornado *or* hurricane.

16 Fill their faces with shame, that they may seek, inquire for, *and* insistently require Your name, O Lord.

17 Let them be put to shame and dismayed forever; yes, let them be put to shame and perish,

18 That they may know that You, Whose name alone is the Lord, are the Most High over all the earth.

PSALM 84

To the Chief Musician; set
to a Philistine lute, or [possibly]
a particular Gittite tune. A Psalm
of the sons of Korah.

HOW LOVELY are Your tabernacles, O Lord of hosts!

2 My soul yearns, yes, even pines *and* is homesick for the courts of the Lord; my heart and my flesh cry out *and* sing for joy to the living God.

3 Yes, the sparrow has found a house, and the swallow a nest for herself, where she may lay her young—even Your altars, O Lord of hosts, my King and my God.

4 Blessed (happy, fortunate, to be envied) are those who dwell in Your house *and* Your presence; they will be singing Your praises all the day long. Selah [pause, and calmly think of that]!

5 Blessed (happy, fortunate, to be envied) is the man whose strength is in You, in whose heart are the highways to Zion.

6 Passing through the Valley of Weeping (Baca), they make it a place of springs; the early rain also fills [the pools] with blessings.

7 They go from strength to strength [increasing in victorious power]; each of them appears before God in Zion.

8 O Lord God of hosts, hear my

prayer; give ear, O God of Jacob! Selah [pause, and calmly think of that]!

9 Behold our shield [the king as Your agent], O God, and look upon the face of Your anointed!

10 For a day in Your courts is better than a thousand [anywhere else]; I would rather be a doorkeeper *and* stand at the threshold in the house of my God than to dwell [at ease] in the tents of wickedness.

11 For the Lord God is a Sun and Shield; the Lord bestows [present] grace *and* favor and [future] glory (honor, splendor, and heavenly bliss)! No good thing will He withhold from those who walk uprightly.

12 O Lord of hosts, blessed (happy, fortunate, to be envied) is the man who trusts in You [leaning and believing on You, committing all and confidently looking to You, and that without fear or misgiving]!

PSALM 85

To the Chief Musician. A Psalm
of the sons of Korah.

LORD, YOU have [at last] been favorable *and* have dealt graciously with Your land [of Canaan]; You have brought back [from Babylon] the captives of Jacob.

2 You have forgiven *and* taken away the iniquity of Your people, You have covered all their sin. Selah [pause, and calmly realize what that means]!

3 You have withdrawn all Your wrath *and* indignation, You have turned away from the blazing anger [which You had let loose].

4 Restore us, O God of our salvation, and cause Your anger toward us to cease [forever].

5 Will You be angry with us forever? Will You prolong Your anger [and disfavor] *and* spread it out to all generations?

6 Will You not revive us again, that Your people may rejoice in You?

7 Show us Your mercy *and* lovingkindness, O Lord, and grant us Your salvation.

8 I will listen [with expectancy] to what God the Lord will say, for He will speak peace to His people, to His saints (those who are in right standing with Him)—but let them not turn again to [self-confident] folly.

9 Surely His salvation is near to those who reverently *and* worshipfully fear Him, [and is ready to be appropriated] that [the manifest presence of God, His] glory may tabernacle *and* abide in our land.

10 Mercy *and* loving-kindness and truth have met together; righteousness and peace have kissed each other.

11 Truth shall spring up from the earth, and righteousness shall look down from heaven.

12 Yes, the Lord will give what is good, and our land will yield its increase.

13 Righteousness shall go before Him and shall make His footsteps a way in which to walk.

PSALM 86

A Prayer of David.

INCLINE YOUR ear, O Lord, and answer me, for I am poor *and* distressed, needy *and* desiring.

2 Preserve my life, for I am godly *and* dedicated; O my God, save Your servant, for I trust in You [leaning and believing on You, committing all and confidently looking to You, without fear or doubt].

3 Be merciful *and* gracious to me, O Lord, for to You do I cry all the day.

4 Make me, Your servant, to rejoice, O Lord, for to You do I lift myself up.

5 For You, O Lord, are good, and ready to forgive [our trespasses, sending them away, letting them go completely and forever]; and You are abundant in mercy *and* loving-kindness to all those who call upon You.

6 Give ear, O Lord, to my prayer; and listen to the cry of my supplications.

7 In the day of my trouble I will call on You, for You will answer me.

8 There is none like unto You among the gods, O Lord, neither are their works like unto Yours.

9 All nations whom You have made shall come and fall down before You, O Lord; and they shall glorify Your name.

10 For You are great and work wonders! You alone are God.

11 Teach me Your way, O Lord, that I may walk *and* live in Your truth; direct *and* unite my heart [solely, reverently] to fear *and* honor Your name. [Ps. 5:11; 69:36.]

12 I will confess *and* praise You, O Lord my God, with my whole (united) heart; and I will glorify Your name forevermore.

13 For great is Your mercy *and* loving-kindness toward me; and You have delivered me from the depths of Sheol [from the exceeding depths of affliction].

14 O God, the proud *and* insolent are risen against me; a rabble of violent *and* ruthless men has sought *and* demanded my life, and they have not set You before them.

15 But You, O Lord, are a God merciful and gracious, slow to anger and abounding in mercy *and* lovingkindness and truth.

16 O turn to me and have mercy *and* be gracious to me; grant strength (might *and* inflexibility to temptation) to Your servant and save the son of Your handmaiden.

17 Show me a sign of [Your evident] goodwill *and* favor, that those who hate me may see it and be put to shame, because You, Lord, [will show Your approval of me when You] help and comfort me.

PSALM 87

A Psalm of the sons of Korah. A song.

O**N THE** holy hills stands the city [of Jerusalem and the temple] God founded.

2 The Lord loves the gates of Zion [through which the crowds of pilgrims enter from all nations] more than all the dwellings of Jacob (Israel).

3 Glorious things are spoken of you, O city of God. Selah [pause, and calmly realize what that means]!

4 I will make mention of Rahab [the poetic name for Egypt] and Babylon as among those who know [the city of God] — behold, Philistia and Tyre, with Ethiopia (Cush) — [saying], This man was born there.

5 Yes, of Zion it shall be said, This man and that man were born in her, for the Most High Himself will establish her.

6 The Lord shall count, when He registers the peoples, that this man was born there. Selah [pause, and calmly think of that]!

7 The singers as well as the players on instruments shall say, All my springs (my sources of life and joy) are in you [city of our God].

PSALM 88

A song. A Psalm of the sons of Korah. To the Chief Musician; set to chant mournfully. A didactic or reflective poem of Heman the Ezrahite.

O **LORD,** the God of my salvation, I have cried to You for help by day; at night I am in Your presence. [Luke 18:7.]

2 Let my prayer come before You *and* really enter into Your presence; incline Your ear to my cry!

3 For I am full of troubles, and my life draws near to Sheol (the place of the dead).

4 I am counted among those who go down into the pit (the grave); I am like

a man who has no help *or* strength [a mere shadow],

5 Cast away among the dead, like the slain that lie in a [nameless] grave, whom You [seriously] remember no more, and they are cut off from Your hand.

6 You have laid me in the depths of the lowest pit, in darkness, in the deeps.

7 Your wrath lies hard upon me, and You have afflicted me with all Your waves. Selah [pause, and calmly think of that]! [Ps. 42:7.]

8 You have put my [familiar] friends far from me; You have made me an abomination to them. I am shut up, and I cannot come forth.

9 My eye grows dim because of sorrow *and* affliction. Lord, I have called daily on You; I have spread forth my hands to You.

10 Will You show wonders to the dead? Shall the departed arise and praise You? Selah [pause, and calmly think of that]!

11 Shall Your steadfast love be declared in the grave? Or Your faithfulness in Abaddon (Sheol, as a place of ruin and destruction)?

12 Shall Your wonders be known in the dark? And Your righteousness in the place of forgetfulness [where the dead forget and are forgotten]?

13 But to You I cry, O Lord; and in the morning shall my prayer come to meet You.

14 Lord, why do You cast me off? Why do You hide Your face from me? [Matt. 27:46.]

15 I am afflicted and close to death from my youth up; while I suffer Your terrors I am distracted [I faint].

16 Your fierce wrath has swept over me; Your terrors have destroyed me.

17 They surround me like a flood all day long; together they have closed in upon me.

18 Lover and friend have You put far from me; my familiar friends are darkness *and* the grave.

PSALM 89
A skillful song, *or* a didactic *or* reflective poem, of Ethan the Ezrahite.

I WILL sing of the mercy *and* loving-kindness of the Lord forever; with my mouth will I make known Your faithfulness from generation to generation.

2 For I have said, Mercy *and* loving-kindness shall be built up forever; Your faithfulness will You establish in the very heavens [unchangeable and perpetual].

3 [You have said] I have made a ᵗcovenant with My chosen one, I have sworn to David My servant,

4 Your Seed I will establish forever, and I will build up your throne for all generations. Selah [pause, and calmly think of that]! [Isa. 9:7; Luke 1:32, 33; Gal. 3:16]

5 Let heaven (the angels) praise Your wonders, O Lord, Your faithfulness also in the assembly of the holy ones (the holy angels).

6 For who in the heavens can be compared to the Lord? Who among the mighty [heavenly beings] can be likened to the Lord?

7 A God greatly feared *and* revered in the council of the holy (angelic) ones, and to be feared *and* worshipfully revered above all those who are round about Him?

8 O Lord God of hosts, who is a

---

t "This covenant most incontestably had Jesus Christ in view. This is the Seed or Posterity Who would sit on the throne and reign forever and ever. David and his family have long since become extinct; none of his race has sat on the Jewish throne for more than two thousand years. But the Christ . . . will reign until all His enemies are put under His feet (Ps. 110:1; I Cor. 15:25, 27; Eph. 1:22); and to this the psalmist says, Selah." (One of many similar 19th-century comments.)

mighty one like unto You, O Lord? And Your faithfulness is round about You [an essential part of You at all times].

9 You rule the raging of the sea; when its waves arise, You still them.

10 You have broken Rahab (Egypt) in pieces; with Your mighty arm You have scattered Your enemies.

11 The heavens are Yours, the earth also is Yours; the world and all that is in it, You have founded them.

12 The north and the south, You have created them; Mount Tabor and Mount Hermon joyously praise Your name.

13 You have a mighty arm; strong is Your hand, Your right hand is soaring high.

14 Righteousness and justice are the foundation of Your throne; mercy *and* loving-kindness and truth go before Your face.

15 Blessed (happy, fortunate, to be envied) are the people who know the joyful sound [who understand and appreciate the spiritual blessings symbolized by the feasts]; they walk, O Lord, in the light *and* favor of Your countenance!

16 In Your name they rejoice all the day, and in Your righteousness they are exalted.

17 For You are the glory of their strength [their proud adornment], and by Your favor our horn is exalted *and* we walk with uplifted faces!

18 For our shield belongs to the Lord, and our king to the Holy One of Israel.

19 Once You spoke in a vision to Your devoted ones and said, I have endowed one who is mighty [a hero, giving him the power to help—to be a champion for Israel]; I have exalted one chosen from among the people.

20 I have found David My servant; with My holy oil have I anointed him, [Acts 13:22.]

21 With whom My hand shall be established *and* ever abide; My arm also shall strengthen him.

22 The enemy shall not exact from him *or* do him violence *or* outwit him, nor shall the wicked afflict *and* humble him.

23 I will beat down his foes before his face and smite those who hate him.

24 My faithfulness and My mercy *and* loving-kindness shall be with him, and in My name shall his horn be exalted [great power and prosperity shall be conferred upon him].

25 I will set his hand in control also on the [Mediterranean] Sea, and his right hand on the rivers [Euphrates with its tributaries].

26 He shall cry to Me, You are my Father, my God, and the Rock of my salvation!

27 Also I will make him the firstborn, the highest of the kings of the earth. [Rev. 1:5.]

28 My mercy *and* loving-kindness will I keep for him forevermore, and My covenant shall stand fast *and* be faithful with him.

29 His *Offspring also will I make to endure forever, and his throne as the days of heaven. [Isa. 9:7; Gal. 3:16.]

30 If his children forsake My law and walk not in My ordinances,

31 If they break *or* profane My statutes and keep not My commandments,

32 Then will I punish their transgression with the rod [of chastisement], and their iniquity with stripes. [II Sam. 7:14.]

33 Nevertheless, My loving-kindness will I not break off from him, nor allow My faithfulness to fail [to lie and be false to him].

34 My covenant will I not break *or* profane, nor alter the thing that is gone out of My lips.

35 Once [for all] have I sworn by My holiness, which cannot be violated; I will not lie to David:

u See footnote on Ps. 89:3.

36 His Offspring shall endure forever, and his throne [shall continue] as the sun before Me. [Isa. 9:7; Gal. 3:16.]

37 It shall be established forever as the moon, the faithful witness in the heavens. Selah [pause, and calmly think of that]! [Rev. 1:5; 3:14.]

38 But [in apparent contradiction to all this] You [even You the faithful Lord] have cast off and rejected; You have been full of wrath against Your anointed.

39 You have despised and loathed and renounced the covenant with Your servant; You have profaned his crown by casting it to the ground.

40 You have broken down all his hedges and his walls; You have brought his strongholds to ruin.

41 All who pass along the road spoil and rob him; he has become the scorn and reproach of his neighbors.

42 You have exalted the right hand of his foes; You have made all his enemies rejoice.

43 Moreover, You have turned back the edge of his sword and have not made him to stand in battle.

44 You have made his glory and splendor to cease and have hurled to the ground his throne.

45 The days of his youth have You shortened; You have covered him with shame. Selah [pause, and calmly think of that]!

46 How long, O Lord? Will You hide Yourself forever? How long shall Your wrath burn like fire?

47 O [earnestly] remember how short my time is and what a mere fleeting life mine is. For what emptiness, falsity, futility, and frailty You have created all men!

48 What man can live and shall not see death, or can deliver himself from the [powerful] hand of Sheol (the place of the dead)? Selah [pause, and calmly consider that]!

49 Lord, where are Your former loving-kindnesses [shown in the reigns of David and Solomon], which You swore to David in Your faithfulness?

50 Remember, Lord, and earnestly imprint [on Your heart] the reproach of Your servants, scorned and insulted, how I bear in my bosom the reproach of all the many and mighty peoples,

51 With which Your enemies have taunted, O Lord, with which they have mocked the footsteps of Your anointed.

52 Blessed be the Lord forevermore! Amen and Amen.

BOOK FOUR

PSALM 90

A Prayer of Moses the man of God.

LORD, YOU have been our dwelling place and our refuge in all generations [says Moses].

2 Before the mountains were brought forth or ever You had formed and given birth to the earth and the world, even from everlasting to everlasting You are God.

3 You turn man back to dust and corruption, and say, Return, O sons of the earthborn [to the earth]!

4 For a thousand years in Your sight are but as yesterday when it is past, or as a watch in the night. [II Pet. 3:8.]

5 You carry away [these disobedient people, doomed to die within forty years] as with a flood; they are as a sleep [vague and forgotten as soon as they are gone]. In the morning they are like grass which grows up—

6 In the morning it flourishes and springs up; in the evening it is mown down and withers.

7 For we [the Israelites in the wilderness] are consumed by Your anger, and by Your wrath are we troubled, overwhelmed, and frightened away.

8 Our iniquities, our secret heart and its sins [which we would so like to conceal even from ourselves], You

have set in the [revealing] light of Your countenance.

9 For all our days [out here in this wilderness, says Moses] pass away in Your wrath; we spend our years as a tale that is told [for we adults know we are doomed to die soon, without reaching Canaan]. [Num. 14:26–35.]

10 The days of our years are ᵛthreescore years and ten (seventy years)—or even, if by reason of strength, fourscore years (eighty years); yet is their pride [in additional years] only labor and sorrow, for it is soon gone, and we fly away.

11 Who knows the power of Your anger? [Who worthily connects this brevity of life with Your recognition of sin?] And Your wrath, who connects it with the reverent and worshipful fear that is due You?

12 So teach us to number our days, that we may get us a heart of wisdom.

13 Turn, O Lord [from Your fierce anger]! How long—? Revoke Your sentence and be compassionate and at ease toward Your servants.

14 O satisfy us with Your mercy and loving-kindness in the morning [now, before we are older], that we may rejoice and be glad all our days.

15 Make us glad in proportion to the days in which You have afflicted us and to the years in which we have suffered evil.

16 Let Your work [the signs of Your power] be revealed to Your servants, and Your [glorious] majesty to their children.

17 And let the beauty and delightfulness and favor of the Lord our God be upon us; confirm and establish the work of our hands—yes, the work of our hands, confirm and establish it.

PSALM 91

HE WHO ᵂdwells in the secret place of the Most High shall remain stable and fixed under the shadow of the Almighty [Whose power no foe can withstand].

2 I will say of the Lord, He is my Refuge and my Fortress, my God; on Him I lean and rely, and in Him I [confidently] trust!

3 For [then] He will deliver you from the snare of the fowler and from the deadly pestilence.

4 [Then] He will cover you with His pinions, and under His wings shall you trust and find refuge; His truth and His faithfulness are a shield and a buckler.

5 You shall not be afraid of the terror of the night, nor of the arrow (the evil plots and slanders of the wicked) that flies by day,

6 Nor of the pestilence that stalks in darkness, nor of the destruction and sudden death that surprise and lay waste at noonday.

7 A thousand may fall at your side, and ten thousand at your right hand, but it shall not come near you.

8 Only a spectator shall you be [yourself inaccessible in the secret place of the Most High] as you witness the reward of the wicked.

9 Because you have made the Lord

---

v This psalm is credited to Moses, who is interceding with God to remove the curse which made it necessary for every Israelite over twenty years of age (when they rebelled against God at Kadesh-barnea) to die before reaching the promised land (Num. 14:26-35). Moses says most of them are dying at seventy years of age. This number has often been mistaken as a set span of life for all mankind. It was not intended to refer to anyone except those Israelites under the curse during that particular forty years. Seventy years never has been the average span of life for humanity. When Jacob, the father of the twelve tribes, had reached 130 years (Gen. 47:9), he complained that he had not attained to the years of his immediate ancestors. In fact, Moses himself lived to be 120 years old, Aaron 123, Miriam several years older, and Joshua 110 years of age. Note as well that in the Millennium a person dying at 100 will still be thought a child (Isa. 65:20).   w The rich promises of this whole chapter are dependent upon one's meeting exactly the conditions of these first two verses (see Exod. 15:26).

your refuge, and the Most High your dwelling place, [Ps. 91:1, 14.]

10 There shall no evil befall you, nor any plague *or* calamity come near your tent.

11 For He will give His angels [especial] charge over you to accompany *and* defend *and* preserve you in all your ways [of obedience and service].

12 They shall bear you up on their hands, lest you dash your foot against a stone. [Luke 4:10, 11; Heb. 1:14.]

13 You shall tread upon the lion and adder; the young lion and the serpent shall you trample underfoot. [Luke 10:19.]

14 Because he has set his love upon Me, therefore will I deliver him; I will set him on high, because he knows *and* understands My name [has a personal knowledge of My mercy, love, and kindness—trusts and relies on Me, knowing I will never forsake him, no, never].

15 He shall call upon Me, and I will answer him; I will be with him in trouble, I will deliver him and honor him.

16 With long life will I satisfy him and show him My salvation.

PSALM 92

A Psalm. A song for the Sabbath day.

IT IS a good *and* delightful thing to give thanks to the Lord, to sing praises [with musical accompaniment] to Your name, O Most High,

2 To show forth Your loving-kindness in the morning and Your faithfulness by night,

3 With an instrument of ten strings and with the lute, with a solemn sound upon the lyre.

4 For You, O Lord, have made me glad by Your works; at the deeds of Your hands I joyfully sing.

5 How great are Your doings, O Lord! Your thoughts are very deep.

6 A man in his rude *and* uncultivat-

ed state knows not, neither does a [self-confident] fool understand this:

7 That though the wicked spring up like grass and all evildoers flourish, they are doomed to be destroyed forever.

8 But You, Lord, are on high forever.

9 For behold, Your adversaries, O Lord, for behold, Your enemies shall perish; all the evildoers shall be scattered.

10 But my horn (emblem of excessive strength and stately grace) You have exalted like that of a wild ox; I am anointed with fresh oil.

11 My eye looks upon those who lie in wait for me; my ears hear the evildoers that rise up against me.

12 The [uncompromisingly] righteous shall flourish like the palm tree [be long-lived, stately, upright, useful, and fruitful]; they shall grow like a cedar in Lebanon [majestic, stable, durable, and incorruptible].

13 Planted in the house of the Lord, they shall flourish in the courts of our God.

14 [Growing in grace] they shall still bring forth fruit in old age; they shall be full of sap [of spiritual vitality] and [rich in the] verdure [of trust, love, and contentment].

15 [They are living memorials] to show that the Lord is upright *and* faithful to His promises; He is my Rock, and there is no unrighteousness in Him. [Rom. 9:14.]

PSALM 93

THE LORD reigns, He is clothed with majesty; the Lord is robed, He has girded Himself with strength *and* power; the world also is established, that it cannot be moved.

2 Your throne is established from of old; You are from everlasting.

3 The floods have lifted up, O Lord, the floods have lifted up their voice; the floods lift up the roaring of their waves.

4 The Lord on high is mightier *and* more glorious than the noise of many waters, yes, than the mighty breakers *and* waves of the sea.

5 Your testimonies are very sure; holiness [apparent in separation from sin, with simple trust and hearty obedience] is becoming to Your house, O Lord, forever.

PSALM 94

O LORD God, You to Whom vengeance belongs, O God, You to Whom vengeance belongs, shine forth!

2 Rise up, O Judge of the earth; render to the proud a fit compensation!

3 Lord, how long shall the wicked, how long shall the wicked triumph *and* exult?

4 They pour out arrogant words, speaking hard things; all the evildoers boast loftily. [Jude 14, 15.]

5 They crush Your people, O Lord, and afflict Your heritage.

6 They slay the widow and the transient stranger and murder the unprotected orphan.

7 Yet they say, The Lord does not see, neither does the God of Jacob notice it.

8 Consider *and* understand, you stupid ones among the people! And you [self-confident] fools, when will you become wise?

9 He Who planted the ear, shall He not hear? He Who formed the eye, shall He not see?

10 He Who disciplines *and* instructs the nations, shall He not punish, He Who teaches man knowledge?

11 The Lord knows the thoughts of man, that they are vain (empty and futile—only a breath). [I Cor. 3:20.]

12 Blessed (happy, fortunate, to be envied) is the man whom You discipline *and* instruct, O Lord, and teach out of Your law,

13 That You may give him power to keep himself calm in the days of adversity, until the [inevitable] pit of corruption is dug for the wicked.

14 For the Lord will not cast off *nor* spurn His people, neither will He abandon His heritage.

15 For justice will return to the [uncompromisingly] righteous, and all the upright in heart will follow it.

16 Who will rise up for me against the evildoers? Who will stand up for me against the workers of iniquity?

17 Unless the Lord had been my help, I would soon have dwelt in [the land where there is] silence.

18 When I said, My foot is slipping, Your mercy *and* loving-kindness, O Lord, held me up.

19 In the multitude of my [anxious] thoughts within me, Your comforts cheer *and* delight my soul!

20 Shall the throne of iniquity have fellowship with You—they who frame *and* hide their unrighteous doings under [the sacred name of] law?

21 They band themselves together against the life of the [consistently] righteous and condemn the innocent to death.

22 But the Lord has become my High Tower *and* Defense, and my God the Rock of my refuge.

23 And He will turn back upon them their own iniquity and will wipe them out by means of their own wickedness; the Lord our God will wipe them out.

PSALM 95

O COME, let us sing to the Lord; let us make a joyful noise to the Rock of our salvation!

2 Let us come before His presence with thanksgiving; let us make a joyful noise to Him with songs of praise!

3 For the Lord is a great God, and a great King above all gods.

4 In His hand are the deep places of the earth; the heights *and* strength of the hills are His also.

5 The sea is His, for He made it; and His hands formed the dry land.

6 O come, let us worship and bow down, let us kneel before the Lord our Maker [in reverent praise and supplication].

7 For He is our God and we are the people of His pasture and the sheep of His hand. Today, if you will hear His voice, [Heb. 3:7–11.]

8 Harden not your hearts as at Meribah and as at Massah in the day of temptation in the wilderness, [Exod. 17:1–7; Num. 20:1–13; Deut. 6:16.]

9 When your fathers tried My patience and tested Me, proved Me, and saw My work [of judgment].

10 Forty years long was I grieved and disgusted with that generation, and I said, It is a people that do err in their hearts, and they do not approve, acknowledge, or regard My ways.

11 Wherefore I swore in My wrath that they would not enter My rest [the land of promise]. [Heb. 4:3–11.]

PSALM 96

O SING to the Lord a new song; sing to the Lord, all the earth!

2 Sing to the Lord, bless (affectionately praise) His name; show forth His salvation from day to day.

3 Declare His glory among the nations, His marvelous works among all the peoples.

4 For great is the Lord and greatly to be praised; He is to be reverently feared and worshiped above all [so-called] gods. [Deut. 6:5; Rev. 14:7.]

5 For all the gods of the nations are [lifeless] idols, but the Lord made the heavens.

6 Honor and majesty are before Him; strength and beauty are in His sanctuary.

7 Ascribe to the Lord, O you families of the peoples, ascribe to the Lord glory and strength.

8 Give to the Lord the glory due His name; bring an offering and come [before Him] into His courts.

9 O worship the Lord in the beauty of holiness; tremble before and reverently fear Him, all the earth.

10 Say among the nations that the Lord reigns; the world also is established, so that it cannot be moved; He shall judge and rule the people righteously and with justice. [Rev. 11:15; 19:6.]

11 Let the heavens be glad, and let the earth rejoice; let the sea roar, and all the things which fill it;

12 Let the field be exultant, and all that is in it! Then shall all the trees of the wood sing for joy

13 Before the Lord, for He comes, for He comes to judge and govern the earth! He shall judge the world with righteousness and justice and the peoples with His faithfulness and truth. [I Chron. 16:23–33; Rev. 19:11.]

PSALM 97

THE LORD reigns, let the earth rejoice; let the multitude of isles and coastlands be glad!

2 Clouds and darkness are round about Him [as at Sinai]; righteousness and justice are the foundation of His throne. [Exod. 19:9.]

3 Fire goes before Him and burns up His adversaries round about.

4 His lightnings illumine the world; the earth sees and trembles.

5 The hills melted like wax at the presence of the Lord, at the presence of the Lord of the whole earth.

6 The heavens declare His righteousness, and all the peoples see His glory.

7 Let all those be put to shame who serve graven images, who boast in idols. Fall prostrate before Him, all you gods. [Heb. 1:6.]

8 Zion heard and was glad, and the daughters of Judah rejoiced [in relief] because of Your judgments, O Lord.

9 For You, Lord, are high above all the earth; You are exalted far above all gods.

10 O you who love the Lord, hate evil; He preserves the lives of His

saints (the children of God), He delivers them out of the hand of the wicked. [Rom. 8:13–17.]

11 Light is sown for the [uncompromisingly] righteous *and* strewn along their pathway, and joy for the upright in heart [the irrepressible joy which comes from consciousness of His favor and protection].

12 Rejoice in the Lord, you [consistently] righteous (upright and in right standing with God), and give thanks at the remembrance of His holiness.

PSALM 98
A Psalm.

O SING to the Lord a new song, for He has done marvelous things; His right hand and His holy arm have wrought salvation for Him.

2 The Lord has made known His salvation; His righteousness has He openly shown in the sight of the nations. [Luke 2:30, 31.]

3 He has [earnestly] remembered His mercy *and* loving-kindness, His truth *and* His faithfulness toward the house of Israel; all the ends of the earth have witnessed the salvation of our God. [Acts 13:47; 28:28.]

4 Make a joyful noise to the Lord, all the earth; break forth and sing for joy, yes, sing praises!

5 Sing praises to the Lord with the lyre, with the lyre and the voice of melody.

6 With trumpets and the sound of the horn make a joyful noise before the King, the Lord!

7 *Let the sea roar, and all that fills* it, the world, and those who dwell in it!

8 Let the rivers clap their hands; together let the hills sing for joy

9 Before the Lord, for He is coming to judge [and rule] the earth; with righteousness will He judge [and rule] the world, and the peoples with equity.

PSALM 99

T HE LORD reigns, let the peoples tremble [with reverential fear]! He sits [enthroned] above the cherubim, let the earth quake!

2 The Lord is great in Zion, and He is high above all the peoples.

3 Let them confess *and* praise Your great name, awesome *and* reverence inspiring! It is holy, *and* holy is He! [Rev. 15:4.]

4 The strength of the king who loves righteousness *and* equity You establish in uprightness; You execute justice and righteousness in Jacob (Israel).

5 Extol the Lord our God and worship at His footstool! Holy is He!

6 Moses and Aaron were among His priests, and Samuel was among those who called upon His name; they called upon the Lord, and He answered them.

7 He spoke to them in the pillar of cloud; they kept His testimonies and the statutes that He gave them. [Ps. 105:9, 10.]

8 You answered them, O Lord our God; You were a forgiving God to them, although avenging their evildoing *and* wicked practices.

9 Extol the Lord our God and worship at His holy hill, for the Lord our God is holy!

PSALM 100
A Psalm of thanksgiving *and* for the thank offering.

M AKE A joyful noise to the Lord, all you lands!

2 Serve the Lord with gladness! *Come before His presence* with singing!

3 Know (perceive, recognize, and understand with approval) that the Lord is God! It is He Who has made us, not we ourselves [and we are His]! We are His people and the sheep of His pasture. [Eph. 2:10.]

4 Enter into His gates with thanks-

giving *and* a thank offering and into His courts with praise! Be thankful *and* say so to Him, bless *and* affectionately praise His name!

5 For the Lord is good; His mercy *and* loving-kindness are everlasting, His faithfulness *and* truth endure to all generations.

PSALM 101

A Psalm of David.

I WILL sing of mercy *and* loving-kindness and justice; to You, O Lord, will I sing.

2 I will behave myself wisely *and* give heed to the blameless way— O when will You come to me? I will walk within my house in integrity *and* with a blameless heart.

3 I will set no base *or* wicked thing before my eyes. I hate the work of them who turn aside [from the right path]; it shall not grasp hold of me.

4 A perverse heart shall depart from me; I will know no evil person *or* thing.

5 Whoso privily slanders his neighbor, him will I cut off [from me]; he who has a haughty look and a proud *and* arrogant heart I cannot *and* I will not tolerate.

6 My eyes shall [look with favor] upon the faithful of the land, that they may dwell with me; he who walks blamelessly, he shall minister to me.

7 He who works deceit shall not dwell in my house; he who tells lies shall not continue in my presence.

8 Morning after morning I will root up all the wicked in the land, that I may eliminate all the evildoers from the city of the Lord.

PSALM 102

A Prayer of the afflicted; when he is overwhelmed *and* faint and pours out his complaint to God.

H EAR MY prayer, O Lord, and let my cry come to You.

2 Hide not Your face from me in the day when I am in distress! Incline Your ear to me; in the day when I call, answer me speedily.

3 For my days consume away like smoke, and my bones burn like a firebrand *or* like a hearth.

4 My heart is smitten like grass *and* withered, so that [in absorption] I forget to eat my food.

5 By reason of my loud groaning [from suffering and trouble] my flesh cleaves to my bones.

6 I am like a melancholy pelican *or* vulture of the wilderness; I am like a [desolate] owl of the waste places.

7 I am sleepless *and* lie awake [mourning], like a bereaved sparrow alone on the housetop.

8 My adversaries taunt *and* reproach me all the day; and they who are angry with me use my name as a curse.

9 For I have eaten the ashes [in which I sat] as if they were bread and have mingled my drink with weeping

10 Because of Your indignation and Your wrath, for You have taken me up and cast me away.

11 My days are like an evening shadow that stretches out *and* declines [with the sun]; and I am withered like grass.

12 But You, O Lord, are enthroned forever; and the fame of Your name endures to all generations.

13 You will arise *and* have mercy *and* loving-kindness for Zion, for it is time to have pity *and* compassion for her; yes, the set time has come [the moment designated]. [Ps. 12:5; 119:126.]

14 For Your servants take [melancholy] pleasure in the stones [of her ruins] and show pity for her dust.

15 So the nations shall fear *and* worshipfully revere the name of the Lord, and all the kings of the earth Your glory. [Ps. 96:9.]

16 When the Lord builds up Zion, He will appear in His glory;

17 He will regard the plea of the

destitute and will not despise their prayer.

18 Let this be recorded for the generation yet unborn, that a people yet to be created shall praise the Lord.

19 For He looked down from the height of His sanctuary, from heaven did the Lord behold the earth,

20 To hear the sighing *and* groaning of the prisoner, to loose those who are appointed to death,

21 So that men may declare the name of the Lord in Zion and His praise in Jerusalem

22 When peoples are gathered together, and the kingdoms, to worship *and* serve the Lord.

23 He has afflicted *and* weakened my strength, humbling *and* bringing me low [with sorrow] in the way; He has shortened my days [aging me prematurely].

24 I said, O my God, take me not away in the midst of my days, You Whose years continue throughout all generations.

25 At the beginning You existed *and* laid the foundations of the earth; the heavens are the work of Your hands.

26 They shall perish, but You shall remain *and* endure; yes, all of them shall wear out *and* become old like a garment. Like clothing You shall change them, and they shall be changed *and* pass away.

27 But You remain the same, and Your years shall have no end. [Heb. 1:10–12.]

28 The children of Your servants shall dwell safely *and* continue, and their descendants shall be established before You.

PSALM 103

[A Psalm of David.]

BLESS (AFFECTIONATELY, gratefully praise) the Lord, O my soul; and all that is [deepest] within me, bless His holy name!

2 Bless (affectionately, gratefully praise) the Lord, O my soul, and forget not [one of] all His benefits—

3 Who forgives [every one of] all your iniquities, Who heals [each one of] all your diseases,

4 Who redeems your life from the pit *and* corruption, Who beautifies, dignifies, *and* crowns you with lovingkindness and tender mercy;

5 Who satisfies your mouth [your necessity and desire at your personal age and situation] with good so that your youth, renewed, is like the eagle's [strong, overcoming, soaring]! [Isa. 40:31.]

6 The Lord executes righteousness *and* justice [not for me only, but] for all who are oppressed.

7 He made known His ways [of righteousness and justice] to Moses, His acts to the children of Israel.

8 The Lord is merciful and gracious, slow to anger and plenteous in mercy *and* loving-kindness. [James 5:11.]

9 He will not always chide *or* be contending, neither will He keep His anger forever *or* hold a grudge.

10 He has not dealt with us after our sins nor rewarded us according to our iniquities.

11 For as the heavens are high above the earth, so great are His mercy *and* loving-kindness toward those who reverently and worshipfully fear Him.

12 As far as the east is from the west, so far has He removed our transgressions from us.

13 As a father loves *and* pities his children, so the Lord loves and pities those who fear Him [with reverence, worship, and awe].

14 For He knows our frame, He [earnestly] remembers *and* imprints [on His heart] that we are dust.

15 As for man, his days are as grass; as a flower of the field, so he flourishes.

16 For the wind passes over it and

it is gone, and its place shall know it no more.

17 But the mercy *and* loving-kindness of the Lord are from everlasting to everlasting upon those who reverently *and* worshipfully fear Him, and His righteousness is to children's children—[Deut. 10:12.]

18 To such as keep His covenant [hearing, receiving, loving, and obeying it] and to those who [earnestly] remember His commandments to do them [imprinting them on their hearts].

19 The Lord has established His throne in the heavens, and His kingdom rules over all.

20 Bless (affectionately, gratefully praise) the Lord, you His angels, you mighty ones who do His commandments, hearkening to the voice of His word.

21 Bless (affectionately, gratefully praise) the Lord, all you His hosts, you His ministers who do His pleasure.

22 Bless the Lord, all His works in all places of His dominion; bless (affectionately, gratefully praise) the Lord, O my soul!

PSALM 104

BLESS (AFFECTIONATELY, gratefully praise) the Lord, O my soul! O Lord my God, You are very great! You are clothed with honor and majesty—

2 [You are the One] Who covers Yourself with light as with a garment, Who stretches out the heavens like a curtain *or* a tent,

3 Who lays the beams of the upper room of His abode in the waters [above the firmament], Who makes the clouds His chariot, Who walks on the wings of the wind,

4 Who makes winds His messengers, flames of fire His ministers. [Heb. 1:7.]

5 You laid the foundations of the earth, that it should not be moved forever. [Job 38:4, 6.]

6 You covered it with the deep as

with a garment; the waters stood above the mountains. [Gen. 1:2; II Pet. 3:5.]

7 At Your rebuke they fled; at the voice of Your thunder they hastened away.

8 The mountains rose, the valleys sank down to the place which You appointed for them.

9 You have set a boundary [for the waters] which they may not pass over, that they turn not again to deluge the earth.

10 He sends forth springs into the valleys; their waters run among the mountains.

11 They give drink to every [wild] beast of the field; the wild asses quench their thirst there.

12 Beside them the birds of the heavens have their nests; they sing among the branches. [Matt. 13:32.]

13 He waters the mountains from His upper rooms; the earth is satisfied *and* abounds with the fruit of His works.

14 He causes vegetation to grow for the cattle, and all that the earth produces for man to cultivate, that he may bring forth food out of the earth—

15 And wine that gladdens the heart of man, to make his face shine more than oil, and bread to support, refresh, *and* strengthen man's heart.

16 The trees of the Lord are watered abundantly *and* are filled with sap, the cedars of Lebanon which He has planted,

17 Where the birds make their nests; as for the stork, the fir trees are her house.

18 The high mountains are for the wild goats; the rocks are a refuge for the conies *and* badgers.

19 [The Lord] appointed the moon for the seasons; the sun knows [the exact time of] its setting.

20 You [O Lord] make darkness and it becomes night, in which creeps forth every wild beast of the forest.

21 The young lions roar after their prey and seek their food from God.

22 When the sun arises, they withdraw themselves and lie down in their dens.

23 Man goes forth to his work and remains at his task until evening.

24 O Lord, how many *and* varied are Your works! In wisdom have You made them all; the earth is full of Your riches *and* Your creatures.

25 Yonder is the sea, great and wide, in which are swarms of innumerable creeping things, creatures both small and great.

26 There go the ships of the sea, and Leviathan (the sea monster), which You have formed to sport in it.

27 These all wait *and* are dependent upon You, that You may give them their food in due season.

28 When You give it to them, they gather it up; You open Your hand, and they are filled with good things.

29 When You hide Your face, they are troubled *and* dismayed; when You take away their breath, they die and return to their dust.

30 When You send forth Your Spirit *and* give them breath, they are created, and You replenish the face of the ground.

31 May the glory of the Lord endure forever; may the Lord rejoice in His works—

32 Who looks on the earth, and it quakes *and* trembles, Who touches the mountains, and they smoke!

33 I will sing to the Lord as long as I live; I will sing praise to my God *while* I have any being.

34 May my meditation be sweet to Him; as for me, I will rejoice in the Lord.

35 Let sinners be consumed from the earth, and let the wicked be no more. Bless (affectionately, gratefully praise) the Lord, O my soul! Praise the Lord! (Hallelujah!)

PSALM 105

O GIVE thanks unto the Lord, call upon His name, make known His doings among the peoples!

2 Sing to Him, sing praises to Him; meditate on *and* talk of all His marvelous deeds *and* devoutly praise them.

3 Glory in His holy name; let the hearts of those rejoice who seek *and* require the Lord [as their indispensable necessity].

4 Seek, inquire of *and* for the Lord, *and* crave Him and His strength (His might and inflexibility to temptation); seek *and* require His face *and* His presence [continually] evermore.

5 [Earnestly] remember the marvelous deeds that He has done, His miracles *and* wonders, the judgments *and* sentences which He pronounced [upon His enemies, as in Egypt]. [Ps. 78:43–51.]

6 O you offspring of Abraham His servant, you children of Jacob, His chosen ones,

7 He is the Lord our God; His judgments are in all the earth.

8 He is [earnestly] mindful of His covenant *and* forever it is imprinted on His heart, the word which He commanded *and* established to a thousand generations,

9 The covenant which He made with Abraham, and His sworn promise to Isaac, [Luke 1:72, 73.]

10 Which He confirmed to Jacob as a statute, to Israel as an everlasting covenant,

11 Saying, Unto you will I give the land of Canaan as your measured portion, possession, *and* inheritance.

12 When they were but a few men in number, in fact, very few, and were temporary residents *and* strangers in it,

13 When they went from one nation to another, from one kingdom to another people,

14 He allowed no man to do them

wrong; in fact, He reproved kings for their sakes, [Gen. 12:17; 20:3–7.]

15 Saying, Touch not My anointed, and do My prophets no harm. [I Chron. 16:8–22.]

16 Moreover, He called for a famine upon the land [of Egypt]; He cut off every source of bread. [Gen. 41:54.]

17 He sent a man before them, even Joseph, who was sold as a servant. [Gen. 45:5; 50:20, 21.]

18 His feet they hurt with fetters; he was laid in chains of iron *and* his soul entered into the iron,

19 Until his word [to his cruel brothers] came true, until the word of the Lord tried *and* tested him.

20 The king sent and loosed him, even the ruler of the peoples, and let him go free.

21 He made Joseph lord of his house and ruler of all his substance, [Gen. 41:40.]

22 To bind his princes at his pleasure and teach his elders wisdom.

23 Israel also came into Egypt; and Jacob sojourned in the land of Ham. [Gen. 46:6.]

24 There [the Lord] greatly increased His people and made them stronger than their oppressors.

25 He turned the hearts [of the Egyptians] to hate His people, to deal craftily with His servants.

26 He sent Moses His servant, and Aaron, whom He had chosen.

27 They showed His signs among them, wonders *and* miracles in the land of Ham (Egypt).

28 He sent [thick] darkness and made the land dark, and they [God's two servants] rebelled not against His word. [Exod. 10:22; Ps. 99:7.]

29 He turned [Egypt's] waters into blood and caused their fish to die. [Exod. 7:20, 21.]

30 Their land brought forth frogs in abundance, even in the chambers of their kings. [Exod. 8:6.]

31 He spoke, and there came swarms of beetles *and* flies and mosquitoes and lice in all their borders. [Exod. 8:17, 24.]

32 He gave them hail for rain, with lightning like flaming fire in their land. [Exod. 9:23, 25.]

33 He smote their vines also and their fig trees and broke the [ice-laden] trees of their borders. [Ps. 78:47.]

34 He spoke, and the locusts came, and the grasshoppers, and that without number, [Exod. 10:4, 13, 14.]

35 And ate up all the vegetation in their land and devoured the fruit of their ground.

36 He smote also all the firstborn in their land, the beginning *and* chief substance of all their strength. [Exod. 12:29; Ps. 78:51.]

37 He brought [Israel] forth also with silver and gold, and there was not one feeble person among their tribes. [Exod. 12:35.]

38 Egypt was glad when they departed, for the fear of them had fallen upon the people. [Exod. 12:33.]

39 The Lord spread a cloud for a covering [by day], and a fire to give light in the night. [Exod. 13:21.]

40 [The Israelites] asked, and He brought quails and satisfied them with the bread of heaven. [Exod. 16:12–15.]

41 He opened the rock, and water gushed out; it ran in the dry places like a river. [Exod. 17:6; Num. 20:11.]

42 For He [earnestly] remembered His holy word *and* promise to Abraham His servant. [Gen. 15:14.]

43 And He brought forth His people with joy, and His chosen ones with gladness *and* singing,

44 And gave them the lands of the nations [of Canaan], and they reaped the fruits of those peoples' labor, [Deut. 6:10, 11.]

45 That they might observe His statutes and keep His laws [hearing, receiving, loving, and obeying them]. Praise the Lord! (Hallelujah!)

PSALM 106

PRAISE THE Lord! (Hallelujah!) O give thanks to the Lord, for He is good; for His mercy *and* loving-kindness endure forever! [I Chron. 16:34.]

2 Who can put into words *and* tell the mighty deeds of the Lord? *Or* who can show forth all the praise [that is due Him]?

3 Blessed (happy, fortunate, to be envied) are those who observe justice [treating others fairly] *and* who do right *and* are in right standing with God at all times.

4 [Earnestly] remember me, O Lord, when You favor Your people! O visit me also when You deliver them, *and* grant me Your salvation!—

5 That I may see *and* share the welfare of Your chosen ones, that I may rejoice in the gladness of Your nation, that I may glory with Your heritage.

6 We have sinned, as did also our fathers; we have committed iniquity, we have done wickedly. [Lev. 26:40–42.]

7 Our fathers in Egypt understood not nor appreciated Your miracles; they did not [earnestly] remember the multitude of Your mercies nor imprint Your loving-kindness [on their hearts], but they were rebellious *and* provoked the Lord at the sea, even at the Red Sea.

8 Nevertheless He saved them for His name's sake [to prove the righteousness of the divine character], that He might make His mighty power known.

9 He rebuked the Red Sea also, and it dried up; so He led them through the depths as through a pastureland. [Exod. 14:21.]

10 And He saved them from the hand of him that hated them, and redeemed them from the hand of the [Egyptian] enemy. [Exod. 14:30.]

11 And the waters covered their adversaries; not one of them was left. [Exod. 14:27, 28; 15:5.]

12 Then [Israel] believed His words [trusting in, relying on them]; they sang His praise.

13 But they hastily forgot His works; they did not [earnestly] wait for His plans [to develop] regarding them,

14 But lusted exceedingly in the wilderness and tempted *and* tried to restrain God [with their insistent desires] in the desert. [Num. 11:4.]

15 And He gave them their request, but sent leanness into their souls *and* [thinned their numbers by] disease and death. [Ps. 78:29–31.]

16 They envied Moses also in the camp, and Aaron [the high priest], the holy one of the Lord. [Num. 16:1–32.]

17 Therefore the earth opened and swallowed up Dathan and closed over the company of Abiram. [Num. 16:31, 32.]

18 And a fire broke out in their company; the flame burned up the wicked. [Num. 16:35, 46.]

19 They made a calf in Horeb and worshiped a molten image. [Exod. 32:4.]

20 Thus they exchanged Him Who was their Glory for the image of an ox that eats grass [they traded their Honor for the image of a calf]!

21 They forgot God their Savior, Who had done such great things in Egypt,

22 Wonders *and* miracles in the land of Ham, dreadful *and* awesome things at the Red Sea.

23 Therefore He said He would destroy them. [And He would have done so] had not Moses, His chosen one, stepped into the breach before Him to turn away His threatening wrath. [Exod. 32:10, 11, 32.]

24 Then they spurned *and* despised the pleasant *and* desirable land [Canaan]; they believed not His word [neither trusting in, relying on, nor holding to it];

25 But they murmured in their tents

and hearkened not to the voice of the Lord.

26 Therefore He lifted up His hand [as if taking an oath] against them, that He would cause them to fall in the wilderness,

27 Cast out their descendants among the nations, and scatter them in the lands [of the earth].

28 They joined themselves also to the [idol] Baal of Peor and ate sacrifices [offered] to the lifeless [gods].

29 Thus they provoked the Lord to anger with their practices, and a plague broke out among them.

30 Then stood up Phinehas [the priest] and executed judgment, and so the plague was stayed. [Num. 25:7, 8.]

31 And that was credited to him for righteousness (right doing and right standing with God) to all generations forever.

32 They angered the Lord also at the waters of Meribah, so that it went ill with Moses for their sakes; [Num. 20:3–13.]

33 For they provoked [Moses'] spirit, so that he spoke unadvisedly with his lips.

34 They did not destroy the [heathen] nations as the Lord commanded them,

35 But mingled themselves with the [idolatrous] nations and learned their ways *and* works

36 And served their idols, which were a snare to them.

37 Yes, they sacrificed their sons and their daughters to demons [II Kings 16:3.]

38 And shed innocent blood, even the blood of their sons and of their daughters, whom they sacrificed to the idols of Canaan; and the land was polluted with their blood.

39 Thus were they defiled by their own works, and they played the harlot *and* practiced idolatry with their own deeds [of idolatrous rites].

40 Therefore was the wrath of the Lord kindled against His people, insomuch that He abhorred *and* rejected His own heritage. [Deut. 32:17.]

41 And He gave them into the hands of the [heathen] nations, and they that hated them ruled over them.

42 Their enemies also oppressed them, and they were brought into subjection under the hand of their foes.

43 Many times did [God] deliver them, but they were rebellious in their counsel and sank low through their iniquity.

44 Nevertheless He regarded their distress when He heard their cry;

45 And He [earnestly] remembered for their sake His covenant and relented their sentence of evil [comforting and easing Himself] according to the abundance of His mercy *and* lovingkindness [when they cried out to Him].

46 He also caused [Israel] to find sympathy among those who had carried them away captive.

47 Deliver us, O Lord our God, and gather us from among the nations, that we may give thanks to Your holy name *and* glory in praising You.

48 Blessed (affectionately and gratefully praised) be the Lord, the God of Israel, from everlasting to everlasting! And let all the people say, Amen! Praise the Lord! (Hallelujah!) [I Chron. 16:35, 36.]

BOOK FIVE

PSALM 107

O GIVE thanks to the Lord, for He is good; for His mercy *and* loving-kindness endure forever!

2 Let the redeemed of the Lord say so, whom He has delivered from the hand of the adversary,

3 And gathered them out of the lands, from the east and from the west, from the north and from the [Red] Sea in the south.

4 Some wandered in the wilderness in a solitary desert track; they found no city for habitation.

5 Hungry and thirsty, they fainted;

their lives were near to being extinguished.

6 Then they cried to the Lord in their trouble, and He delivered them out of their distresses.

7 He led them forth by the straight *and* right way, that they might go to a city where they could establish their homes.

8 Oh, that men would praise [and confess to] the Lord for His goodness *and* loving-kindness and His wonderful works to the children of men!

9 For He satisfies the longing soul and fills the hungry soul with good.

10 Some sat in darkness and in the shadow of death, being bound in affliction and in irons, [Luke 1:79.]

11 Because they had rebelled against the words of God and spurned the counsel of the Most High.

12 Therefore He bowed down their hearts with hard labor; they stumbled *and* fell down, and there was none to help.

13 Then they cried to the Lord in their trouble, and He saved them out of their distresses.

14 He brought them out of darkness and the shadow of death and broke apart the bonds that held them. [Ps. 68:6; Acts 12:7; 16:26.]

15 Oh, that men would praise [and confess to] the Lord for His goodness *and* loving-kindness and His wonderful works to the children of men!

16 For He has broken the gates of bronze and cut the bars of iron apart.

17 Some are fools [made ill] because of the way of their transgressions and are afflicted because of their iniquities.

18 They loathe every kind of food, and they draw near to the gates of death.

19 Then they cry to the Lord in their trouble, and He delivers them out of their distresses.

20 He sends forth His word and heals them and rescues them from the pit *and* destruction. [II Kings 20:4, 5; Matt. 8:8.]

21 Oh, that men would praise [and confess to] the Lord for His goodness *and* loving-kindness and His wonderful works to the children of men! [Heb. 13:15.]

22 And let them sacrifice the sacrifices of thanksgiving and rehearse His deeds with shouts of joy *and* singing!

23 Some go down to the sea *and* travel over it in ships to do business in great waters;

24 These see the works of the Lord and His wonders in the deep.

25 For He commands and raises up the stormy wind, which lifts up the waves of the sea.

26 [Those aboard] mount up to the heavens, they go down again to the deeps; their courage melts away because of their plight.

27 They reel to and fro and stagger like a drunken man and are at their wits' end [all their wisdom has come to nothing].

28 Then they cry to the Lord in their trouble, and He brings them out of their distresses.

29 He hushes the storm to a calm *and* to a gentle whisper, so that the waves of the sea are still. [Ps. 89:9; Matt. 8:26.]

30 Then the men are glad because of the calm, and He brings them to their desired haven.

31 Oh, that men would praise [and confess to] the Lord for His goodness *and* loving-kindness and His wonderful works to the children of men!

32 Let them exalt Him also in the congregation of the people and praise Him in the company of the elders.

33 He turns rivers into a wilderness, water springs into a thirsty ground, [I Kings 17:1, 7.]

34 A fruitful land into a barren, salt waste, because of the wickedness of those who dwell in it. [Gen. 13:10; 14:3; 19:25.]

35 He turns a wilderness into a pool

of water and a dry ground into water springs; [Isa. 41:18.]

36 And there He makes the hungry to dwell, that they may prepare a city for habitation,

37 And sow fields, and plant vineyards which yield fruits of increase.

38 He blesses them also, so that they are multiplied greatly, and allows not their cattle to decrease.

39 When they are diminished and bowed down through oppression, trouble, and sorrow,

40 He pours contempt upon princes and causes them to wander in waste places where there is no road.

41 Yet He raises the poor *and* needy from affliction and makes their families like a flock.

42 The upright shall see it and be glad, but all iniquity shall shut its mouth.

43 Whoso is wise [if there be any truly wise] will observe *and* heed these things; and they will diligently consider the mercy *and* loving-kindness of the Lord.

PSALM 108
A song. A Psalm of David.

O GOD, my heart is fixed (steadfast, in the confidence of faith); I will sing, yes, I will sing praises, even with my glory [all the faculties and powers of one created in Your image]!

2 Awake, harp and lyre; I myself will wake very early—I will waken the dawn!

3 I will praise *and* give thanks to You, O Lord, among the peoples; and I will sing praises unto You among the nations.

4 For Your mercy *and* loving-kindness are great *and* high as the heavens! Your truth *and* faithfulness reach to the skies! [Ps. 57:7–11.]

5 Be exalted, O God, above the heavens, and let Your glory be over all the earth.

6 That Your beloved [followers]

may be delivered, save with Your right hand and answer us! [or me]!

7 God has promised in His holiness [regarding the establishment of David's dynasty]: I will rejoice, I will distribute [Canaan among My people], dividing Shechem and [the western region and allotting the eastern region which contains] the Valley of Succoth.

8 Gilead is Mine, Manasseh is Mine; Ephraim also is My stronghold *and* the defense of My head; Judah is My scepter *and* lawgiver. [Gen. 49:10.]

9 Moab is My washbasin; over Edom [My slave] My shoe I cast [to be cleaned]; over Philistia I shout [in triumph].

10 Who will bring me [David] into the strong, fortified city [of Petra]? Who will lead me into Edom?

11 Have You not cast us off, O God? And will You not go forth, O God, with our armies?

12 Give us help against the adversary, for vain is the help of man.

13 Through *and* with God we shall do valiantly, for He it is Who shall tread down our adversaries. [Ps. 60:5–12.]

PSALM 109
To the Chief Musician. A Psalm of David.

O GOD of my praise! Keep not silence,

2 For the mouths of the wicked and the mouth of deceit are opened against me; they have spoken to me *and* against me with lying tongues.

3 They have compassed me about also with words of hatred and have fought against me without a cause.

4 In return for my love they are my adversaries, but I resort to prayer.

5 And they have rewarded *and* laid upon me evil for good, and hatred for my love.

6 Set a wicked man over him [as a judge], and let [a malicious] accuser stand at his right hand.

7 When [the wicked] is judged, let him be condemned, and let his prayer [for leniency] be turned into a sin.

8 Let his days be few; and let another take his office and charge. [Acts 1:20.]

9 Let his children be fatherless and his wife a widow.

10 Let his children be continual vagabonds [as was Cain] and beg; let them seek their bread and be driven far from their ruined homes. [Gen. 4:12.]

11 Let the creditor and extortioner seize all that he has; and let strangers (barbarians and foreigners) plunder the fruits of his labor.

12 Let there be none to extend or continue mercy and kindness to him, neither let there be any to have pity on his fatherless children.

13 Let his posterity be cut off, and in the generation following let their names be blotted out.

14 Let the iniquity of his fathers be remembered by the Lord; and let not the sin of his mother be blotted out.

15 Let them be before the Lord continually, that He may cut off the memory of them from the earth!—

16 Because the man did not [earnestly] remember to show mercy, but pursued and persecuted the poor and needy man, and the broken in heart [he was ready] to slay.

17 Yes, he loved cursing, and it came [back] upon him; he delighted not in blessing, and it was far from him.

18 He clothed himself also with cursing as with his garment, and it seeped into his inward [life] like water, and like oil into his bones.

19 Let it be to him as the raiment with which he covers himself and as the girdle with which he is girded continually.

20 Let this be the reward of my adversaries from the Lord, and of those who speak evil against my life.

21 But You deal with me and act for me, O God the Lord, for Your name's sake; because Your mercy and loving-kindness are good, O deliver me.

22 For I am poor and needy, and my heart is wounded and stricken within me.

23 I am gone like the shadow when it lengthens and declines; I toss up and down and am shaken off as the locust.

24 My knees are weak and totter from fasting; and my body is gaunt and has no fatness.

25 I have become also a reproach and a taunt to others; when they see me, they shake their heads. [Matt. 26:39.]

26 Help me, O Lord my God; O save me according to Your mercy and loving-kindness!—

27 That they may know that this is Your hand, that You, Lord, have done it.

28 Let them curse, but do You bless. When adversaries arise, let them be put to shame, but let Your servant rejoice.

29 Let my adversaries be clothed with shame and dishonor, and let them cover themselves with their own disgrace and confusion as with a robe.

30 I will give great praise and thanks to the Lord with my mouth; yes, and I will praise Him among the multitude.

31 For He will stand at the right hand of the poor and needy, to save him from those who condemn his life.

PSALM 110
A Psalm of David.

THE LORD (God) says to my Lord (the Messiah), Sit at My right hand, until I make Your adversaries Your footstool. [Matt. 26:64; Acts 2:34; I Cor. 15:25; Col. 3:1; Heb. 12:2.]

2 The Lord will send forth from Zion the scepter of Your strength; rule, then, in the midst of Your foes. [Rom. 11:26, 27.]

3 Your people will offer themselves willingly in the day of Your power, in the beauty of holiness *and* in holy array out of the womb of the morning; to You [will spring forth] Your young men, who are as the dew.

4 The Lord has sworn and will not revoke *or* change it: You are a priest forever, after the manner *and* order of Melchizedek. [Heb. 5:10; 7:11, 15, 21.]

5 The Lord at Your right hand will shatter kings in the day of His indignation.

6 He will execute judgment [in overwhelming punishment] upon the nations; He will fill the valleys with the dead bodies, He will crush the [chief] heads over lands many *and* far extended. [Ezek. 38:21, 22; 39:11, 12.]

7 He will drink of the brook by the way; therefore will He lift up His head [triumphantly].

PSALM 111

PRAISE THE Lord! (Hallelujah!) I will praise and give thanks to the Lord with my whole heart in the council of the upright and in the congregation.

2 The works of the Lord are great, sought out by all those who have delight in them.

3 His work is honorable and glorious, and His righteousness endures forever.

4 He has made His wonderful works to be remembered; the Lord is gracious, merciful, *and* full of loving compassion.

5 He has given food *and* provision to those who reverently *and* worshipfully fear Him; He will remember His covenant forever *and* imprint it [on His mind]. [Deut. 10:12; Ps. 96:9.]

6 He has declared *and* shown to His people the power of His works in giving them the heritage of the nations [of Canaan].

7 The works of His hands are [absolute] truth and justice [faithful and right]; and all His decrees *and* precepts are sure (fixed, established, and trustworthy).

8 They stand fast *and* are established forever and ever and are done in [absolute] truth and uprightness.

9 He has sent redemption to His people; He has commanded His covenant to be forever; holy is His name, inspiring awe, reverence, *and* godly fear.

10 The reverent fear *and* worship of the Lord is the beginning of ˣWisdom *and* skill [the preceding and the first essential, the prerequisite and the alphabet]; a good understanding, wisdom, *and* meaning have all those who do [the will of the Lord]. Their praise of Him endures forever. [Job. 28:28; Prov. 1:7; Matt. 22:37, 38; Rev. 14:7.]

PSALM 112

PRAISE THE Lord! (Hallelujah!) Blessed (happy, fortunate, to be envied) is the man who fears (reveres and worships) the Lord, who delights greatly in His commandments. [Deut. 10:12.]

2 His [spiritual] offspring shall be mighty upon earth; the generation of the upright shall be blessed.

3 Prosperity *and* welfare are in his house, and his righteousness endures forever.

4 Light arises in the darkness for the upright, gracious, compassionate, *and* just [who are in right standing with God].

5 It is well with the man who deals generously and lends, who conducts his affairs with justice. [Ps. 37:26; Luke 6:35; Col. 4:5.]

6 He will not be moved forever; the [uncompromisingly] righteous (the upright, in right standing with God)

ˣ See footnote on Job 28:12.

shall be in everlasting remembrance. [Prov. 10:7.]

7 He shall not be afraid of evil tidings; his heart is firmly fixed, trusting (leaning on and being confident) in the Lord.

8 His heart is established *and* steady, he will not be afraid while he waits to see his desire established upon his adversaries.

9 He has distributed freely [he has given to the poor and needy]; his righteousness (uprightness and right standing with God) endures forever; his horn shall be exalted in honor. [II Cor. 9:9.]

10 The wicked man will see it and be grieved *and* angered, he will gnash his teeth and disappear [in despair]; the desire of the wicked shall perish *and* come to nothing.

PSALM 113

PRAISE THE Lord! (Hallelujah!) Praise, O servants of the Lord, praise the name of the Lord!

2 Blessed be the name of the Lord from this time forth and forever

3 From the rising of the sun to the going down of it *and* from east to west, the name of the Lord is to be praised!

4 The Lord is high above all nations, and His glory above the heavens!

5 Who is like the Lord our God, Who has His seat on high,

6 Who humbles Himself to regard the heavens and the earth! [Ps. 138:6; Isa. 57:15.]

7 [The Lord] raises the poor out of the dust *and* lifts the needy from the ash heap *and* the dung hill,

8 That He may seat them with princes, even with the princes of His people.

9 He makes the barren woman to be a homemaker *and* a joyful mother of [spiritual] children. Praise the Lord! (Hallelujah!)

PSALM 114

WHEN ISRAEL came forth out of Egypt, the house of Jacob from a people of strange language,

2 Judah became [God's] sanctuary (the Holy Place of His habitation), and Israel His dominion. [Exod. 29:45, 46; Deut. 27:9.]

3 The [Red] Sea looked and fled; the Jordan [River] was turned back. [Exod. 14:21; Josh. 3:13, 16; Ps. 77:16.]

4 The mountains skipped like rams, the little hills like lambs.

5 What ails you, O [Red] Sea, that you flee? O Jordan, that you turn back?

6 You mountains, that you skip like rams, and you little hills, like lambs?

7 Tremble, O earth, at the presence of the Lord, at the presence of the God of Jacob,

8 Who turned the rock into a pool of water, the flint into a fountain of waters. [Exod. 17:6; Num. 20:11.]

PSALM 115

NOT TO us, O Lord, not to us but to Your name give glory, for Your mercy *and* loving-kindness and for the sake of Your truth *and* faithfulness!

2 Why should the nations say, Where is now their God?

3 But our God is in heaven; He does whatever He pleases.

4 The idols of the nations are silver and gold, the work of men's hands.

5 They have mouths, but they speak not; eyes have they, but they see not;

6 They have ears, but they hear not; noses have they, but they smell not;

7 They have hands, but they handle not; feet have they, but they walk not; neither can they make a sound with their throats.

8 They who make idols are like them; so are all who trust in *and* lean on them. [Ps. 135:15–18.]

9 O Israel, trust *and* take refuge in

the Lord! [Lean on, rely on, and be confident in Him!] He is their Help and their Shield.

10 O house of Aaron [the priesthood], trust in and lean on the Lord! He is their Help and their Shield.

11 You who [reverently] fear the Lord, trust in and lean on the Lord! He is their Help and their Shield.

12 The Lord has been mindful of us, He will bless us: He will bless the house of Israel, He will bless the house of Aaron [the priesthood],

13 He will bless those who reverently and worshipfully fear the Lord, both small and great. [Ps. 103:11; Rev. 11:18; 19:5.]

14 May the Lord give you increase more and more, you and your children.

15 May you be blessed of the Lord, Who made heaven and earth!

16 The heavens are the Lord's heavens, but the earth has He given to the children of men.

17 The dead praise not the Lord, neither any who go down into silence.

18 But we will bless (affectionately and gratefully praise) the Lord from this time forth and forever. Praise the Lord! (Hallelujah!)

PSALM 116

I LOVE the Lord, because He has heard [and now hears] my voice and my supplications.

2 Because He has inclined His ear to me, therefore will I call upon Him as long as I live.

3 The cords and sorrows of death were around me, and the terrors of Sheol (the place of the dead) had laid hold of me; I suffered anguish and grief (trouble and sorrow).

4 Then called I upon the name of the Lord: O Lord, I beseech You, save my life and deliver me!

5 Gracious is the Lord, and [rigidly] righteous; yes, our God is merciful.

6 The Lord preserves the simple; I was brought low, and He helped and saved me.

7 Return to your rest, O my soul, for the Lord has dealt bountifully with you. [Matt. 11:29.]

8 For You have delivered my life from death, my eyes from tears, and my feet from stumbling and falling.

9 I will walk before the Lord in the land of the living.

10 I believed (trusted in, relied on, and clung to my God), and therefore have I spoken [even when I said], I am greatly afflicted. [II Cor. 4:13.]

11 I said in my haste, All men are deceitful and liars.

12 What shall I render to the Lord for all His benefits toward me? [How can I repay Him for all His bountiful dealings?]

13 I will lift up the cup of salvation and deliverance and call on the name of the Lord.

14 I will pay my vows to the Lord, yes, in the presence of all His people.

15 Precious (important and no light matter) in the sight of the Lord is the death of His saints (His loving ones).

16 O Lord, truly I am Your servant; I am Your servant, the son of Your handmaid; You have loosed my bonds.

17 I will offer to You the sacrifice of thanksgiving and will call on the name of the Lord.

18 I will pay my vows to the Lord, yes, in the presence of all His people,

19 In the courts of the Lord's house—in the midst of you, O Jerusalem. Praise the Lord! (Hallelujah!)

PSALM 117

O PRAISE the Lord, all you nations! Praise Him, all you people! [Rom. 15:11.]

2 For His mercy and loving-kindness are great toward us, and the truth and faithfulness of the Lord endure forever. Praise the Lord! (Hallelujah!)

PSALM 118

O GIVE thanks to the Lord, for He is good; for His mercy and loving-kindness endure forever!

2 Let Israel now say that His mercy and loving-kindness endure forever.

3 Let the house of Aaron [the priesthood] now say that His mercy and loving-kindness endure forever.

4 Let those now who reverently and worshipfully fear the Lord say that His mercy and loving-kindness endure forever.

5 Out of my distress I called upon the Lord; the Lord answered me and set me free and in a large place.

6 The Lord is on my side; I will not fear. What can man do to me? [Heb. 13:6.]

7 The Lord is on my side and takes my part, He is among those who help me; therefore shall I see my desire established upon those who hate me.

8 It is better to trust and take refuge in the Lord than to put confidence in man.

9 It is better to trust and take refuge in the Lord than to put confidence in princes.

10 All nations (the surrounding tribes) compassed me about, but in the name of the Lord I will cut them off!

11 They compassed me about, yes, they surrounded me on every side; but in the name of the Lord I will cut them off!

12 They swarmed about me like bees, they blaze up and are extinguished like a fire of thorns; in the name of the Lord I will cut them off! [Deut. 1:44.]

13 You [my adversary] thrust sorely at me that I might fall, but the Lord helped me.

14 The Lord is my Strength and Song; and He has become my Salvation.

15 The voice of rejoicing and salvation is in the tents and private dwellings of the [uncompromisingly] righteous: the right hand of the Lord does valiantly and achieves strength!

16 The right hand of the Lord is exalted; the right hand of the Lord does valiantly and achieves strength!

17 I shall not die but live, and shall declare the works and recount the illustrious acts of the Lord.

18 The Lord has chastened me sorely, but He has not given me over to death. [II Cor. 6:9.]

19 Open to me the [temple] gates of righteousness; I will enter through them, and I will confess and praise the Lord.

20 This is the gate of the Lord; the [uncompromisingly] righteous shall enter through it. [Ps. 24:7.]

21 I will confess, praise, and give thanks to You, for You have heard and answered me; and You have become my Salvation and Deliverer.

22 The stone which the builders rejected has become the chief cornerstone.

23 This is from the Lord and is His doing; it is marvelous in our eyes. [Matt. 21:42; Acts 4:11; I Pet. 2:7.]

24 This is the day which the Lord has brought about; we will rejoice and be glad in it.

25 Save now, we beseech You, O Lord; send now prosperity, O Lord, we beseech You, and give to us success!

26 Blessed is he who comes in the name of the Lord; we bless you from the house of the Lord [you who come into His sanctuary under His guardianship]. [Mark 11:9, 10.]

27 The Lord is God, Who has shown and given us light [He has illuminated us with grace, freedom, and joy]. Decorate the festival with leafy boughs and bind the sacrifices to be offered with thick cords [all over the priest's court, right up] to the horns of the altar.

28 You are my God, and I will confess, praise, and give thanks to You; You are my God, I will extol You.

29 O give thanks to the Lord, for He is good; for His mercy *and* loving-kindness endure forever.

PSALM 119

BLESSED (HAPPY, fortunate, to be envied) are the undefiled (the upright, truly sincere, and blameless) in the way [of the revealed will of God], who walk (order their conduct and conversation) in the law of the Lord (the whole of God's revealed will).

2 Blessed (happy, fortunate, to be envied) are they who keep His testimonies, and who seek, inquire for *and* of Him *and* crave Him with the whole heart.

3 Yes, they do no unrighteousness [no willful wandering from His precepts]; they walk in His ways. [I John 3:9; 5:18.]

4 You have commanded us to keep Your precepts, that we should observe them diligently.

5 Oh, that my ways were directed *and* established to observe Your statutes [hearing, receiving, loving, and obeying them]!

6 Then shall I not be put to shame [by failing to inherit Your promises] when I have respect to all Your commandments.

7 I will praise *and* give thanks to You with uprightness of heart when I learn [by sanctified experiences] Your righteous judgments [Your decisions against and punishments for particular lines of thought and conduct].

8 I will keep Your statutes; O forsake me not utterly.

9 How shall a young man cleanse his way? By taking heed *and* keeping watch [on himself] according to Your word [conforming his life to it].

10 With my whole heart have I sought You, inquiring for *and* of You *and* yearning for You; Oh, let me not wander *or* step aside [either in ignorance or willfully] from Your commandments. [II Chron. 15:15.]

11 Your word have I laid up in my heart, that I might not sin against You.

12 Blessed are You, O Lord; teach me Your statutes.

13 With my lips have I declared *and* recounted all the ordinances of Your mouth.

14 I have rejoiced in the way of Your testimonies as much as in all riches.

15 I will meditate on Your precepts and have respect to Your ways [the paths of life marked out by Your law]. [Ps. 104:34.]

16 I will delight myself in Your statutes; I will not forget Your word.

17 Deal bountifully with Your servant, that I may live; and I will observe Your word [hearing, receiving, loving, and obeying it]. [Ps. 119:97–101.]

18 Open my eyes, that I may behold wondrous things out of Your law.

19 I am a stranger *and* a temporary resident on the earth; hide not Your commandments from me. [Gen. 47:9; I Chron. 29:15; Ps. 39:12; II Cor. 5:6; Heb. 11:13.]

20 My heart is breaking with the longing that it has for Your ordinances *and* judgments at all times.

21 You rebuke the proud *and* arrogant, the accursed ones, who err *and* wander from Your commandments.

22 Take away from me reproach and contempt, for I keep Your testimonies.

23 Princes also sat *and* talked against me, but Your servant meditated on Your statutes.

24 Your testimonies also are my delight and my counselors.

25 My earthly life cleaves to the dust; revive *and* stimulate me according to Your word! [Ps. 143:11.]

26 I have declared my ways *and* opened my griefs to You, and You listened to me; teach me Your statutes.

27 Make me understand the way of Your precepts; so shall I meditate on *and* talk of Your wondrous works. [Ps. 145:5, 6.]

28 My life dissolves *and* weeps itself away for heaviness; raise me up *and* strengthen me according to [the promises of] Your word.

29 Remove from me the way of falsehood *and* unfaithfulness [to You], and graciously impart Your law to me.

30 I have chosen the way of truth *and* faithfulness; Your ordinances have I set before me.

31 I cleave to Your testimonies; O Lord, put me not to shame!

32 I will [not merely walk, but] run the way of Your commandments, when You give me a heart that is willing.

33 Teach me, O Lord, the way of Your statutes, and I will keep it to the end [steadfastly].

34 Give me understanding, that I may keep Your law; yes, I will observe it with my whole heart. [Prov. 2:6; James 1:5.]

35 Make me go in the path of Your commandments, for in them do I delight.

36 Incline my heart to Your testimonies and not to covetousness (robbery, sensuality, unworthy riches). [Ezek. 33:31; Mark 7:21, 22; I Tim. 6:10; Heb. 13:5.]

37 Turn away my eyes from beholding vanity (idols and idolatry); and restore me to vigorous life *and* health in Your ways.

38 Establish Your word *and* confirm Your promise to Your servant, which is for those who reverently fear *and* devotedly worship You. [Deut. 10:12; Ps. 96:9.]

39 Turn away my reproach which I fear *and* dread, for Your ordinances are good.

40 Behold, I long for Your precepts; in Your righteousness give me renewed life.

41 Let Your mercy *and* lovingkindness come also to me, O Lord, even Your salvation according to Your promise;

42 Then shall I have an answer for those who taunt *and* reproach me, for I lean on, rely on, *and* trust in Your word.

43 And take not the word of truth utterly out of my mouth, for I hope in Your ordinances.

44 I will keep Your law continually, forever and ever [hearing, receiving, loving, and obeying it].

45 And I will walk at liberty *and* at ease, for I have sought and inquired for [and desperately required] Your precepts.

46 I will speak of Your testimonies also before kings and will not be put to shame. [Ps. 138:1; Matt. 10:18, 19; Acts 26:1, 2.]

47 For I will delight myself in Your commandments, which I love.

48 My hands also will I lift up [in fervent supplication] to Your commandments, which I love, and I will meditate on Your statutes.

49 Remember [fervently] the word *and* promise to Your servant, in which You have caused me to hope.

50 This is my comfort *and* consolation in my affliction: that Your word has revived me *and* given me life. [Rom. 15:4.]

51 The proud have had me greatly in derision, yet have I not declined in my interest in *or* turned aside from Your law.

52 When I have [earnestly] recalled Your ordinances from of old, O Lord, I have taken comfort.

53 Burning indignation, terror, *and* sadness seize upon me because of the wicked, who forsake Your law.

54 Your statutes have been my songs in the house of my pilgrimage.

55 I have [earnestly] remembered Your name, O Lord, in the night, and I have observed Your law.

56 This I have had [as the gift of Your grace and as my reward]: that I have kept Your precepts [hearing, receiving, loving, and obeying them].

57 You are my portion, O Lord; I have promised to keep Your words.

58 I entreated Your favor with my whole heart; be merciful *and* gracious to me according to Your promise.

59 I considered my ways; I turned my feet to [obey] Your testimonies.

60 I made haste and delayed not to keep Your commandments.

61 Though the cords of the wicked have enclosed *and* ensnared me, I have not forgotten Your law.

62 At midnight I will rise to give thanks to You because of Your righteous ordinances.

63 I am a companion of all those who fear, revere, *and* worship You, and of those who observe *and* give heed to Your precepts.

64 The earth, O Lord, is full of Your mercy *and* loving-kindness; teach me Your statutes.

65 You have dealt well with Your servant, O Lord, according to Your promise.

66 Teach me good judgment, wise *and* right discernment, and knowledge, for I have believed (trusted, relied on, and clung to) Your commandments.

67 Before I was afflicted I went astray, but now Your word do I keep [hearing, receiving, loving, and obeying it].

68 You are good *and* kind and do good; teach me Your statutes.

69 The arrogant *and* godless have put together a lie against me, but I will keep Your precepts with my whole heart.

70 Their hearts are as fat as grease [their minds are dull and brutal], but I delight in Your law.

71 It is good for me that I have been afflicted, that I might learn Your statutes.

72 The law from Your mouth is better to me than thousands of gold and silver pieces.

73 Your hands have made me, cunningly fashioned *and* established me; give me understanding, that I may learn Your commandments.

74 Those who reverently *and* worshipfully fear You will see me and be glad, because I have hoped in Your word *and* tarried for it.

75 I know, O Lord, that Your judgments are right *and* righteous, and that in faithfulness You have afflicted me. [Heb. 12:10.]

76 Let, I pray You, Your merciful kindness *and* steadfast love be for my comfort, according to Your promise to Your servant.

77 Let Your tender mercy *and* loving-kindness come to me that I may live, for Your law is my delight!

78 Let the proud be put to shame, for they dealt perversely with me without a cause; but I will meditate on Your precepts.

79 Let those who reverently *and* worshipfully fear You turn to me, and those who have known Your testimonies.

80 Let my heart be sound (sincere and wholehearted and blameless) in Your statutes, that I may not be put to shame.

81 My soul languishes *and* grows faint for Your salvation, but I hope in Your word.

82 My eyes fail, watching for [the fulfillment of] Your promise. I say, When will You comfort me?

83 For I have become like a bottle [a wineskin blackened and shriveled] in the smoke [in which it hangs], yet do I not forget Your statutes.

84 How many are the days of Your servant [which he must endure]? When will You judge those who pursue and persecute me? [Rev. 6:10.]

85 The godless *and* arrogant have dug pitfalls for me, men who do not conform to Your law.

86 All Your commandments are faithful *and* sure. [The godless] pursue *and* persecute me with falsehood; help me [Lord]!

87 They had almost consumed me upon earth, but I forsook not Your precepts.

88 According to Your steadfast

love give life to me; then I will keep the testimony of Your mouth [hearing, receiving, loving, and obeying it].

89 Forever, O Lord, Your word is settled in heaven [stands firm as the heavens]. [Ps. 89:2; Matt. 24:34, 35; I Pet. 1:25.]

90 Your faithfulness is from generation to generation; You have established the earth, and it stands fast.

91 All [the whole universe] are Your servants; therefore they continue this day according to Your ordinances. [Jer. 33:25.]

92 Unless Your law had been my delight, I would have perished in my affliction.

93 I will never forget Your precepts, [how can I?] for it is by them You have quickened me (granted me life).

94 I am Yours, therefore save me [Your own]; for I have sought (inquired of and for) Your precepts and required them [as my urgent need]. [Ps. 42:1.]

95 The wicked wait for me to destroy me, but I will consider Your testimonies.

96 I have seen that everything [human] has its limits and end [no matter how extensive, noble, or excellent]; but Your commandment is exceedingly broad and extends without limits [into eternity]. [Rom. 3:10–19.]

97 Oh, how love I Your law! It is my meditation all the day. [Ps. 1:2.]

98 You, through Your commandment, make me wiser than my enemies, for [Your words] are ever before me.

99 I have better understanding and deeper insight than all my teachers, because Your testimonies are my meditation. [II Tim. 3:15.]

100 I understand more than the aged, because I keep Your precepts [hearing, receiving, loving, and obeying them].

101 I have restrained my feet from every evil way, that I might keep Your word [hearing, receiving, loving, and obeying it]. [Prov. 1:15.]

102 I have not turned aside from Your ordinances, for You Yourself have taught me.

103 How sweet are Your words to my taste, sweeter than honey to my mouth! [Ps. 19:10; Prov. 8:11.]

104 Through Your precepts I get understanding; therefore I hate every false way.

105 Your word is a lamp to my feet and a light to my path. [Prov. 6:23.]

106 I have sworn [an oath] and have confirmed it, that I will keep Your righteous ordinances [hearing, receiving, loving, and obeying them]. [Neh. 10:29.]

107 I am sorely afflicted; renew and quicken me [give me life], O Lord, according to Your word!

108 Accept, I beseech You, the freewill offerings of my mouth, O Lord, and teach me Your ordinances. [Hos. 14:2; Heb. 13:15.]

109 My life is continually in my hand, yet I do not forget Your law.

110 The wicked have laid a snare for me, yet I do not stray from Your precepts.

111 Your testimonies have I taken as a heritage forever, for they are the rejoicing of my heart. [Deut. 33:4.]

112 I have inclined my heart to perform Your statutes forever, even to the end.

113 I hate the thoughts of undecided [in religion], double-minded people, but Your law do I love.

114 You are my hiding place and my shield; I hope in Your word. [Ps. 32:7; 91:1.]

115 Depart from me, you evildoers, that I may keep the commandments of my God [hearing, receiving, loving, and obeying them]. [Ps. 6:8; 139:19; Matt. 7:23.]

116 Uphold me according to Your promise, that I may live; and let me not be put to shame in my hope! [Ps. 25:2; Rom. 5:5; 9:33; 10:11.]

117 Hold me up, that I may be safe and have regard for Your statutes continually!

118 You spurn *and* set at nought all those who stray from Your statutes, for their own lying deceives them *and* their tricks are in vain.

119 You put away *and* count as dross all the wicked of the earth [for there is no true metal in them]; therefore I love Your testimonies.

120 My flesh trembles *and* shudders for fear *and* reverential, worshipful awe of You, and I am afraid *and* in dread of Your judgments.

121 I have done justice and righteousness; leave me not to those who would oppress me.

122 Be surety for Your servant for good [as Judah was surety for the safety of Benjamin]; let not the proud oppress me. [Gen. 43:9.]

123 My eyes fail, watching for Your salvation and for the fulfillment of Your righteous promise.

124 Deal with Your servant according to Your mercy *and* loving-kindness, and teach me Your statutes.

125 I am Your servant; give me understanding (discernment and comprehension), that I may know (discern and be familiar with the character of) Your testimonies.

126 It is time for the Lord to act; they have frustrated Your law.

127 Therefore I love Your commandments more than [resplendent] gold, yes, more than [perfectly] refined gold.

128 Therefore I esteem as right all, yes, all Your precepts; I hate every false way.

129 Your testimonies are wonderful [far exceeding anything conceived by man]; therefore my [penitent] self keeps them [hearing, receiving, loving, and obeying them].

130 The entrance *and* unfolding of Your words give light; their unfolding gives understanding (discernment and comprehension) to the simple.

131 I opened my mouth and panted [with eager desire], for I longed for Your commandments.

132 Look upon me, be merciful unto me, *and* show me favor, as is Your way to those who love Your name.

133 Establish my steps *and* direct them by [means of] Your word; let not any iniquity have dominion over me.

134 Deliver me from the oppression of man; so will I keep Your precepts [hearing, receiving, loving, and obeying them]. [Luke 1:74.]

135 Make Your face shine [with pleasure] upon Your servant, and teach me Your statutes. [Ps. 4:6.]

136 Streams of water run down my eyes, because men do not keep Your law [they hear it not, nor receive it, love it, or obey it].

137 [Rigidly] righteous are You, O Lord, and upright are Your judgments *and* all expressions of Your will.

138 You have commanded *and* appointed Your testimonies in righteousness and in great faithfulness.

139 My zeal has consumed me *and* cut me off, because my adversaries have forgotten Your words.

140 Your word is very pure (tried and well refined); therefore Your servant loves it.

141 I am small (insignificant) and despised, but I do not forget Your precepts.

142 Your righteousness is an everlasting righteousness, and Your law is truth. [Ps. 19:9; John 17:17.]

143 Trouble and anguish have found *and* taken hold on me, yet Your commandments are my delight.

144 Your righteous testimonies are everlasting *and* Your decrees are binding to eternity; give me understanding and I shall live [give me discernment and comprehension and I shall not die].

145 I cried with my whole heart; hear me, O Lord; I will keep Your

statutes [I will hear, receive, love, and obey them].

146 I cried to You; save me, that I may keep Your testimonies [hearing, receiving, loving, and obeying them].

147 I anticipated the dawning of the morning and cried [in childlike prayer]; I hoped in Your word.

148 My eyes anticipate the night watches and I am awake before the cry of the watchman, that I may meditate on Your word.

149 Hear my voice according to Your steadfast love; O Lord, quicken me and give me life according to Your [righteous] decrees.

150 They draw near who follow after wrong thinking and persecute me with wickedness; they are far from Your law.

151 You are near, O Lord [nearer to me than my foes], and all Your commandments are truth.

152 Of old have I known Your testimonies, and for a long time, [therefore it is a thoroughly established conviction] that You have founded them forever. [Luke 21:33.]

153 Consider my affliction and deliver me, for I do not forget Your law.

154 Plead my cause and redeem me; revive me and give me life according to Your word.

155 Salvation is far from the wicked, for they seek not nor hunger for Your statutes.

156 Great are Your tender mercy and loving-kindness, O Lord; give me life according to Your ordinances.

157 Many are my persecutors and my adversaries, yet I do not swerve from Your testimonies.

158 I behold the treacherous and am grieved and loathe them, because they do not respect Your law [neither hearing, receiving, loving, nor obeying it].

159 Consider how I love Your precepts; revive me and give life to me, O Lord, according to Your loving-kindness!

160 The sum of Your word is truth [the total of the full meaning of all Your individual precepts]; and every one of Your righteous decrees endures forever.

161 Princes pursue and persecute me without cause, but my heart stands in awe of Your words [dreading violation of them far more than the force of prince or potentate]. [I Sam. 24:11, 14; 26:18.]

162 I rejoice at Your word as one who finds great spoil.

163 I hate and abhor falsehood, but Your law do I love.

164 Seven times a day and all day long do I praise You because of Your righteous decrees.

165 Great peace have they who love Your law; nothing shall offend them or make them stumble. [Prov. 3:2; Isa. 32:17.]

166 I am hoping and waiting [eagerly] for Your salvation, O Lord, and I do Your commandments. [Gen. 49:18.]

167 Your testimonies have I kept [hearing, receiving, loving, and obeying them]; I love them exceedingly!

168 I have observed Your precepts and Your testimonies, for all my ways are [fully known] before You.

169 Let my mournful cry and supplication come [near] before You, O Lord; give me understanding (discernment and comprehension) according to Your word [of assurance and promise].

170 Let my supplication come before You; deliver me according to Your word!

171 My lips shall pour forth praise [with thanksgiving and renewed trust] when You teach me Your statutes.

172 My tongue shall sing [praise for the fulfillment] of Your word, for all Your commandments are righteous.

173 Let Your hand be ready to help me, for I have chosen Your precepts.

174 I have longed for Your salva-

tion, O Lord, and Your law is my delight.

175 Let me live that I may praise You, and let Your decrees help me.

176 I have gone astray like a lost sheep; seek, inquire for, *and* demand Your servant, for I do not forget Your commandments. [Isa. 53:6; Luke 15:4; I Pet. 2:25.]

PSALM 120

A Song of ⁷Ascents.

IN MY distress I cried to the Lord, and He answered me.

2 Deliver me, O Lord, from lying lips and from deceitful tongues.

3 What shall be given to you? Or what more shall be done to you, you deceitful tongue?—

4 Sharp arrows of a [mighty] warrior, with [glowing] coals of the broom tree!

5 Woe is me that I sojourn with Meshech, that I dwell beside the tents of Kedar [as if among notoriously barbarous people]! [Gen. 10:2; 25:13; Jer. 49:28, 29.]

6 My life has too long had its dwelling with him who hates peace.

7 I am for peace; but when I speak, they are for war.

PSALM 121

A Song of ⁷Ascents.

I WILL lift up my eyes to the hills [around Jerusalem, to sacred Mount Zion and Mount Moriah]—From whence shall my help come? [Jer. 3:23.]

2 My help comes from the Lord, Who made heaven and earth.

3 He will not allow your foot to slip *or* to be moved; He Who keeps you will not slumber. [I Sam. 2:9; Ps. 127:1; Prov. 3:23, 26; Isa. 27:3.]

4 Behold, He who keeps Israel will neither slumber nor sleep.

5 The Lord is your keeper; the Lord is your shade on your right hand [the side not carrying a shield]. [Isa. 25:4.]

6 The sun shall not smite you by day, nor the moon by night. [Ps. 91:5; Isa. 49:10; Rev. 7:16.]

7 The Lord will keep you from all evil; He will keep your life.

8 The Lord will keep your going out and your coming in from this time forth and forevermore. [Deut. 28:6; Prov. 2:8; 3:6.]

PSALM 122

A Song of ⁷Ascents. Of David.

I WAS glad when they said to me, Let us go to the house of the Lord! [Isa. 2:3; Zech. 8:21.]

2 Our feet are standing within your gates, O Jerusalem!—

3 Jerusalem, which is built as a city that is compacted together—

4 To which the tribes go up, even the tribes of the Lord, as was decreed *and* as a testimony for Israel, to give thanks to the name of the Lord.

5 For there the thrones of judgment were set, the thrones of the house of David.

6 Pray for the peace of Jerusalem! May they prosper who love you [the Holy City]!

7 May peace be within your walls and prosperity within your palaces!

8 For my brethren and companions' sake, I will now say, Peace be within you!

9 For the sake of the house of the Lord our God, I will seek, inquire for, *and* require your good.

y It is possible that the fifteen psalms known as the "Songs of Degrees or Ascents" were sung by the caravans of pilgrims going up to attend the annual feasts at Jerusalem. But it is equally possible that the title has reference to some peculiarity in connection with the music or the manner of using it.   z See Psalm 120 title footnote.

PSALM 123
A Song of [a]Ascents.

UNTO YOU do I lift up my eyes, O You Who are enthroned in heaven.

2 Behold, as the eyes of servants look to the hand of their master, and as the eyes of a maid to the hand of her mistress, so our eyes look to the Lord our God, until He has mercy *and* loving-kindness for us.

3 Have mercy on us, O Lord, have mercy on *and* loving-kindness for us, for we are exceedingly satiated with contempt.

4 Our life is exceedingly filled with the scorning *and* scoffing of those who are at ease and with the contempt of the proud (irresponsible tyrants who disregard God's law).

PSALM 124
A Song of [a]Ascents. Of David.

IF IT had not been the Lord Who was on our side—now may Israel say—

2 If it had not been the Lord Who was on our side when men rose up against us,

3 Then they would have quickly swallowed us up alive when their wrath was kindled against us;

4 Then the waters would have overwhelmed us *and* swept us away, the torrent would have gone over us;

5 Then the proud waters would have gone over us.

6 Blessed be the Lord, Who has not given us as prey to their teeth!

7 We are like a bird escaped from the snare of the fowlers; the snare is broken, and we have escaped!

8 Our *help* is in the name of the Lord, Who made heaven and earth.

PSALM 125
A Song of [a]Ascents.

THOSE WHO trust in, lean on, *and* confidently hope in the Lord are like Mount Zion, which cannot be moved but abides *and* stands fast forever.

2 As the mountains are round about Jerusalem, so the Lord is round about His people from this time forth and forever.

3 For the scepter of wickedness shall not rest upon the land of the [uncompromisingly] righteous, lest the righteous (God's people) stretch forth their hands to iniquity *and* apostasy.

4 Do good, O Lord, to those who are good, and to those who are right [with You and all people] in their hearts.

5 As for such as turn aside to their crooked ways [of indifference to God], the Lord will lead them forth with the workers of iniquity. Peace be upon Israel!

PSALM 126
A Song of [a]Ascents.

WHEN THE Lord brought back the captives [who returned] to Zion, we were like those who dream [it seemed so unreal]. [Ps. 53:6; Acts 12:9.]

2 Then were our mouths filled with laughter, and our tongues with singing. Then they said among the nations, The Lord has done great things for them.

3 The Lord has done great things for us! We are glad!

4 Turn to freedom our captivity *and* restore our fortunes, O Lord, as the streams in the South (the Negeb) [are restored by the torrents].

5 They who sow in tears shall reap in joy and singing.

6 He who goes forth bearing seed and weeping [at needing his precious supply of grain for sowing] shall doubtless come again with rejoicing, bringing his sheaves with him.

a See Psalm 120 title footnote.

PSALM 127

A Song of [b]Ascents. Of Solomon.

EXCEPT THE Lord builds the house, they labor in vain who build it; except the Lord keeps the city, the watchman wakes but in vain. [Ps. 121:1, 3, 5.]

2 It is vain for you to rise up early, to take rest late, to eat the bread of [anxious] toil—for He gives [blessings] to His beloved in sleep.

3 Behold, children are a heritage from the Lord, the fruit of the womb a reward. [Deut. 28:4.]

4 As arrows are in the hand of a warrior, so are the children of one's youth.

5 Happy, blessed, and fortunate is the man whose quiver is filled with them! They will not be put to shame when they speak with their adversaries [in gatherings] at the [city's] gate.

PSALM 128

A Song of [b]Ascents.

BLESSED (HAPPY, fortunate, to be envied) is everyone who fears, reveres, and worships the Lord, who walks in His ways and lives according to His commandments. [Ps. 1:1, 2.]

2 For you shall eat [the fruit] of the labor of your hands; happy (blessed, fortunate, enviable) shall you be, and it shall be well with you.

3 Your wife shall be like a fruitful vine in the innermost parts of your house; your children shall be like olive plants round about your table.

4 Behold, thus shall the man be blessed who reverently and worshipfully fears the Lord.

5 May the Lord bless you out of Zion [His sanctuary], and may you see the prosperity of Jerusalem all the days of your life;

6 Yes, may you see your children's children. Peace be upon Israel!

PSALM 129

A Song of [b]Ascents.

MANY A time and much have they afflicted me from my youth up—let Israel now say—

2 Many a time and much have they afflicted me from my youth up, yet they have not prevailed against me.

3 The plowers plowed upon my back; they made long their furrows.

4 The Lord is [uncompromisingly] righteous; He has cut asunder the thick cords by which the wicked [enslaved us].

5 Let them all be put to shame and turned backward who hate Zion.

6 Let them be as the grass upon the housetops, which withers before it grows up,

7 With which the mower fills not his hand, nor the binder of sheaves his bosom—

8 While those who go by do not say, The blessing of the Lord be upon you! We bless you in the name of the Lord!

PSALM 130

A Song of [b]Ascents.

OUT OF the depths have I cried to You, O Lord.

2 Lord, hear my voice; let Your ears be attentive to the voice of my supplications.

3 If You, Lord, should keep account of and treat [us according to our] sins, O Lord, who could stand? [Ps. 143:2; Rom. 3:20; Gal. 2:16.]

4 But there is forgiveness with You [just what man needs], that You may be reverently feared and worshiped. [Deut. 10:12.]

5 I wait for the Lord, I expectantly wait, and in His word do I hope.

6 I am looking and waiting for the Lord more than watchmen for the morning, I say, more than watchmen for the morning.

b See Psalm 120 title footnote.

7 O Israel, hope in the Lord! For with the Lord there is mercy *and* loving-kindness, and with Him is plenteous redemption.

8 And He will redeem Israel from all their iniquities.

PSALM 131

A Song of *c*Ascents. Of David.

LORD, MY heart is not haughty, nor my eyes lofty; neither do I exercise myself in matters too great or in things too wonderful for me.

2 Surely I have calmed and quieted my soul; like a weaned child with his mother, like a weaned child is my soul within me [ceased from fretting].

3 O Israel, hope in the Lord from this time forth and forever.

PSALM 132

A Song of *c*Ascents.

LORD, [earnestly] remember to David's credit all his humiliations *and* hardships *and* endurance—

2 How he swore to the Lord and vowed to the Mighty One of Jacob:

3 Surely I will not enter my dwelling house or get into my bed—

4 I will not permit my eyes to sleep *or* my eyelids to slumber,

5 Until I have found a place for the Lord, a habitation for the Mighty One of Jacob. [Acts 7:46.]

6 Behold, at Ephratah we [first] heard of [the discovered ark]; we found it in the fields of the wood [at Kiriath-jearim]. [I Sam. 6:21.]

7 Let us go into His tabernacle; let us worship at His footstool.

8 Arise, O Lord, to Your resting-place, You and the ark [the symbol] of Your strength.

9 Let Your priests be clothed with righteousness (right living and right standing with God); and let Your saints shout for joy!

10 For Your servant David's sake, turn not away the face of Your anointed *and* reject not Your own king.

11 The Lord swore to David in truth; He will not turn back from it: One of the fruit of your body I will set upon your throne. [Ps. 89:3, 4; Luke 1:69; Acts 2:30, 31.]

12 If your children will keep My covenant and My testimony that I shall teach them, their children also shall sit upon your throne forever.

13 For the Lord has chosen Zion, He has desired it for His habitation:

14 This is My resting-place forever [says the Lord]; here will I dwell, for I have desired it.

15 I will surely *and* abundantly bless her provision; I will satisfy her poor with bread.

16 Her priests also will I clothe with salvation, and her saints shall shout aloud for joy.

17 There will I make a horn spring forth *and* bud for David; I have ordained *and* prepared a lamp for My anointed [fulfilling the promises of old]. [I Kings 11:36; 15:4; II Chron. 21:7; Luke 1:69.]

18 His enemies will I clothe with shame, but upon himself shall his crown flourish.

PSALM 133

A Song of *c*Ascents. Of David.

BEHOLD, HOW good and how pleasant it is for brethren to dwell together in unity!

2 It is like the precious ointment poured on the head, that ran down on the beard, even the beard of Aaron [the first high priest], that came down upon the collar *and* skirts of his garments [consecrating the whole body]. [Exod. 30:25, 30.]

3 It is like the dew of [lofty] Mount Hermon and the dew that comes on the hills of Zion; for there the Lord has commanded the blessing, even life for-

evermore [upon the high and the lowly].

PSALM 134

A Song of *d* Ascents.

BEHOLD, BLESS (affectionately and gratefully praise) the Lord, all you servants of the Lord, [singers] who by night stand in the house of the Lord. [I Chron. 9:33.]

2 Lift up your hands in holiness *and* to the sanctuary and bless the Lord [affectionately and gratefully praise Him]!

3 The Lord bless you out of Zion, even He Who made heaven and earth.

PSALM 135

PRAISE THE Lord! (Hallelujah!) Praise the name of the Lord; praise Him, O you servants of the Lord!

2 You who stand in the house of the Lord, in the courts of the house of our God,

3 Praise the Lord! For the Lord is good; sing praises to His name, for He is gracious *and* lovely!

4 For the Lord has chosen [the descendants of] Jacob for Himself, Israel for His peculiar possession *and* treasure. [Deut. 7:6.]

5 For I know that the Lord is great and that our Lord is above all gods.

6 Whatever the Lord pleases, that has He done in the heavens and on earth, in the seas and all deeps—

7 Who causes the vapors to arise from the ends of the earth, Who makes lightnings for the rain, Who brings the wind out of His storehouses;

8 Who smote the firstborn of Egypt, both of man and beast; [Exod. 12:12, 29; Ps. 78:51; 136:10.]

9 Who sent signs and wonders into the midst of you, O Egypt, upon Pharaoh and all his servants;

10 Who smote nations many *and* great and slew mighty kings—

11 Sihon king of the Amorites, Og king of Bashan, and all the kingdoms of Canaan.

12 [The Lord] gave their land as a heritage, a heritage to Israel His people.

13 Your name, O Lord, endures forever, Your fame, O Lord, throughout all ages.

14 For the Lord will judge *and* vindicate His people, and He will delay His judgments [manifesting His righteousness and mercy] *and* take into favor His servants [those who meet His terms of separation unto Him]. [Heb. 10:30.]

15 The idols of the nations are silver and gold, the work of men's hands.

16 [Idols] have mouths, but they speak not; eyes have they, but they see not;

17 They have ears, but they hear not, nor is there any breath in their mouths.

18 Those who make [idols] are like them; so is everyone who trusts in *and* relies on them. [Ps. 115:4–8.]

19 Bless (affectionately and gratefully praise) the Lord, O house of Israel; bless the Lord, O house of Aaron [God's ministers].

20 Bless the Lord, O house of Levi [the dedicated tribe]; you who reverently *and* worshipfully fear the Lord, bless the Lord [affectionately and gratefully praise Him]! [Deut. 6:5; Ps. 31:23.]

21 Blessed out of Zion be the Lord, Who dwells [with us] at Jerusalem! Praise the Lord! (Hallelujah!)

PSALM 136

O GIVE thanks to the Lord, for He is good; for His mercy *and* loving-kindness endure forever.

2 O give thanks to the God of gods, for His mercy *and* loving-kindness endure forever.

3 O give thanks to the Lord of

d See Psalm 120 title footnote.

lords, for His mercy *and* loving-kindness endure forever—

4 To Him Who alone does great wonders, for His mercy *and* loving-kindness endure forever;

5 To Him Who by wisdom *and* understanding made the heavens, for His mercy *and* loving-kindness endure forever;

6 To Him Who stretched out the earth upon the waters, for His mercy *and* loving-kindness endure forever;

7 To Him Who made the great lights, for His mercy *and* loving-kindness endure forever—

8 The sun to rule over the day, for His mercy *and* loving-kindness endure forever;

9 The moon and stars to rule by night, for His mercy *and* loving-kindness endure forever;

10 To Him Who smote Egypt in their firstborn, for His mercy *and* loving-kindness endure forever; [Exod. 12:29.]

11 And brought out Israel from among them, for His mercy *and* loving-kindness endure forever; [Exod. 12:51; 13:3, 17.]

12 With a strong hand and with an outstretched arm, for His mercy *and* loving-kindness endure forever;

13 To Him Who divided the Red Sea into parts, for His mercy *and* loving-kindness endure forever; [Exod. 14:21, 22.]

14 And made Israel to pass through the midst of it, for His mercy *and* loving-kindness endure forever;

15 But shook off *and* overthrew Pharaoh and his host into the Red Sea, for His mercy *and* loving-kindness endure forever;

16 To Him Who led His people through the wilderness, for His mercy *and* loving-kindness endure forever;

17 To Him Who smote great kings, for His mercy *and* loving-kindness endure forever;

18 And slew famous kings, for His mercy *and* loving-kindness endure forever—[Deut. 29:7.]

19 Sihon king of the Amorites, for His mercy *and* loving-kindness endure forever; [Num. 21:21–24.]

20 And Og king of Bashan, for His mercy *and* loving-kindness endure forever; [Num. 21:33–35.]

21 And gave their land as a heritage, for His mercy *and* loving-kindness endure forever;

22 Even a heritage to Israel His servant, for His mercy *and* loving-kindness endure forever; [Josh. 12:1.]

23 To Him Who [earnestly] remembered us in our low estate *and* imprinted us [on His heart], for His mercy *and* loving-kindness endure forever;

24 And rescued us from our enemies, for His mercy *and* loving-kindness endure forever;

25 To Him Who gives food to all flesh, for His mercy *and* loving-kindness endure forever;

26 O give thanks to the God of heaven, for His mercy *and* loving-kindness endure forever!

PSALM 137

BY THE rivers of Babylon, there we [captives] sat down, yes, we wept when we [earnestly] remembered Zion [the city of our God imprinted on our hearts].

2 On the willow trees in the midst of [Babylon] we hung our harps.

3 For there they who led us captive required of us a song with words, and our tormentors *and* they who wasted us required of us mirth, saying, Sing us one of the songs of Zion.

4 How shall we sing the Lord's song in a strange land?

5 If I forget you, O Jerusalem, let my right hand forget its skill [with the harp.]

6 Let my tongue cleave to the roof of my mouth if I remember you not, if I prefer not Jerusalem above my chief joy! [Ezek. 3:26.]

7 Remember, O Lord, against the Edomites, that they said in the day of Jerusalem's fall, Down, down to the ground with her!

8 O Daughter of Babylon [you devastator, you!], who [ought to be and] shall be destroyed, happy *and* blessed shall he be who requites you as you have served us. [Isa. 13:1–22; Jer. 25:12, 13.]

9 Happy *and* blessed shall he be who takes and dashes your little ones against the rock!

PSALM 138
[A Psalm] of David.

I WILL confess *and* praise You [O God] with my whole heart; before the gods will I sing praises to You.

2 I will worship toward Your holy temple and praise Your name for Your loving-kindness and for Your truth *and* faithfulness; for You have exalted above all else Your name and Your word *and* You have magnified Your word above all Your name!

3 In the day when I called, You answered me; and You strengthened me with strength (might and inflexibility to temptation) in my inner self.

4 All the kings of the land shall give You credit *and* praise You, O Lord, for they have heard of the promises of Your mouth [which were fulfilled].

5 Yes, they shall sing of the ways of the Lord *and* joyfully celebrate His mighty acts, for great is the glory of the Lord.

6 For though the Lord is high, yet has He respect to the lowly [bringing them into fellowship with Him]; but the proud *and* haughty He knows *and* recognizes [only] at a distance. [Prov. 3:34; James 4:6; I Pet. 5:5.]

7 Though I walk in the midst of trouble, You will revive me; You will stretch forth Your hand against the wrath of my enemies, and Your right hand will save me. [Ps. 23:3, 4.]

8 The Lord will perfect that which

concerns me; Your mercy *and* lovingkindness, O Lord, endure forever—forsake not the works of Your own hands. [Ps. 57:2; Phil. 1:6.]

PSALM 139
To the Chief Musician. A Psalm of David.

O LORD, you have searched me [thoroughly] and have known me.

2 You know my downsitting and my uprising; You understand my thought afar off. [Matt. 9:4; John 2:24, 25.]

3 You sift *and* search out my path and my lying down, and You are acquainted with all my ways.

4 For there is not a word in my tongue [still unuttered], but, behold, O Lord, You know it altogether. [Heb. 4:13.]

5 You have beset me *and* shut me in—behind and before, and You have laid Your hand upon me.

6 Your [infinite] knowledge is too wonderful for me; it is high above me, I cannot reach it.

7 Where could I go from Your Spirit? Or where could I flee from Your presence?

8 If I ascend up into heaven, You are there; if I make my bed in Sheol (the place of the dead), behold, You are there. [Rom. 11:33.]

9 If I take the wings of the morning or dwell in the uttermost parts of the sea,

10 Even there shall Your hand lead me, and Your right hand shall hold me.

11 If I say, Surely the darkness shall cover me and the night shall be [the only] light about me,

12 Even the darkness hides nothing from You, but the night shines as the day; the darkness and the light are both alike to You. [Dan. 2:22.]

13 For You did form my inward parts; You did knit me together in my mother's womb.

14 I will confess *and* praise You *for You are fearful and wonderful and* for the awful wonder of my birth! Wonderful are Your works, and that my inner self knows right well.

15 My frame was not hidden from You when I was being formed in secret [and] intricately *and* curiously wrought [as if embroidered with various colors] in the depths of the earth [a region of darkness and mystery].

16 Your eyes saw my unformed substance, and in Your book all the days [of my life] were written before ever they took shape, when as yet there was none of them.

17 How precious *and* weighty also are Your thoughts to me, O God! How vast is the sum of them! [Ps. 40:5.]

18 If I could count them, they would be more in number than the sand. When I awoke, [could I count to the end] I would still be with You.

19 If You would [only] slay the wicked, O God, and the men of blood depart from me—[Isa. 11:4.]

20 Who speak against You wickedly, Your enemies who take Your name in vain! [Jude 15.]

21 Do I not hate them, O Lord, who hate You? And am I not grieved *and* do I not loathe those who rise up against You?

22 I hate them with perfect hatred; they have become my enemies.

23 Search me [thoroughly], O God, and know my heart! Try me and know my thoughts!

24 And see if there is any wicked *or* hurtful way in me, *and* lead me in the *way everlasting.*

PSALM 140
To the Chief Musician. A Psalm of David.

DELIVER ME, O Lord, from evil men; preserve me from violent men;

2 They devise mischiefs in their heart; continually they gather together *and* stir up wars.

3 They sharpen their tongues like a serpent's; adders' poison is under their lips. Selah [pause, and calmly think of that]! [Rom. 3:13.]

4 Keep me, O Lord, from the hands of the wicked; preserve me from the violent men who have purposed to thrust aside my steps.

5 The proud have hidden a snare for me; they have spread cords as a net by the wayside, they have set traps for me. Selah [pause, and calmly think of that]!

6 I said to the Lord, You are my God; give ear to the voice of my supplications, O Lord.

7 O God the Lord, the Strength of my salvation, You have covered my head in the day of battle.

8 Grant not, O Lord, the desires of the wicked; further not their wicked plot *and* device, lest they exalt themselves. Selah [pause, and calmly think of that]!

9 Those who are fencing me in raise their heads; may the mischief of their own lips *and* the very things they desire for me come upon them.

10 Let burning coals fall upon them; let them be cast into the fire, into floods of water *or* deep water pits, from which they shall not rise.

11 Let not a man of slanderous tongue be established in the earth; let evil hunt the violent man to overthrow him [let calamity follow his evildoings].

12 I know *and* rest in confidence upon it that the Lord will maintain the cause of the afflicted, and will secure justice for the poor *and* needy [of His believing children].

13 Surely the [uncompromising-

ly] righteous shall give thanks to Your name; the upright shall dwell in Your presence (before Your very face).

PSALM 141
A Psalm of David.

LORD, I call upon You; hasten to me. Give ear to my voice when I cry to You.

2 Let my prayer be set forth as incense before You, the lifting up of my hands as the evening sacrifice. [I Tim. 2:8; Rev. 8:3, 4.]

3 Set a guard, O Lord, before my mouth; keep watch at the door of my lips.

4 Incline my heart not to submit or consent to any evil thing or to be occupied in deeds of wickedness with men who work iniquity; and let me not eat of their dainties.

5 Let the righteous man smite and correct me — it is a kindness. Oil so choice let not my head refuse or discourage; for even in their evils or calamities shall my prayer continue. [Prov. 9:8; 19:25; 25:12; Gal. 6:1.]

6 When their rulers are overthrown in stony places, [their followers] shall hear my words, that they are sweet (pleasant, mild, and just).

7 The unburied bones [of slaughtered rulers] shall lie scattered at the mouth of Sheol, [as unregarded as] the lumps of soil behind the plowman when he breaks open the ground. [II Cor. 1:9.]

8 But my eyes are toward You, O God the Lord; in You do I trust and take refuge; pour not out my life nor leave it destitute and bare.

9 Keep me from the trap which they have laid for me, and the snares of evildoers.

10 Let the wicked fall together into their own nets, while I pass over them and escape.

PSALM 142
A skillful song, or a didactic or reflective poem, of David; when he was in the cave. A Prayer.

I CRY to the Lord with my voice; with my voice to the Lord do I make supplication.

2 I pour out my complaint before Him; I tell before Him my trouble.

3 When my spirit was overwhelmed and fainted [throwing all its weight] upon me, then You knew my path. In the way where I walk they have hidden a snare for me.

4 Look on the right hand [the point of attack] and see; for there is no man who knows me [to appear for me]. Refuge has failed me and I have no way to flee; no man cares for my life or my welfare.

5 I cried to You, O Lord; I said, You are my refuge, my portion in the land of the living.

6 Attend to my loud cry, for I am brought very low; deliver me from my persecutors, for they are stronger than I.

7 Bring my life out of prison, that I may confess, praise, and give thanks to Your name; the righteous will surround me and crown themselves because of me, for You will deal bountifully with me.

PSALM 143
A Psalm of David.

HEAR MY prayer, O Lord, give ear to my supplications! In Your faithfulness answer me, and in Your righteousness.

2 And enter not into judgment with Your servant, for in Your sight no man living is [in himself] righteous or justified. [Ps. 130:3; Rom. 3:20–26; Gal. 2:16.]

3 For the enemy has pursued and persecuted my soul, he has crushed my life down to the ground; he has made me to dwell in dark places as those who have been long dead.

4 Therefore is my spirit overwhelmed *and* faints within me [wrapped in gloom]; my heart within my bosom grows numb.

5 I remember the days of old; I meditate on all Your doings; I ponder the work of Your hands.

6 I spread forth my hands to You; my soul thirsts after You like a thirsty land [for water]. Selah [pause, and calmly think of that]!

7 Answer me speedily, O Lord, for my spirit fails; hide not Your face from me, lest I become like those who go down into the pit (the grave).

8 Cause me to hear Your lovingkindness in the morning, for on You do I lean *and* in You do I trust. Cause me to know the way wherein I should walk, for I lift up my inner self to You.

9 Deliver me, O Lord, from my enemies; I flee to You to hide me.

10 Teach me to do Your will, for You are my God; let Your good Spirit lead me into a level country *and* into the land of uprightness.

11 Save my life, O Lord, for Your name's sake; in Your righteousness, bring my life out of trouble *and* free me from distress.

12 And in your mercy *and* lovingkindness, cut off my enemies and destroy all those who afflict my inner self, for I am Your servant.

PSALM 144

[A Psalm] of David.

BLESSED BE the Lord, my Rock *and* my keen *and* firm Strength, Who teaches *my* hands to war and my *fingers* to fight—

2 My Steadfast Love and my Fortress, my High Tower and my Deliverer, my Shield and He in Whom I trust *and* take refuge, Who subdues my people under me.

3 Lord, what is man that You take notice of him? Or [the] son of man that You take account of him? [Job 7:17; Ps. 8:4; Heb. 2:6.]

4 Man is like vanity *and* a breath; his days are as a shadow that passes away.

5 Bow Your heavens, O Lord, and come down; touch the mountains, and they shall smoke.

6 Cast forth lightning and scatter [my enemies]; send out Your arrows and embarrass *and* frustrate them.

7 Stretch forth Your hand from above; rescue me and deliver me out of great waters, from the hands of hostile aliens (tribes around us)

8 Whose mouths speak deceit and whose right hands are right hands [raised in taking] fraudulent oaths.

9 I will sing a new song to You, O God; upon a harp, an instrument of ten strings, will I offer praises to You.

10 You are He Who gives salvation to kings, Who rescues David His servant from the hurtful sword [of evil].

11 Rescue me and deliver me out of the power of [hostile] alien [tribes] whose mouths speak deceit and whose right hands are right hands [raised in taking] fraudulent oaths.

12 When our sons shall be as plants grown large in their youth *and* our daughters as sculptured corner pillars hewn like those of a palace;

13 When our garners are full, affording all manner of store, and our sheep bring forth thousands and ten thousands in our pastures;

14 When our oxen are well loaded; *when* there is no invasion [of hostile armies] and no going forth [against besiegers—when there is no murder or manslaughter] and no outcry in our streets;

15 Happy *and* blessed are the people who are in such a case; yes, happy (blessed, fortunate, prosperous, to be envied) are the people whose God is the Lord!

PSALM 145

[A Psalm] of praise. Of David.

I WILL extol You, my God, O King;
and I will bless Your name forever
and ever [with grateful, affectionate
praise].

2 Every day [with its new reasons]
will I bless You [affectionately and
gratefully praise You]; yes, I will
praise Your name forever and ever.

3 Great is the Lord and highly to be
praised; and His greatness is [so vast
and deep as to be] unsearchable. [Job
5:9; 9:10; Rom. 11:33.]

4 One generation shall laud Your
works to another and shall declare
Your mighty acts.

5 On the glorious splendor of Your
majesty and on Your wondrous works
I will meditate.

6 Men shall speak of the might of
Your tremendous *and* terrible acts, and
I will declare Your greatness.

7 They shall pour forth [like a foun-
tain] the fame of Your great *and* abundant goodness and shall sing aloud of
Your rightness *and* justice.

8 The Lord is gracious and full of
compassion, slow to anger and
abounding in mercy *and* loving-kindness.

9 The Lord is good to all, and His
tender mercies are over all His works
[the entirety of things created].

10 All Your works shall praise
You, O Lord, and Your loving ones
shall bless You [affectionately and
gratefully shall Your saints confess
and praise You]!

11 They shall speak of the glory of
Your kingdom and talk of Your power,

12 To make known to the sons of
men God's mighty deeds and the glorious majesty of His kingdom.

13 Your kingdom is an everlasting
kingdom, and Your dominion endures
throughout all generations.

14 The Lord upholds all those [of
His own] who are falling and raises up
all those who are bowed down.

15 The eyes of all wait for You
[looking, watching, and expecting]
and You give them their food in due
season.

16 You open Your hand and satisfy
every living thing with favor.

17 The Lord is [rigidly] righteous
in all His ways and gracious *and* merciful in all His works.

18 The Lord is near to all who call
upon Him, to all who call upon Him
sincerely *and* in truth.

19 He will fulfill the desires of
those who reverently *and* worshipfully
fear Him; He also will hear their cry
and will save them.

20 The Lord preserves all those
who love Him, but all the wicked will
He destroy.

21 My mouth shall speak the praise
of the Lord; and let all flesh bless (affectionately and gratefully praise) His
holy name forever and ever.

PSALM 146

PRAISE THE Lord! (Hallelujah!)
Praise the Lord, O my soul!

2 While I live will I praise the Lord;
I will sing praises to my God while I
have any being.

3 Put not your trust in princes, in a
son of man, in whom there is no help.

4 When his breath leaves him, he
returns to his earth; in that very day his
[previous] thoughts, plans, *and* purposes perish. [I Cor. 2:6.]

5 Happy (blessed, fortunate, enviable) is he who has the God of [special
revelation to] Jacob for his help,
whose hope is in the Lord his God,
[Gen. 32:30.]

6 Who made heaven and earth, the
sea, and all that is in them, Who keeps
truth *and* is faithful forever,

7 Who executes justice for the oppressed, Who gives food to the hungry. The Lord sets free the prisoners,

8 The Lord opens the eyes of the
blind, the Lord lifts up those who are
bowed down, the Lord loves the [un-
compromisingly] righteous (those up-

right in heart and in right standing with Him). [Luke 13:13; John 9:7, 32.]

9 The Lord protects *and* preserves the strangers *and* temporary residents, He upholds the fatherless and the widow *and* sets them upright, but the way of the wicked He makes crooked (turns upside down and brings to ruin).

10 The Lord shall reign forever, even Your Lord, O Zion, from generation to generation. Praise the Lord! (Hallelujah!) [Ps. 10:16; Rev. 11:15.]

PSALM 147

PRAISE the Lord! For it is good to sing praises to our God, for He is gracious *and* lovely; praise is becoming *and* appropriate.

2 The Lord is building up Jerusalem; He is gathering together the exiles of Israel.

3 He heals the brokenhearted and binds up their wounds [curing their pains and their sorrows]. [Ps. 34:18; Isa. 57:15; 61:1; Luke 4:18.]

4 He determines *and* counts the number of the stars; He calls them all by their names.

5 Great is our Lord and of great power; His understanding is inexhaustible *and* boundless.

6 The Lord lifts up the humble *and* downtrodden; He casts the wicked down to the ground.

7 Sing to the Lord with thanksgiving; sing praises with the harp *or* the lyre to our God!—

8 Who covers the heavens with clouds, Who prepares rain for the earth, Who makes grass to grow on the mountains.

9 He gives to the beast his food, and to the *young* ravens that for which they cry.

10 He delights not in the strength of the horse, nor does He take pleasure in the legs of a man.

11 The Lord takes pleasure in those who reverently *and* worshipfully fear Him, in those who hope in His mercy *and* loving-kindness. [Ps. 145:20.]

12 Praise the Lord, O Jerusalem! Praise your God, O Zion!

13 For He has strengthened and made hard the bars of your gates, and He has blessed your children within you.

14 He makes peace in your borders; He fills you with the finest of the wheat.

15 He sends forth His commandment to the earth; His word runs very swiftly.

16 He gives [to the earth] snow like [a blanket of] wool; He scatters the hoarfrost like ashes.

17 He casts forth His ice like crumbs; who can stand before His cold?

18 He sends out His word, and melts [ice and snow]; He causes His wind to blow, and the waters flow.

19 He declares His word to Jacob, His statutes and His ordinances to Israel. [Mal. 4:4.]

20 He has not dealt so with any [other] nation; they have not known (understood, appreciated, given heed to, and cherished) His ordinances. Praise the Lord! (Hallelujah!) [Ps. 79:6; Jer. 10:25.]

PSALM 148

PRAISE THE Lord! Praise the Lord from the heavens, praise Him in the heights!

2 Praise Him, all His angels, praise Him, all His hosts!

3 Praise Him, sun and moon, praise Him, all you stars of light!

4 Praise Him, you highest heavens and you waters above the heavens!

5 Let them praise the name of the Lord, for He commanded and they were created.

6 He also established them forever and ever; He made a decree which shall not pass away [He fixed their bounds which cannot be passed over].

7 Praise the Lord from the earth, you sea monsters and all deeps!

8 You lightning, hail, fog, *and*

frost, you stormy wind fulfilling His orders!

9 Mountains and all hills, fruitful trees and all cedars!

10 Beasts and all cattle, creeping things and flying birds!

11 Kings of the earth and all peoples, princes and all rulers and judges of the earth!

12 Both young men and maidens, old men and children!

13 Let them praise and exalt the name of the Lord, for His name alone is exalted and supreme! His glory and majesty are above earth and heaven!

14 He has lifted up a horn for His people [giving them power, prosperity, dignity, and preeminence], a song of praise for all His godly ones, for the people of Israel, who are near to Him. Praise the Lord! (Hallelujah!) [Ps. 75:10; Eph. 2:17.]

PSALM 149

P RAISE THE Lord! Sing to the Lord a new song, praise Him in the assembly of His saints!

2 Let Israel rejoice in Him, their Maker; let Zion's children triumph and be joyful in their King! [Zech. 9:9; Matt. 21:5.]

3 Let them praise His name in chorus and choir and with the [single or group] dance; let them sing praises to Him with the tambourine and lyre!

4 For the Lord takes pleasure in His people; He will beautify the humble with salvation and adorn the wretched with victory.

5 Let the saints be joyful in the glory and beauty [which God confers upon them]; let them sing for joy upon their beds.

6 Let the high praises of God be in their throats and a two-edged sword in their hands, [Heb. 4:12; Rev. 1:16.]

7 To wreak vengeance upon the nations and chastisement upon the peoples,

8 To bind their kings with chains, and their nobles with fetters of iron,

9 To execute upon them the judgment written. He [the Lord] is the honor of all His saints. Praise the Lord! (Hallelujah!)

PSALM 150

P RAISE THE Lord! Praise God in His sanctuary; praise Him in the heavens of His power!

2 Praise Him for His mighty acts; praise Him according to the abundance of His greatness! [Deut. 3:24; Ps. 145:5, 6.]

3 Praise Him with trumpet sound; praise Him with lute and harp!

4 Praise Him with tambourine and [single or group] dance; praise Him with stringed and wind instruments or flutes!

5 Praise Him with resounding cymbals; praise Him with loud clashing cymbals!

6 Let everything that has breath and every breath of life praise the Lord! Praise the Lord! (Hallelujah!)

Proverbs

THE
PROVERBS

CHAPTER 1

THE PROVERBS (truths obscurely expressed, maxims, and parables) of Solomon son of David, king of Israel:

2 [a]That people may know skillful *and* godly [b]Wisdom and instruction, discern *and* comprehend the words of understanding *and* insight,

3 Receive instruction in wise dealing *and* the discipline of wise thoughtfulness, righteousness, justice, and integrity,

4 That prudence may be given to the simple, and knowledge, discretion, *and* discernment to the youth—

5 The wise also will hear and increase in learning, and the person of understanding will acquire skill *and* attain to sound counsel [so that he may be able to steer his course rightly]— [Prov. 9:9.]

6 That people may understand a proverb and a figure of speech *or* an enigma with its interpretation, and the words of the wise and their dark sayings *or* riddles.

7 The reverent *and* worshipful fear of the Lord is the beginning *and* the principal *and* choice part of knowledge [its starting point and its essence]; but fools despise skillful *and* godly Wisdom, instruction, *and* discipline. [Ps. 111:10.]

8 My son, hear the instruction of your father; reject not *nor* forsake the teaching of your mother.

9 For they are a [victor's] chaplet (garland) of grace upon your head and chains *and* pendants [of gold worn by kings] for your neck.

10 My son, if sinners entice you, do not consent. [Ps. 1:1; Eph. 5:11.]

11 If they say, Come with us; let us lie in wait [to shed] blood, let us ambush the innocent without cause [and show that his piety is in vain];

12 Let us swallow them up alive as does Sheol (the place of the dead), and whole, as those who go down into the pit [of the dead];

13 We shall find *and* take all kinds of precious goods [when our victims are put out of the way], we shall fill our houses with plunder;

14 Throw in your lot with us [they insist] *and* be a sworn brother *and* comrade; let us all have one purse in common—

15 My son, do not walk in the way with them; restrain your foot from their path;

16 For their feet run to evil, and they make haste to shed blood.

17 For in vain is the net spread in the sight of any bird!

18 But [when these men set a trap for others] they are lying in wait for their own blood; they set an ambush for their own lives.

19 So are the ways of everyone who is greedy of gain; such [greed for plunder] takes away the lives of its possessors. [Prov. 15:27; I Tim. 6:10.]

---

a Over the doors of the school of Plato these words were written in Greek, "Let no one enter who is not a geometrician." But Solomon opens wide the doors of his proverbs with a special message of welcome to the unlearned, the simple, the foolish, the young, and even to the wise—that all "will hear and increase in learning" (Prov. 1:5).   b A key term in the book of Proverbs, "Wisdom" is capitalized throughout, as God's design for living and as a reminder of Christ, Whom the apostle Paul calls "the wisdom of God . . . in Whom are hid all the treasures of wisdom and knowledge" (I Cor. 1:24; Col. 2:3 KJV).

20 ᶜWisdom cries aloud in the street, she raises her voice in the markets;

21 She cries at the head of the noisy intersections [in the chief gathering places]; at the entrance of the city gates she speaks:

22 How long, O simple ones [open to evil], will you love being simple? And the scoffers delight in scoffing and [self-confident] fools hate knowledge?

23 If you will turn (repent) *and* give heed to my reproof, behold, I [ᵈWisdom] will pour out my spirit upon you, I will make my words known to you. [Isa. 11:2; Eph. 1:17–20.]

24 Because I have called you *and* have refused [to answer], have stretched out my hand and no man has heeded it, [Isa. 65:11, 12; 66:4; Jer. 7:13, 14; Zech. 7:11–13.]

25 And you treated as nothing all my counsel and would accept none of my reproof,

26 I also will laugh at your calamity; I will mock when the thing comes that shall cause you terror and panic—

27 When your panic comes as a storm *and* desolation and your calamity comes on as a whirlwind, when distress and anguish come upon you.

28 Then will they call upon me [Wisdom] but I will not answer; they will seek me early *and* diligently but they will not find me. [Job 27:9; 35:12, 13; Isa. 1:15, 16; Jer. 11:11; Mic. 3:4; James 4:3.]

29 Because they hated knowledge and did not choose the reverent *and* worshipful fear of the Lord, [Prov. 8:13.]

30 Would accept none of my counsel, and despised all my reproof,

31 Therefore shall they eat of the fruit of their own way and be satiated with their own devices.

32 For the backsliding of the simple

shall slay them, and the careless ease of [self-confident] fools shall destroy them. [Isa. 32:6.]

33 But whoso hearkens to me [Wisdom] shall dwell securely *and* in confident trust and shall be quiet, without fear *or* dread of evil.

CHAPTER 2

MY SON, if you will receive my words and treasure up my commandments within you,

2 Making your ear attentive to skillful *and* godly ᶜWisdom *and* inclining and directing your heart *and* mind to understanding [applying all your powers to the quest for it];

3 Yes, if you cry out for insight and raise your voice for understanding,

4 If you seek [Wisdom] as for silver and search for skillful *and* godly Wisdom as for hidden treasures,

5 Then you will understand the reverent *and* worshipful fear of the Lord and find the knowledge of [our omniscient] God. [Prov. 1:7.]

6 For the Lord gives skillful *and* godly Wisdom; from His mouth come knowledge and understanding.

7 He hides away sound *and* godly Wisdom *and* stores it for the righteous (those who are upright and in right standing with Him); He is a shield to those who walk uprightly *and* in integrity,

8 That He may guard the paths of justice; yes, He preserves the way of His saints. [I Sam. 2:9; Ps. 66:8, 9.]

9 Then you will understand righteousness, justice, and fair dealing [in every area and relation]; yes, you will understand every good path.

10 For skillful *and* godly Wisdom shall enter into your heart, and knowledge shall be pleasant to you;

11 Discretion shall watch over you, understanding shall keep you,

12 To deliver you from the way of

c Wisdom here is personified. Read "the Wisdom of God" instead of "Wisdom" and see the wonderful power of this book.   d See footnotes on Prov. 1:2 and 1:20.   e See footnote on Prov. 1:2.

evil *and* the evil men, from men who speak perverse things *and* are liars,

13 Men who forsake the paths of uprightness to walk in the ways of darkness,

14 Who rejoice to do evil and delight in the perverseness of evil,

15 Who are crooked in their ways, wayward *and* devious in their paths.

16 [Discretion shall watch over you, understanding shall keep you] to deliver you from the alien woman, from the outsider with her flattering words, [Prov. 2:11.]

17 Who forsakes the husband *and* guide of her youth and forgets the covenant of her God.

18 For her house sinks down to death and her paths to the spirits [of the dead].

19 None who go to her return again, neither do they attain *or* regain the paths of life.

20 So may you walk in the way of good men, and keep to the paths of the [consistently] righteous (the upright, in right standing with God).

21 For the upright shall dwell in the land, and the men of integrity, blameless *and* complete [in God's sight], shall remain in it;

22 But the wicked shall be cut off from the earth, and the treacherous shall be rooted out of it.

CHAPTER 3

MY SON, forget not my law *or* teaching, but let your heart keep my commandments;

2 For length of days and tranquility of a life [worth living] and tranquility [inward and outward and continuing through old age till death], these shall they add to you.

3 Let not mercy and kindness [shutting out all hatred and selfishness] and truth [shutting out all deliberate hypocrisy *or* falsehood] forsake you; bind them about your neck, write them

upon the tablet of your heart. [Col. 3:9–12.]

4 So shall you find favor, good understanding, *and* high esteem in the sight [or judgment] of God and man. [Luke 2:52.]

5 Lean on, trust in, *and* be confident in the Lord with all your heart *and* mind and do not rely on your own insight *or* understanding.

6 In all your ways know, recognize, *and* acknowledge Him, and He will direct *and* make straight *and* plain your paths.

7 Be not wise in your own eyes; reverently fear *and* worship the Lord and turn [entirely] away from evil. [Prov. 8:13.]

8 It shall be health to your nerves *and* sinews, and marrow *and* moistening to your bones.

9 Honor the Lord with your capital *and* sufficiency [from righteous labors] and with the firstfruits of all your income; [Deut. 26:2; Mal. 3:10; Luke 14:13, 14.]

10 So shall your storage places be filled with plenty, and your vats shall be overflowing with new wine. [Deut. 28:8.]

11 My son, do not despise *or* shrink from the chastening of the Lord [His correction by punishment *or* by subjection to suffering or trial]; neither be weary of *or* impatient about *or* loathe *or* abhor His reproof, [Ps. 94:12; Heb. 12:5, 6; Rev. 3:19.]

12 For whom the Lord loves He corrects, even as a father corrects the son in whom he delights.

13 Happy (blessed, fortunate, enviable) is the man who finds skillful *and* godly Wisdom, and the man who gets understanding [drawing it forth from God's Word and life's experiences],

14 For the gaining of it is better than the gaining of silver, and the profit of it better than fine gold.

15 Skillful *and* godly /Wisdom is

f See footnote on Prov. 1:20.

more precious than rubies; and nothing you can wish for is to be compared to her. [Job 28:12–18.]

16 Length of days is in her right hand, and in her left hand are riches and honor. [Prov. 8:12–21; I Tim. 4:8.]

17 Her ways are highways of pleasantness, and all her paths are peace.

18 She is a tree of life to those who lay hold on her; and happy (blessed, fortunate, to be envied) is everyone who holds her fast.

19 The Lord by skillful and godly Wisdom has founded the earth; by understanding He has established the heavens. [Col. 1:16.]

20 By His knowledge the deeps were broken up, and the skies distill the dew.

21 My son, let them not escape from your sight, but keep sound and godly Wisdom and discretion,

22 And they will be life to your inner self, and a gracious ornament to your neck (your outer self).

23 Then you will walk in your way securely and in confident trust, and you shall not dash your foot or stumble. [Ps. 91:11, 12; Prov. 10:9.]

24 When you lie down, you shall not be afraid; yes, you shall lie down, and your sleep shall be sweet.

25 Be not afraid of sudden terror and panic, nor of the stormy blast or the storm and ruin of the wicked when it comes [for you will be guiltless],

26 For the Lord shall be your confidence, firm and strong, and shall keep your foot from being caught [in a trap or some hidden danger].

27 Withhold not good from those to whom it is due [its rightful owners], when it is in the power of your hand to do it. [Rom. 13:7; Gal. 6:10.]

28 Do not say to your neighbor, Go, and come again; and tomorrow I will give it—when you have it with you. [Lev. 19:13; Deut. 24:15.]

29 Do not contrive or dig up or cultivate evil against your neighbor, who dwells trustingly and confidently beside you.

30 Contend not with a man for no reason—when he has done you no wrong. [Rom. 12:18.]

31 Do not resentfully envy and be jealous of an unscrupulous, grasping man, and choose none of his ways. [Ps. 37:1; 73:3; Prov. 24:1.]

32 For the perverse are an abomination [extremely disgusting and detestable] to the Lord; but His confidential communion and secret counsel are with the [uncompromisingly] righteous (those who are upright and in right standing with Him). [Ps. 25:14.]

33 The curse of the Lord is in and on the house of the wicked, but He declares blessed (joyful and favored with blessings) the home of the just and consistently righteous. [Ps. 37:22; Zech. 5:4; Mal. 2:2.]

34 Though He scoffs at the scoffers and scorns the scorners, yet He gives His undeserved favor to the low [in rank], the humble, and the afflicted. [James 4:6; I Pet. 5:5.]

35 The wise shall inherit glory (all honor and good) but shame is the highest rank conferred on [self-confident] fools. [Isa. 32:6.]

CHAPTER 4

HEAR, MY sons, the instruction of a father, and pay attention in order to gain and to know intelligent discernment, comprehension, and interpretation [of spiritual matters].

2 For I give you good doctrine [what is to be received]; do not forsake my teaching.

3 When I [Solomon] was a son with my father [David], tender and the only son in the sight of my mother [Bathsheba],

4 He taught me and said to me, Let your heart hold fast my words; keep my commandments and live. [I Chron. 28:9; Eph. 6:4.]

5 Get skillful and godly Wisdom, get understanding (discernment, com-

prehension, and interpretation); do not forget and do not turn back from the words of my mouth.

6 Forsake not [Wisdom], and she will keep, defend, *and* protect you; love her, and she will guard you.

7 The beginning of Wisdom is: get Wisdom (skillful and godly Wisdom)! [For skillful *and* godly Wisdom is the principal thing.] And with all you have gotten, get understanding (discernment, comprehension, and interpretation). [James 1:5.]

8 Prize Wisdom highly *and* exalt her, and she will exalt *and* promote you; she will bring you to honor when you embrace her.

9 She shall give to your head a wreath of gracefulness; a crown of beauty *and* glory will she deliver to you.

10 Hear, O my son, and receive my sayings, and the years of your life shall be many.

11 I have taught you in the way of skillful *and* godly Wisdom [which is comprehensive insight into the ways and purposes of God]; I have led you in paths of uprightness.

12 When you walk, your steps shall not be hampered [your path will be clear and open]; and when you run, you shall not stumble.

13 Take firm hold of instruction, do not let go; guard her, for she is your life.

14 Enter not into the path of the wicked, and go not in the way of evil men.

15 Avoid it, do not go on it; turn from it and pass on.

16 For they cannot sleep unless they have caused trouble *or* vexation; their sleep is taken away unless they have caused someone to fall.

17 For they eat the bread of wickedness and drink the wine of violence.

18 But the path of the [uncompromisingly] just *and* righteous is like the light of dawn, that shines more and more (brighter and clearer) until [it reaches its full strength and glory in] the perfect day [to be prepared]. [II Sam. 23:4; Matt. 5:14; Phil. 2:15.]

19 The way of the wicked is like deep darkness; they do not know over what they stumble. [John 12:35.]

20 My son, attend to my words; consent *and* submit to my sayings.

21 Let them not depart from your sight; keep them in the center of your heart.

22 For they are life to those who find them, healing *and* health to all their flesh.

23 Keep *and* guard your heart with all vigilance *and* above all that you guard, for out of it flow the springs of life.

24 Put away from you false *and* dishonest speech, and willful *and* contrary talk put far from you.

25 Let your eyes look right on [with fixed purpose], and let your gaze be straight before you.

26 Consider well the path of your feet, and let all your ways be established *and* ordered aright.

27 Turn not aside to the right hand or to the left; remove your foot from evil.

CHAPTER 5

MY SON, be attentive to my Wisdom [godly Wisdom learned by actual and costly experience], and incline your ear to my understanding [of what is becoming and prudent for you],

2 That you may exercise proper discrimination *and* discretion and your lips may guard *and* keep knowledge *and* the wise answer [to temptation].

3 For the lips of a loose woman drip honey as a honeycomb, and her mouth is smoother than oil; [Ezek. 20:30; Col. 2:8–10; II Pet. 2:14–17.]

4 But in the end she is bitter as wormwood, sharp as a two-edged *and* devouring sword.

5 Her feet go down to death; her

steps take hold of Sheol (Hades, the place of the dead).

6 She loses sight of *and* walks not in the path of life; her ways wind about aimlessly, and you cannot know them.

7 Now therefore, my sons, listen to me, and depart not from the words of my mouth.

8 Let your way in life be far from her, and come not near the door of her house [avoid the very scenes of temptation], [Prov. 4:15; Rom. 16:17; I Thess. 5:19–22.]

9 Lest you give your honor to others and your years to those without mercy,

10 Lest strangers [and false teachings] take their fill of your strength *and* wealth and your labors go to the house of an alien [from God]—

11 And you groan *and* mourn when your end comes, when your flesh and body are consumed,

12 And you say, How I hated instruction *and* discipline, and my heart despised reproof!

13 I have not obeyed the voice of my teachers nor submitted *and* consented to those who instructed me.

14 [The extent and boldness of] my sin involved almost all evil [in the estimation] of the congregation *and* the community.

15 *ᵍ* Drink waters out of your own cistern [of a pure marriage relationship], and fresh running waters out of your own well.

16 Should your offspring be dispersed abroad as water brooks in the streets?

17 [Confine yourself to your own wife] let your children be for you

alone, and not the children of strangers with you.

18 Let your fountain [of human life] be blessed [with the rewards of fidelity], and rejoice in the wife of your youth.

19 Let her be as the loving hind and pleasant doe [tender, gentle, attractive]—let her bosom satisfy you at all times, and always be transported with delight in her love.

20 Why should you, my son, be infatuated with a loose woman, embrace the bosom of an outsider, *and* go astray?

21 For the ways of man are directly before the eyes of the Lord, and He [Who would have us live soberly, chastely, and godly] carefully weighs all man's goings. [II Chron. 16:9; Job 31:4; 34:21; Prov. 15:3; Jer. 16:17; Hos. 7:2; Heb. 4:13.]

22 His own iniquities shall ensnare the wicked man, and he shall be held with the cords of his sin.

23 He will die for lack of discipline *and* instruction, and in the greatness of his folly he will go astray *and* be lost.

CHAPTER 6

MY SON, if you have become security for your neighbor, if you have given your pledge for a stranger *or* another,

2 You are snared with the words of your lips, you are caught by the speech of your mouth.

3 Do this now [at once and earnestly], my son, and deliver yourself when you have put yourself into the *ʰ*power of your neighbor; go, bestir *and* humble yourself, and beg your neighbor [to pay his debt and thereby release you].

---

g All of the Ten Commandments are reflected in the book of Proverbs; here it is the seventh, "You shall not commit adultery."   h The Bible consistently teaches that one is not to forsake a friend, and this passage is not to be otherwise construed. But it is one thing to lend a friend money, and quite another thing to promise to pay his debts for him if he fails to do so himself. It might cost one, under the rigid customary laws governing debt, his money, his land, his bed, and his clothing—and if these were not sufficient, he and his wife and children could be sold as slaves, not to be released until the next Year of Jubilee—fifty years after the previous one. God's Word is very plain on the subject of not underwriting another person's debts (see Prov. 11:15; 17:18; 22:26).

4 Give not [unnecessary] sleep to your eyes, nor slumber to your eyelids;

5 Deliver yourself, as a roe *or* gazelle from the hand of the hunter, and as a bird from the hand of the fowler.

6 Go to the ant, you sluggard; consider her ways and be wise!—[Job 12:7.]

7 Which, having no chief, overseer, or ruler,

8 Provides her food in the summer and gathers her supplies in the harvest.

9 How long will you sleep, O sluggard? When will you arise out of your sleep? [Prov. 24:33, 34.]

10 Yet a little sleep, a little slumber, a little folding of the hands to lie down *and* sleep—

11 So will your poverty come like a robber *or* one who travels [with slowly but surely approaching steps] and your want like an armed man [making you helpless]. [Prov. 10:4; 13:4; 20:4.]

12 A worthless person, a wicked man, is he who goes about with a perverse (contrary, wayward) mouth.

13 He winks with his eyes, he speaks by shuffling *or* tapping with his feet, he makes signs [to mislead and deceive] *and* teaches with his fingers.

14 Willful *and* contrary in his heart, he devises trouble, vexation, *and* evil continually; he lets loose discord and sows it.

15 Therefore upon him shall the crushing weight of calamity come suddenly; suddenly shall he be broken, and that without remedy.

16 These six things the Lord hates, indeed, seven are an abomination to Him:

17 A proud look [the spirit that makes one overestimate himself and underestimate others], a lying tongue, and hands that shed innocent blood, [Ps. 120:2, 3.]

18 A heart that manufactures wicked thoughts *and* plans, feet that are swift in running to evil,

19 A false witness who breathes out lies [even under oath], and he who sows discord among his brethren.

20 My son, keep your father's [God-given] commandment and forsake not the law of [God] your mother [taught you]. [Eph. 6:1–3.]

21 Bind them continually upon your heart and tie them about your neck. [Prov. 3:3; 7:3.]

22 When you go, they [the words of your parents' God] shall lead you; when you sleep, they shall keep you; and when you waken, they shall talk with you.

23 For the commandment is a lamp, and the whole teaching [of the law] is light, and reproofs of discipline are the way of life, [Ps. 19:8; 119:105.]

24 To keep you from the evil woman, from the flattery of the tongue of a loose woman.

25 Lust not after her beauty in your heart, neither let her capture you with her eyelids.

26 For on account of a harlot a man is brought to a piece of bread, and the adulteress stalks *and* snares [as with a hook] the precious life [of a man].

27 Can a man take fire in his bosom and his clothes not be burned?

28 Can one go upon hot coals and his feet not be burned?

29 So he who cohabits with his neighbor's wife [will be tortured with evil consequences and just retribution]; he who touches her shall not be innocent *or* go unpunished.

30 Men do not despise a thief if he steals to satisfy himself when he is hungry;

31 But if he is found out, he must restore seven times [what he stole]; he must give the whole substance of his house [if necessary—to meet his fine].

32 But whoever commits adultery with a woman lacks heart *and* understanding (moral principle and prudence); he who does it is destroying his own life.

33 Wounds and disgrace will he

get, and his reproach will not be wiped away.

34 For jealousy makes [the wronged] man furious; therefore he will not spare in the day of vengeance [upon the detected one].

35 He will not consider any ransom [offered to buy him off from demanding full punishment]; neither will he be satisfied, though you offer him many gifts *and* bribes.

CHAPTER 7

MY SON, keep my words; lay up within you my commandments [for use when needed] *and* treasure them.

2 Keep my commandments and live, and keep my law *and* teaching as the apple (the pupil) of your eye.

3 Bind them on your fingers; write them on the tablet of your heart.

4 Say to skillful and godly Wisdom, You are my sister, and regard understanding *or* insight as your intimate friend—

5 That they may keep you from the loose woman, from the adventuress who flatters with *and* makes smooth her words.

6 For at the window of my house I looked out through my lattice.

7 And among the simple (emptyheaded and emptyhearted) ones, I perceived among the youths a young man void of good sense,

8 Sauntering through the street near the [loose woman's] corner; and he went the way to her house

9 In the twilight, in the evening; night black and dense was falling [over the young man's life].

10 And behold, there met him a woman, dressed as a harlot and sly *and* cunning of heart.

11 She is turbulent *and* willful; her feet stay not in her house;

12 Now in the streets, now in the marketplaces, she sets her ambush at every corner.

13 So she caught him and kissed him and with impudent face she said to him,

14 Sacrifices of peace offerings were due from me; this day I paid my vows.

15 So I came forth to meet you [that you might share with me the feast from my offering]; diligently I sought your face, and I have found you.

16 I have spread my couch with rugs *and* cushions of tapestry, with striped sheets of fine linen of Egypt.

17 I have perfumed my bed with myrrh, aloes, and cinnamon.

18 Come, let us take our fill of love until morning; let us console *and* delight ourselves with love.

19 For the man is not at home; he is gone on a long journey;

20 He has taken a bag of money with him and will come home at the day appointed [at the full moon].

21 With much justifying *and* enticing argument she persuades him, with the allurements of her lips she leads him [to overcome his conscience and his fears] *and* forces him along.

22 Suddenly he [yields and] follows her reluctantly like an ox moving to the slaughter, like one in fetters going to the correction [to be given] to a fool *or* [i] *like a dog enticed by food to the muzzle*

23 Till a dart [of passion] pierces *and* inflames his vitals; then like a bird fluttering straight into the net [he hastens], not knowing that it will cost him his life.

24 Listen to me now therefore, O you sons, and be attentive to the words of my mouth.

25 Let not your heart incline toward her ways, do not stray into her paths.

26 For she has cast down many wounded; indeed, all her slain are a mighty host. [Neh. 13:26.]

---

i *The Septuagint* (Greek translation of the Old Testament) so reads at this point.

27 Her house is the way to Sheol (Hades, the place of the dead), going down to the chambers of death.

CHAPTER 8

DOES NOT skillful *and* godly Wisdom cry out, and understanding raise her voice [in contrast to the loose woman]?

2 On the top of the heights beside the way, where the paths meet, stands Wisdom [skillful and godly];

3 At the gates at the entrance of the town, at the coming in at the doors, she cries out:

4 To you, O men, I call, and my voice is directed to the sons of men.

5 O you simple *and* thoughtless ones, understand prudence; you [self-confident] fools, be of an understanding heart. [Isa. 32:6.]

6 Hear, for I will speak excellent *and* princely things; and the opening of my lips shall be for right things.

7 For my mouth shall utter truth, and wrongdoing is detestable *and* loathsome to my lips.

8 All the words of my mouth are righteous (upright and in right standing with God); there is nothing contrary to truth or crooked in them.

9 They are all plain to him who understands [and opens his heart], and right to those who find knowledge [and live by it].

10 Receive my instruction in preference to [striving for] silver, and knowledge rather than choice gold.

11 For skillful *and* godly Wisdom is better than rubies *or* pearls, and all the things that may be desired are not to be compared to it. [Job 28:15; Ps. 19:10; 119:127.]

12 I, Wisdom [from God], make prudence my dwelling, and I find out knowledge *and* discretion. [James 1:5.]

13 The reverent fear *and* worshipful awe of the Lord [includes] the hatred of evil; pride, arrogance, the evil

way, and perverted *and* twisted speech I hate.

14 I have counsel and sound knowledge, I have understanding, I have might *and* power.

15 By me kings reign and rulers decree justice. [Dan. 2:21; Rom. 13:1.]

16 By me princes rule, and nobles, even all the judges *and* governors of the earth.

17 I love those who love me, and those who seek me early *and* diligently shall find me. [I Sam. 2:30; Ps. 91:14; John 14:21; James 1:5.]

18 Riches and honor are with me, enduring wealth and righteousness (uprightness in every area and relation, and right standing with God). [Prov. 3:16; Matt. 6:33.]

19 My fruit is better than gold, yes, than refined gold, and my increase than choice silver.

20 I [Wisdom] walk in the way of righteousness (moral and spiritual rectitude in every area and relation), in the midst of the paths of justice,

21 That I may cause those who love me to inherit [true] riches and that I may fill their treasuries.

22 The Lord formed *and* brought me [Wisdom] forth at the beginning of His way, before His acts of old.

23 I [Wisdom] was inaugurated *and* ordained from everlasting, from the beginning, before ever the earth existed. [John 1:1; I Cor. 1:24.]

24 When there were no deeps, I was brought forth, when there were no fountains laden with water.

25 Before the mountains were settled, before the hills, I was brought forth, [Job 15:7, 8.]

26 While as yet He had not made the land or the fields or the first of the dust of the earth.

27 When He prepared the heavens, I [Wisdom] was there; when He drew a circle upon the face of the deep *and* stretched out the firmament over it,

28 When He made firm the skies

above, when He established the fountains of the deep,

29 When He gave to the sea its limit *and* His decree that the waters should not transgress [across the boundaries set by] His command, when He appointed the foundations of the earth— [Job 38:10, 11; Ps. 104:6–9; Jer. 5:22.]

30 Then I [Wisdom] was *j* beside Him as a master *and* director of the work; and I was daily His delight, rejoicing before Him always, [Matt. 3:17; John 1:2, 18.]

31 Rejoicing in His inhabited earth and delighting in the sons of men. [Ps. 16:3.]

32 Now therefore listen to me, O you sons; for blessed (happy, fortunate, to be envied) are those who keep my ways. [Ps. 119:1, 2; 128:1, 2; Luke 11:28.]

33 Hear instruction and be wise, and do not refuse *or* neglect it.

34 Blessed (happy, fortunate, to be envied) is the man who listens to me, watching daily at my gates, waiting at the posts of my doors.

35 For whoever finds me [Wisdom] finds life and draws forth *and* obtains favor from the Lord.

36 But he who misses me *or* sins against me wrongs *and* injures himself; all who hate me love *and* court death.

CHAPTER 9

WISDOM HAS built her house; she has hewn out *and* set up her seven [perfect number of] pillars.

2 She has killed her beasts, she has mixed her [spiritual] wine; she has also set her table. [Matt. 22:2–4.]

3 She has sent out her maids to cry from the highest places of the town:

4 Whoever is simple (easily led astray and wavering), let him turn in here! As for him who lacks understanding, [God's] Wisdom says to him,

5 Come, eat of my bread and drink of the [spiritual] wine which I have mixed. [Isa. 55:1; John 6:27.]

6 Leave off, simple ones [forsake the foolish and simpleminded] and live! And walk in the way of insight *and* understanding.

7 He who rebukes a scorner heaps upon himself abuse, and he who reproves a wicked man gets for himself bruises.

8 Reprove not a scorner, lest he hate you; reprove a wise man, and he will love you. [Ps. 141:5.]

9 Give instruction to a wise man and he will be yet wiser; teach a righteous man (one upright and in right standing with God) and he will increase in learning.

10 The reverent *and* worshipful fear of the Lord is the beginning (the chief and choice part) of Wisdom, and the knowledge of the Holy One is insight *and* understanding.

11 For by me [Wisdom from God] your days shall be multiplied, and the years of your life shall be increased.

12 If you are wise, you are wise for yourself; if you scorn, you alone will bear it *and* pay the penalty.

13 The foolish woman is noisy; she is simple *and* open to all forms of evil, she [willfully and recklessly] knows nothing whatever [of eternal value].

14 For she sits at the door of her house *or* on a seat in the conspicuous places of the town,

15 Calling to those who pass by, who go uprightly on their way:

16 Whoever is simple (wavering and easily led astray), let him turn in here! And as for him who lacks understanding, she says to him,

17 Stolen waters (pleasures) are sweet [because they are forbidden]; and bread eaten in secret is pleasant. [Prov. 20:17.]

18 But he knows not that the shades of the dead are there [specters haunt-

---

j See Wisdom here present and involved at creation as an attribute of God.

ing the scene of past transgressions], and that her invited guests are [already sunk] in the depths of Sheol (the lower world, Hades, the place of the dead).

CHAPTER 10

THE PROVERBS of Solomon: A wise son makes a glad father, but a foolish *and* self-confident son is the grief of his mother.

2 Treasures of wickedness profit nothing, but righteousness (moral and spiritual rectitude in every area and relation) delivers from death.

3 The Lord will not allow the [uncompromisingly] righteous to famish, but He thwarts the desire of the wicked. [Ps. 34:9, 10; 37:25.]

4 He becomes poor who works with a slack *and* idle hand, but the hand of the diligent makes rich.

5 He who gathers in summer is a wise son, but he who sleeps in harvest is a son who causes shame.

6 Blessings are upon the head of the [uncompromisingly] righteous (the upright, in right standing with God) but the mouth of the wicked conceals violence.

7 The memory of the [uncompromisingly] righteous is a blessing, but the name of the wicked shall rot. [Ps. 112:6; 9:5.]

8 The wise in heart will accept *and* obey commandments, but the foolish of lips will fall headlong.

9 He who walks uprightly walks securely, but he who takes a crooked way shall be found out *and* punished.

10 He who winks with the eye [craftily and with malice] causes sorrow; the foolish of lips will fall headlong *but* *k he who boldly reproves makes peace.*

11 The mouth of the [uncompromisingly] righteous man is a well of

life, but the mouth of the wicked conceals violence.

12 Hatred stirs up contentions, but love covers all transgressions.

13 On the lips of him who has discernment skillful *and* godly *l Wisdom is found, but discipline *and* the rod are for the back of him who is without sense *and* understanding.

14 Wise men store up knowledge [in mind and heart], but the mouth of the foolish is a present destruction.

15 The rich man's wealth is his strong city; the poverty of the poor is their ruin. [Ps. 52:7; I Tim. 6:17.]

16 The earnings of the upright (the upright, in right standing with God) lead to life, but the profit of the wicked leads to further sin. [Rom. 6:21; I Tim. 6:10.]

17 He who heeds instruction *and* correction [not only himself] in the way of life [but also] is a way of life for others. And he who neglects *or* refuses reproof [not only himself] goes astray [but also] causes to err *and* is a path toward ruin for others.

18 He who hides hatred is of lying lips, and he who utters slander is a [self-confident] fool. [Prov. 26:24-26.]

19 In a multitude of words transgression is not lacking, but he who restrains his lips is prudent.

20 The tongues of those who are upright *and* in right standing with God are as choice silver; the minds of those who are wicked *and* out of harmony with God are of little value.

21 The lips of the [uncompromisingly] righteous feed *and* guide many, but fools die for want of understanding *and* heart.

22 The blessing of the Lord—it makes [truly] rich, and He adds no sorrow with it [neither does toiling increase it].

k *The Septuagint* (Greek translation of the Old Testament) so reads at this point.   **l** Recall that "Wisdom" is capitalized throughout the book of Proverbs as a reminder of its divine implications. See footnotes on Prov. 1:2 and Prov. 1:20.

23 It is as sport to a [self-confident] fool to do wickedness, but to have skillful *and* godly Wisdom is pleasure *and* relaxation to a man of understanding.

24 The thing a wicked man fears shall come upon him, but the desire of the [uncompromisingly] righteous shall be granted.

25 When the whirlwind passes, the wicked are no more, but the [uncompromisingly] righteous have an everlasting foundation. [Ps. 125:1; Matt. 7:24–27.]

26 As vinegar to the teeth and as smoke to the eyes, so is the sluggard to those who employ *and* send him.

27 The reverent *and* worshipful fear of the Lord prolongs one's days, but the years of the wicked shall be made short.

28 The hope of the [uncompromisingly] righteous (the upright, in right standing with God) is gladness, but the expectation of the wicked (those who are out of harmony with God) comes to nothing.

29 The way of the Lord is strength *and* a stronghold to the upright, but it is destruction to the workers of iniquity.

30 The [consistently] righteous shall never be removed, but the wicked shall not inhabit the earth [eventually]. [Ps. 37:22; 125:1.]

31 The mouths of the righteous (those harmonious with God) bring forth skillful *and* godly Wisdom, but the perverse tongue shall be cut down [like a barren and rotten tree].

32 The lips of the [uncompromisingly] righteous know [and therefore utter] what is acceptable, but the mouth of the wicked knows [and therefore speaks only] what is obstinately willful *and* contrary.

CHAPTER 11

A FALSE balance *and* unrighteous dealings are extremely offensive *and* shamefully sinful to the Lord, but a just weight is His delight. [Lev. 19:35, 36; Prov. 16:11.]

2 When swelling *and* pride come, then emptiness *and* shame come also, but with the humble (those who are lowly, who have been pruned or chiseled by trial, and renounce self) are skillful *and* godly Wisdom *and* soundness.

3 The integrity of the upright shall guide them, but the willful contrariness *and* crookedness of the treacherous shall destroy them.

4 Riches provide no security in any day of wrath *and* judgment, but righteousness (uprightness and right standing with God) delivers from death. [Prov. 10:2; Zeph. 1:18.]

5 The righteousness of the blameless shall rectify *and* make plain their way *and* keep it straight, but the wicked shall fall by their own wickedness.

6 The righteousness of the upright [their rectitude in every area and relation] shall deliver them, but the treacherous shall be taken in their own iniquity *and* greedy desire.

7 When the wicked man dies, his hope [for the future] perishes; and the expectation of the godless comes to nothing.

8 The [uncompromisingly] righteous is delivered out of trouble, and the wicked gets into it instead.

9 With his mouth the godless man destroys his neighbor, but through knowledge *and* superior discernment shall the righteous be delivered.

10 When it goes well with the [uncompromisingly] righteous, the city rejoices, but when the wicked perish, there are shouts of joy.

11 By the blessing of the influence of the upright *and* God's favor [because of them] the city is exalted, but it is overthrown by the mouth of the wicked.

12 He who belittles *and* despises his neighbor lacks sense, but a man of understanding keeps silent.

13 He who goes about as a talebear-

er reveals secrets, but he who is trustworthy *and* faithful in spirit keeps the matter hidden.

14 Where no wise guidance is, the people fall, but in the multitude of counselors there is safety.

15 He who becomes security for an outsider shall smart for it, but he who hates suretyship is secure [from its penalties].

16 A gracious *and* good woman wins honor [for her husband], and violent men win riches *but ᵐa woman who hates righteousness is a throne of dishonor for him.*

17 The merciful, kind, *and* generous man benefits himself [for his deeds return to bless him], but he who is cruel *and* callous [to the wants of others] brings on himself retribution.

18 The wicked man earns deceitful wages, but he who sows righteousness (moral and spiritual rectitude in every area and relation) shall have a sure reward [permanent and satisfying]. [Hos. 10:12; Gal. 6:8, 9; James 3:18.]

19 He who is steadfast in righteousness (uprightness and right standing with God) attains to life, but he who pursues evil does it to his own death.

20 They who are willfully contrary in heart are extremely disgusting *and* shamefully vile in the eyes of the Lord, but such as are blameless *and* wholehearted in their ways are His delight!

21 Assuredly [I pledge it] the wicked shall not go unpunished, but the multitude of the [uncompromisingly] righteous shall be delivered.

22 As a ring of gold in a swine's snout, so is a fair woman who is without discretion.

23 The desire of the [consistently] righteous brings only good, but the expectation of the wicked brings wrath.

24 There are those who [generously] scatter abroad, and yet increase more; there are those who withhold more than is fitting *or* what is justly due, but it results only in want.

25 The liberal person shall be enriched, and he who waters shall himself be watered. [II Cor. 9:6–10.]

26 The people curse him who holds back grain [when the public needs it], but a blessing [from God and man] is upon the head of him who sells it.

27 He who diligently seeks good seeks [God's] favor, but he who searches after evil, it shall come upon him.

28 He who leans on, trusts in, *and* is confident in his riches shall fall, but the [uncompromisingly] righteous shall flourish like a green bough.

29 He who troubles his own house shall inherit the wind, and the foolish shall be servant to the wise of heart.

30 The fruit of the [uncompromisingly] righteous is a tree of life, and he who is wise captures human lives [for God, as a fisher of men—he gathers and receives them for eternity]. [Matt. 4:19; I Cor. 9:19; James 5:20.]

31 Behold, the [uncompromisingly] righteous shall be recompensed on earth; how much more the wicked and the sinner! *And ᵐif the righteous are barely saved, what will become of the ungodly and wicked?* [I Pet. 4:18.]

CHAPTER 12

WHOEVER LOVES instruction *and* correction loves knowledge, but he who hates reproof is like a brute beast, stupid *and* indiscriminating.

2 A good man obtains favor from the Lord, but a man of wicked devices He condemns.

3 A man shall not be established by wickedness, but the root of the [uncompromisingly] righteous shall never be moved.

4 A virtuous *and* worthy wife [earnest and strong in character] is a crowning joy to her husband, but she

m *The Septuagint* (Greek translation of the Old Testament) so reads at this point.

who makes him ashamed is as rottenness in his bones. [Prov. 31:23; I Cor. 11:7.]

5 The thoughts and purposes of the [consistently] righteous are honest and reliable, but the counsels and designs of the wicked are treacherous.

6 The words of the wicked lie in wait for blood, but the mouth of the upright shall deliver them and the innocent ones [thus endangered].

7 The wicked are overthrown and are not, but the house of the [uncompromisingly] righteous shall stand.

8 A man shall be commended according to his Wisdom [godly Wisdom, which is comprehensive insight into the ways and purposes of God], but he who is of a perverse heart shall be despised.

9 Better is he who is lightly esteemed but works for his own support than he who assumes honor for himself and lacks bread.

10 A [consistently] righteous man regards the life of his beast, but even the tender mercies of the wicked are cruel. [Deut. 25:4.]

11 He who tills his land shall be satisfied with bread, but he who follows worthless pursuits is lacking in sense and is without understanding.

12 The wicked desire the booty of evil men, but the root of the [uncompromisingly] righteous yields [richer fruitage].

13 The wicked is [dangerously] snared by the transgression of his lips, but the [uncompromisingly] righteous shall come out of trouble.

14 From the fruit of his words a man shall be satisfied with good, and the work of a man's hands shall come back to him [as a harvest].

15 The way of a fool is right in his own eyes, but he who listens to counsel is wise. [Prov. 3:7; 9:9; 21:2.]

16 A fool's wrath is quickly and openly known, but a prudent man ignores an insult.

17 He who breathes out truth shows forth righteousness (uprightness and right standing with God), but a false witness utters deceit.

18 There are those who speak rashly, like the piercing of a sword, but the tongue of the wise brings healing.

19 Truthful lips shall be established forever, but a lying tongue is [credited] but for a moment.

20 Deceit is in the hearts of those who devise evil, but for the counselors of peace there is joy.

21 No [actual] evil, misfortune, or calamity shall come upon the righteous, but the wicked shall be filled with evil, misfortune, and calamity. [Job 5:19; Ps. 91:3; Prov. 12:13; Isa. 46:4; Jer. 1:8; Dan. 6:27; II Tim. 4:18.]

22 Lying lips are extremely disgusting and hateful to the Lord, but they who deal faithfully are His delight. [Prov. 6:17; 11:20; Rev. 22:15.]

23 A prudent man is reluctant to display his knowledge, but the heart of [self-confident] fools proclaims their folly. [Isa. 32:6.]

24 The hand of the diligent will rule, but the slothful will be put to forced labor.

25 Anxiety in a man's heart weighs it down, but an encouraging word makes it glad. [Ps. 50:4; Prov. 15:13.]

26 The [consistently] righteous man is a guide to his neighbor, but the way of the wicked causes others to go astray.

27 The slothful man does not catch his game or roast it once he kills it, but the diligent man gets precious possessions.

28 Life is in the way of righteousness (moral and spiritual rectitude in every area and relation), and in its pathway there is no death but immortality (perpetual, eternal life). [John 3:36; 4:36; 8:51; 11:26; I Cor. 15:54; Gal. 6:8.]

CHAPTER 13

A WISE son heeds [and is the fruit of] his father's instruction and correction, but a scoffer listens not to rebuke.

2 A good man eats good from the fruit of his mouth, but the desire of the treacherous is for violence.

3 He who guards his mouth keeps his life, but he who opens wide his lips comes to ruin.

4 The appetite of the sluggard craves and gets nothing, but the appetite of the diligent is abundantly supplied. [Prov. 10:4.]

5 A [consistently] righteous man hates lying and deceit, but a wicked man is loathsome [his very breath spreads pollution] and he comes [surely] to shame.

6 Righteousness (rightness and justice in every area and relation) guards him who is upright in the way, but wickedness plunges into sin and overthrows the sinner.

7 One man considers himself rich, yet has nothing [to keep permanently]; another man considers himself poor, yet has great [and indestructible] riches. [Prov. 12:9; Luke 12:20, 21.]

8 A rich man can buy his way out of threatened death by paying a ransom, but the poor man does not even have to listen to threats [from the envious].

9 The light of the [uncompromisingly] righteous [is within him—it grows brighter and] rejoices, but the lamp of the wicked [furnishes only a derived, temporary light and] shall be put out shortly.

10 By pride and insolence comes only contention, but with the well-advised is skillful and godly Wisdom.

11 Wealth [not earned but] won in haste or unjustly or from the production of things for vain or detrimental use [such riches] will dwindle away, but he who gathers little by little will increase [his riches].

12 Hope deferred makes the heart

sick, but when the desire is fulfilled, it is a tree of life.

13 Whoever despises the word and counsel [of God] brings destruction upon himself, but he who [reverently] fears and respects the commandment [of God] is rewarded.

14 The teaching of the wise is a fountain of life, that one may avoid the snares of death.

15 Good understanding wins favor, but the way of the transgressor is hard [like the barren, dry soil or the impassable swamp].

16 Every prudent man deals with knowledge, but a [self-confident] fool exposes and flaunts his folly.

17 A wicked messenger falls into evil, but a faithful ambassador brings healing.

18 Poverty and shame come to him who refuses instruction and correction, but he who heeds reproof is honored.

19 Satisfied desire is sweet to a person; therefore it is hateful and exceedingly offensive to [self-confident] fools to give up evil [upon which they have set their hearts].

20 He who walks [as a companion] with wise men is wise, but he who associates with [self-confident] fools is [a fool himself and] shall smart for it. [Isa. 32:6.]

21 Evil pursues sinners, but the consistently upright and in right standing with God is recompensed with good.

22 A good man leaves an inheritance [of moral stability and goodness] to his children's children, and the wealth of the sinner [finds its way eventually] into the hands of the righteous, for whom it was laid up.

23 Much food is in the tilled land of the poor, but there are those who are destroyed because of injustice.

24 He who spares his rod [of discipline] hates his son, but he who loves him disciplines diligently and pun-

ishes him early. [Prov. 19:18; 22:15; 23:13; 29:15, 17.]

25 The [uncompromisingly] righteous eats to his own satisfaction, but the stomach of the wicked is in want.

CHAPTER 14

EVERY WISE woman builds her house, but the foolish one tears it down with her own hands.

2 He who walks in uprightness reverently and worshipfully fears the Lord, but he who is contrary and devious in his ways despises Him.

3 In the ⁿfool's own mouth is a rod [to shame] his pride, but the wise men's lips preserve them.

4 Where no oxen are, the grain crib is empty, but much increase [of crops] comes by the strength of the ox.

5 A faithful witness will not lie, but a false witness breathes out falsehoods.

6 A scoffer seeks Wisdom in vain [for his very attitude blinds and deafens him to it], but knowledge is easy to him who [being teachable] understands.

7 Go from the presence of a foolish and self-confident man, for you will not find knowledge on his lips.

8 The Wisdom [godly Wisdom, which is comprehensive insight into the ways and purposes of God] of the prudent is to understand his way, but the folly of [self-confident] fools is to deceive.

9 Fools make a mock of sin and sin mocks the fools [who are its victims; a sin offering made by them only mocks them, bringing them disappointment and disfavor], but among the upright there is the favor of God. [Prov. 10:23.]

10 The heart knows its own bitterness, and no stranger shares its joy.

11 The house of the wicked shall be overthrown, but the tent of the upright shall flourish.

12 There is a way which seems right to a man and appears straight before him, but at the end of it is the way of death.

13 Even in laughter the heart is sorrowful, and the end of mirth is heaviness and grief.

14 The backslider in heart [from God and from fearing God] shall be filled with [the fruit of] his own ways, and a good man shall be satisfied with [the fruit of] his ways [with the holy thoughts and actions which his heart prompts and in which he delights].

15 The simpleton believes every word he hears, but the prudent man looks and considers well where he is going.

16 A wise man suspects danger and cautiously avoids evil, but the fool bears himself insolently and is [presumptuously] confident.

17 He who foams up quickly and flies into a passion deals foolishly, and a man of wicked plots and plans is hated.

18 The simple acquire folly, but the prudent are crowned with knowledge.

19 The evil men bow before the good, and the wicked [stand suppliantly] at the gates of the [uncompromisingly] righteous.

20 The poor is hated even by his own neighbor, but the rich has many friends.

21 He who despises his neighbor sins [against God, his fellowman, and himself], but happy (blessed and fortunate) is he who is kind and merciful to the poor.

22 Do they not err who devise evil and wander from the way of life? But loving-kindness and mercy, loyalty

---

ⁿ The word "fool" in the Old Testament seldom, if ever, is used to describe the feebleminded, imbecile, idiot, or moron. Rather, it always has within it the meaning of a **rebel**, especially against God and the laws of order, decency, and justice. Notice in Proverbs how many such characteristics of rebelliousness are listed against the fool, and see God's attitude toward them.

and faithfulness, shall be to those who devise good.

23 In all labor there is profit, but idle talk leads only to poverty.

24 The crown of the wise is their wealth of Wisdom, but the foolishness of [self-confident] fools is [nothing but] folly.

25 A truthful witness saves lives, but a deceitful witness speaks lies [and endangers lives].

26 In the reverent *and* worshipful fear of the Lord there is strong confidence, and His children shall always have a place of refuge.

27 Reverent *and* worshipful fear of the Lord is a fountain of life, that one may avoid the snares of death. [John 4:10, 14.]

28 In a multitude of people is the king's glory, but in a lack of people is the prince's ruin.

29 He who is slow to anger has great understanding, but he who is hasty of spirit exposes *and* exalts his folly. [Prov. 16:32; James 1:19.]

30 A calm *and* undisturbed mind *and* heart are the life *and* health of the body, but envy, jealousy, *and* wrath are like rottenness of the bones.

31 He who oppresses the poor reproaches, mocks, *and* insults his Maker, but he who is kind *and* merciful to the needy honors Him. [Prov. 17:5; Matt. 25:40, 45.]

32 The wicked is overthrown through his wrongdoing *and* calamity, but the [consistently] righteous has hope *and* confidence even in death.

33 Wisdom rests [silently] in the mind *and* heart of him who has understanding, but that which is in the inward part of [self-confident] fools is made known. [Isa. 32:6.]

34 Uprightness *and* right standing with God (moral and spiritual rectitude in every area and relation) elevate a nation, but sin is a reproach to any people.

35 The king's favor is toward a wise *and* discreet servant, but his wrath is against him who does shamefully. [Matt. 24:45, 47.]

CHAPTER 15

A SOFT answer turns away wrath, but grievous words stir up anger. [Prov. 25:15.]

2 The tongue of the wise utters knowledge rightly, but the mouth of the [self-confident] fool pours out folly.

3 The eyes of the Lord are in every place, keeping watch upon the evil and the good. [Job 34:21; Prov. 5:21; Jer. 16:17; 32:19; Heb. 4:13.]

4 A gentle tongue [with its healing power] is a tree of life, but willful contrariness in it breaks down the spirit.

5 A fool despises his father's instruction *and* correction, but he who regards reproof acquires prudence.

6 In the house of the [uncompromisingly] righteous is great [priceless] treasure, but with the income of the wicked is trouble *and* vexation.

7 The lips of the wise disperse knowledge [sifting it as chaff from the grain]; not so the minds *and* hearts of the self-confident *and* foolish.

8 The sacrifice of the wicked is an abomination, hateful *and* exceedingly offensive to the Lord, but the prayer of the upright is His delight! [Isa. 1:11; Jer. 6:20; Amos 5:22.]

9 The way of the wicked is an abomination, *extremely* disgusting *and* shamefully vile to the Lord, but He loves him who pursues righteousness (moral and spiritual rectitude in every area and relation).

10 There is severe discipline for him who forsakes God's way; and he who hates reproof will die [physically, morally, and spiritually].

11 Sheol (the place of the dead) and Abaddon (the abyss, the final place of the accuser Satan) are both before the Lord—how much more, then, the hearts of the children of men? [Job 26:6; Ps. 139:8; Rev. 9:2; 20:1, 2.]

12 A scorner has no love for one

who rebukes him; neither will he go to the wise [for counsel].

13 A glad heart makes a cheerful countenance, but by sorrow of heart the spirit is broken. [Prov. 17:22.]

14 The mind of him who has understanding seeks knowledge and inquires after and craves it, but the mouth of the [self-confident] fool feeds on folly. [Isa. 32:6.]

15 All the days of the desponding and afflicted are made evil [by anxious thoughts and forebodings], but he who has a glad heart has a continual feast [regardless of circumstances].

16 Better is little with the reverent, worshipful fear of the Lord than great and rich treasure and trouble with it. [Ps. 37:16; Prov. 16:8; I Tim. 6:6.]

17 Better is a dinner of herbs where love is than a fatted ox and hatred with it. [Prov. 17:1.]

18 A hot-tempered man stirs up strife, but he who is slow to anger appeases contention.

19 The way of the sluggard is overgrown with thorns [it pricks, lacerates, and entangles him], but the way of the righteous is plain and raised like a highway.

20 A wise son makes a glad father, but a self-confident and foolish man despises his mother and puts her to shame.

21 Folly is pleasure to him who is without heart and sense, but a man of understanding walks uprightly [making straight his course]. [Eph. 5:15.]

22 Where there is no counsel, purposes are frustrated, but with many counselors they are accomplished.

23 A man has joy in making an apt answer, and a word spoken at the right moment—how good it is!

24 The path of the wise leads upward to life, that he may avoid [the gloom] in the depths of Sheol [Hades, the place of the dead]. [Phil. 3:20; Col. 3:1, 2.]

25 The Lord tears down the house of the proud, but He makes secure the boundaries of the [consecrated] widow.

26 The thoughts of the wicked are shamefully vile and exceedingly offensive to the Lord, but the words of the pure are pleasing words to Him.

27 He who is greedy for unjust gain troubles his own household, but he who hates bribes will live. [Isa. 5:8; Jer. 17:11.]

28 The mind of the [uncompromisingly] righteous studies how to answer, but the mouth of the wicked pours out evil things. [I Pet. 3:15.]

29 The Lord is far from the wicked, but He hears the prayer of the [consistently] righteous (the upright, in right standing with Him).

30 The light in the eyes [of him whose heart is joyful] rejoices the hearts of others, and good news nourishes the bones.

31 The ear that listens to the reproof [that leads to or gives] life will remain among the wise.

32 He who refuses and ignores instruction and correction despises himself, but he who heeds reproof gets understanding.

33 The reverent and worshipful fear of the Lord brings instruction in Wisdom, and humility comes before honor.

CHAPTER 16

THE PLANS of the mind and orderly thinking belong to man, but from the Lord comes the [wise] answer of the tongue.

2 All the ways of a man are pure in his own eyes, but the Lord weighs the spirits (the thoughts and intents of the heart). [I Sam. 16:7; Heb. 4:12.]

3 Roll your works upon the Lord [commit and trust them wholly to Him; He will cause your thoughts to become agreeable to His will, and] so shall your plans be established and succeed.

4 The Lord has made everything [to accommodate itself to and contribute] to

its own end *and* His own purpose—even the wicked [are fitted for their role] for the day of calamity *and* evil.

5 Everyone proud *and* arrogant in heart is disgusting, hateful, *and* exceedingly offensive to the Lord; be assured [I pledge it] they will not go unpunished. [Prov. 8:13; 11:20–21.]

6 By mercy *and* love, truth *and* fidelity [to God and man—not by sacrificial offerings], iniquity is purged out of the heart, and by the reverent, worshipful fear of the Lord men depart from *and* avoid evil.

7 When a man's ways please the Lord, He makes even his enemies to be at peace with him.

8 Better is a little with righteousness (uprightness in every area and relation and right standing with God) than great revenues with injustice. [Ps. 37:16; Prov. 15:16.]

9 A man's mind plans his way, but the Lord directs his steps *and* makes them sure. [Ps. 37:23; Prov. 20:24; Jer. 10:23.]

10 Divinely directed decisions are on the lips of the king; his mouth should not transgress in judgment.

11 A just balance *and* scales are the Lord's; all the weights of the bag are His work [established on His eternal principles].

12 It is an abomination [to God and men] for kings to commit wickedness, for a throne is established *and* made secure by righteousness (moral and spiritual rectitude in every area and relation).

13 Right *and* just lips are the delight of a king, and he loves him who speaks what is right.

14 The wrath of a king is as messengers of death, but a wise man will pacify it.

15 In the light of the king's countenance is life, and his favor is as a cloud bringing the spring rain.

16 How much better it is to get skillful *and* godly Wisdom than gold! And to get understanding is to be cho-

sen rather than silver. [Prov. 8:10, 19.]

17 The highway of the upright turns aside from evil; he who guards his way preserves his life.

18 Pride goes before destruction, and a haughty spirit before a fall.

19 Better it is to be of a humble spirit with the meek *and* poor than to divide the spoil with the proud.

20 He who deals wisely *and* heeds [God's] word *and* counsel shall find good, and whoever leans on, trusts in, *and* is confident in the Lord—happy, blessed, *and* fortunate is he.

21 The wise in heart are called prudent, understanding, *and* knowing, *and* winsome speech increases learning [in both speaker and listener].

22 Understanding is a wellspring of life to those who have it, but to give instruction to fools is folly.

23 The mind of the wise instructs his mouth, and adds learning *and* persuasiveness to his lips.

24 Pleasant words are as a honeycomb, sweet to the mind and healing to the body.

25 There is a way that seems right to a man *and* appears straight before him, but at the end of it is the way of death.

26 The appetite of the laborer works for him, for [the need of] his mouth urges him on.

27 A worthless man devises *and* digs up mischief, and in his lips there is as a scorching fire.

28 A perverse man sows strife, and a whisperer separates close friends. [Prov. 17:9.]

29 The exceedingly grasping, covetous, *and* violent man entices his neighbor, leading him in a way that is not good.

30 He who shuts his eyes to devise perverse things and who compresses his lips [as if in concealment] brings evil to pass.

31 The hoary head is a crown of beauty *and* glory if it is found in the way of righteousness (moral and spiri-

tual rectitude in every area and relation). [Prov. 20:29.]

32 He who is slow to anger is better than the mighty, he who rules his [own] spirit than he who takes a city.

33 The lot is cast into the lap, but the decision is wholly of the Lord [even the events that seem accidental are really ordered by Him].

CHAPTER 17

BETTER IS a dry morsel with quietness than a house full of feasting [on offered sacrifices] with strife.

2 A wise servant shall have rule over a son who causes shame, and shall share in the inheritance among the brothers.

3 The refining pot is for silver and the furnace for gold, but the Lord tries the hearts. [Ps. 26:2; Prov. 27:21; Jer. 17:10; Mal. 3:3.]

4 An evildoer gives heed to wicked lips; and a liar listens to a mischievous tongue.

5 Whoever mocks the poor reproaches his Maker, and he who is glad at calamity shall not be held innocent or go unpunished. [Job 31:29; Prov. 14:31; Obad. 12.]

6 Children's children are the crown of old men, and the glory of children is their fathers. [Ps. 127:3; 128:3.]

7 Fine or arrogant speech does not befit [an empty-headed] fool—much less do lying lips befit a prince.

8 A bribe is like a bright, precious stone that dazzles the eyes and affects the mind of him who gives it; [as if by magic] he prospers, whichever way he turns.

9 He who covers and forgives an offense seeks love, but he who repeats or harps on a matter separates even close friends.

10 A reproof enters deeper into a man of understanding than a hundred lashes into a [self-confident] fool. [Isa. 32:6.]

11 An evil man seeks only rebellion; therefore a stern and pitiless messenger shall be sent against him.

12 Let [the brute ferocity of] a bear robbed of her whelps meet a man rather than a [self-confident] fool in his folly [when he is in a rage]. [Hos. 13:8.]

13 Whoever rewards evil for good, evil shall not depart from his house. [Ps. 109:4, 5; Jer. 18:20.]

14 The beginning of strife is as when water first trickles [from a crack in a dam]; therefore stop contention before it becomes worse and quarreling breaks out.

15 He who justifies the wicked and he who condemns the righteous are both an abomination [exceedingly disgusting and hateful] to the Lord. [Exod. 23:7; Prov. 24:24; Isa. 5:23.]

16 Of what use is money in the hand of a [self-confident] fool to buy skillful and godly Wisdom—when he has no understanding or heart for it?

17 A friend loves at all times, and is born, as is a brother, for adversity.

18 A man void of good sense gives a pledge and becomes security for another in the presence of his neighbor.

19 He who loves strife and is quarrelsome loves transgression and involves himself in guilt; he who raises high his gateway and is boastful and arrogant invites destruction.

20 He who has a wayward and crooked mind finds no good, and he who has a willful and contrary tongue will fall into calamity. [James 3:8.]

21 He who becomes the parent of a [self-confident] fool does it to his sorrow, and the father of [an empty-headed] fool has no joy [in him].

22 A happy heart is good medicine and a cheerful mind works healing, but a broken spirit dries up the bones. [Prov. 12:25; 15:13, 15.]

23 A wicked man receives a bribe out of the bosom (pocket) to pervert the ways of justice.

24 A man of understanding sets skillful and godly Wisdom before his

face, but the eyes of a [self-confident] fool are on the ends of the earth.

25 A self-confident and foolish son is a grief to his father and bitterness to her who bore him.

26 Also, to punish or fine the righteous is not good, nor to smite the noble for their uprightness.

27 He who has knowledge spares his words, and a man of understanding has a cool spirit. [James 1:19.]

28 Even a fool when he holds his peace is considered wise; when he closes his lips he is esteemed a man of understanding.

CHAPTER 18

HE WHO willfully separates and estranges himself [from God and man] seeks his own desire and pretext to break out against all wise and sound judgment.

2 A [self-confident] fool has no delight in understanding but only in revealing his personal opinions and himself.

3 When the wicked comes in [to the depth of evil], he becomes a contemptuous despiser [of all that is pure and good], and with inner baseness comes outer shame and reproach.

4 The words of a [discreet and wise] man's mouth are like deep waters [plenteous and difficult to fathom], and the fountain of skillful and godly Wisdom is like a gushing stream [sparkling, fresh, pure, and life-giving].

5 To respect the person of the wicked and be partial to him, so as to deprive the [consistently] righteous of justice, is not good.

6 A [self-confident] fool's lips bring contention, and his mouth invites a beating.

7 A [self-confident] fool's mouth is

his ruin, and his lips are a snare to himself.

8 The words of a whisperer or talebearer are as dainty morsels; they go down into the innermost parts of the body.

9 He who is loose and slack in his work is brother to him who is a destroyer and °he who does not use his endeavors to heal himself is brother to him who commits suicide.

10 The name of the Lord is a strong tower; the [consistently] righteous man [upright and in right standing with God] runs into it and is safe, high [above evil] and strong.

11 The rich man's wealth is his strong city, and as a high protecting wall in his own imagination and conceit.

12 Haughtiness comes before disaster, but humility before honor.

13 He who answers a matter before he hears the facts—it is folly and shame to him. [John 7:51.]

14 The strong spirit of a man sustains him in bodily pain or trouble, but a weak and broken spirit who can raise up or bear?

15 The mind of the prudent is ever getting knowledge, and the ear of the wise is ever seeking (inquiring for and craving) knowledge.

16 A man's gift makes room for him and brings him before great men. [Gen. 32:20; I Sam. 25:27; Prov. 17:8; 21:14.]

17 He who states his case first seems right, until his rival comes and cross-examines him.

18 To cast lots puts an end to disputes and decides between powerful contenders.

19 A brother offended is harder to be won over than a strong city, and [their] contentions separate them like the bars of a castle.

o This verse so reads in *The Septuagint* (Greek translation of the Old Testament). Its statement squarely addresses the problem of whether one has a moral right to neglect his body by "letting nature take its unhindered course" in illness.

20 A man's [moral] self shall be filled with the fruit of his mouth; and with the consequence of his words he must be satisfied [whether good or evil].

21 Death and life are in the power of the tongue, and they who indulge in it shall eat the fruit of it [for death or life]. [Matt. 12:37.]

22 He who finds a [true] wife finds a good thing and obtains favor from the Lord. [Prov. 19:14; 31:10.]

23 The poor man uses entreaties, but the rich answers roughly.

24 The man of many friends [a friend of all the world] will prove himself a bad friend, but there is a friend who sticks closer than a brother.

CHAPTER 19

BETTER IS a poor man who walks in his integrity than a rich man who is perverse in his speech and is a [self-confident] fool.

2 Desire without knowledge is not good, and to be overhasty is to sin *and* miss the mark.

3 The foolishness of man subverts his way [ruins his affairs]; then his heart is resentful *and* frets against the Lord.

4 Wealth makes many friends, but the poor man is avoided by his neighbor. [Prov. 14:20.]

5 A false witness shall not be unpunished, and he who breathes out lies shall not escape. [Exod. 23:1; Deut. 19:16–19; Prov. 6:19; 21:28.]

6 Many will entreat the favor of a liberal man, and every man is a friend to him who gives gifts.

7 All the brothers *of a poor man* detest him—how much more do his friends go far from him! He pursues them with words, but they are gone.

8 He who gains Wisdom loves his own life; he who keeps understanding shall prosper *and* find good.

9 A false witness shall not be unpunished, and he who breathes forth lies shall perish.

10 Luxury is not fitting for a [self-confident] fool—much less for a slave to rule over princes.

11 Good sense makes a man restrain his anger, and it is his glory to overlook a transgression *or* an offense.

12 The king's wrath is as terrifying as the roaring of a lion, but his favor is as [refreshing as] dew upon the grass. [Hos. 14:5.]

13 A self-confident *and* foolish son is the [multiplied] calamity of his father, and the contentions of a wife are like a continual dripping [of water through a chink in the roof].

14 House and riches are the inheritance from fathers, but a wise, understanding, *and* prudent wife is from the Lord. [Prov. 18:22.]

15 Slothfulness casts one into a deep sleep, and the idle person shall suffer hunger.

16 He who keeps the commandment [of the Lord] keeps his own life, but he who despises His ways shall die. [Luke 10:28; 11:28.]

17 He who has pity on the poor lends to the Lord, and that which he has given He will repay to him. [Prov. 28:27; Eccl. 11:1; Matt. 10:42; 25:40; II Cor. 9:6–8; Heb. 6:10.]

18 Discipline your son while there is hope, but do not [indulge your angry resentments by undue chastisements and] set yourself to his ruin.

19 A man of great wrath shall suffer the penalty; for if you deliver him [from the consequences], he will [feel free to] cause you to do it again.

20 Hear counsel, receive instruction, *and* accept correction, that you may be wise in the time to come.

21 Many plans are in a man's mind, but it is the Lord's purpose for him that will stand. [Job 23:13; Ps. 33:10, 11; Isa. 14:26, 27; 46:10; Acts 5:39; Heb. 6:17.]

22 That which is desired in a man is loyalty *and* kindness [and his glory and delight are his giving], but a poor man is better than a liar.

23 The reverent, worshipful fear of the Lord leads to life, and he who has it rests satisfied; he cannot be visited with [actual] evil. [Job 5:19; Ps. 91:3; Prov. 12:13; Isa. 46:4; Jer. 1:8; Dan. 6:27; II Tim. 4:8.]

24 The sluggard buries his hand in the dish, and will not so much as bring it to his mouth again.

25 Strike a scoffer, and the simple will learn prudence; reprove a man of understanding, and he will increase in knowledge.

26 He who does violence to his father and chases away his mother is a son who causes shame and brings reproach.

27 Cease, my son, to hear instruction only to ignore it and stray from the words of knowledge.

28 A worthless witness scoffs at justice, and the mouth of the wicked swallows iniquity.

29 Judgments are prepared for scoffers, and stripes for the backs of [self-confident] fools. [Isa. 32:6.]

CHAPTER 20

WINE IS a mocker, strong drink a riotous brawler; and whoever errs or reels because of it is not wise. [Prov. 23:29, 30; Isa. 28:7; Hos. 4:11.]

2 The terror of a king is as the roaring of a lion; whoever provokes him to anger or angers himself against him sins against his own life.

3 It is an honor for a man to cease from strife and keep aloof from it, but every fool will quarrel.

4 The sluggard does not plow when winter sets in; therefore he begs in harvest and has nothing.

5 Counsel in the heart of man is like water in a deep well, but a man of understanding draws it out. [Prov. 18:4.]

6 Many a man proclaims his own loving-kindness and goodness, but a faithful man who can find?

7 The righteous man walks in his integrity; blessed (happy, fortunate, enviable) are his children after him.

8 A king who sits on the throne of judgment winnows out all evil [like chaff] with his eyes.

9 Who can say, I have made my heart clean, I am pure from my sin? [I Kings 8:46; II Chron. 6:36; Job 9:30; 14:4; Ps. 51:5; I John 1:8.]

10 Diverse weights [one for buying and another for selling] and diverse measures—both of them are exceedingly offensive and abhorrent to the Lord. [Deut. 25:13; Mic. 6:10, 11.]

11 Even a child is known by his acts, whether [or not] what he does is pure and right.

12 The hearing ear and the seeing eye—the Lord has made both of them.

13 Love not sleep, lest you come to poverty; open your eyes and you will be satisfied with bread.

14 It is worthless, it is worthless! says the buyer; but when he goes his way, then he boasts [about his bargain].

15 There is gold, and a multitude of pearls, but the lips of knowledge are a vase of preciousness [the most precious of all]. [Job 28:12, 16–19; Prov. 3:15; 8:11.]

16 [The judge tells the creditor] Take the garment of one who is surety for a stranger; and hold him in pledge when he is security for foreigners.

17 Food gained by deceit is sweet to a man, but afterward his mouth will be filled with gravel.

18 Purposes and plans are established by counsel; and [only] with good advice make or carry on war.

19 He who goes about as a talebearer reveals secrets; therefore associate not with him who talks too freely. [Rom. 16:17, 18.]

20 Whoever curses his father or his mother, his lamp shall be put out in complete darkness.

21 An inheritance hastily gotten [by greedy, unjust means] at the begin-

ning, in the end it will not be blessed. [Prov. 28:20; Hab. 2:6.]

22 Do not say, I will repay evil; wait [expectantly] for the Lord, and He will rescue you. [II Sam. 16:12; Rom. 12:17–19; I Thess. 5:15; I Pet. 3:9.]

23 Diverse and deceitful weights are shamefully vile and abhorrent to the Lord, and false scales are not good.

24 Man's steps are ordered by the Lord. How then can a man understand his way?

25 It is a snare to a man to utter a vow [of consecration] rashly and [not until] afterward inquire [whether he can fulfill it].

26 A wise king winnows out the wicked [from among the good] and brings the threshing wheel over them [to separate the chaff from the grain].

27 The spirit of man [that factor in human personality which proceeds immediately from God] is the lamp of the Lord, searching all his innermost parts. [I Cor. 2:11.]

28 Loving-kindness and mercy, truth and faithfulness, preserve the king, and his throne is upheld by [the people's] loyalty.

29 The glory of young men is their strength, and the beauty of old men is their gray head [suggesting wisdom and experience].

30 Blows that wound cleanse away evil, and strokes [for correction] reach to the innermost parts.

CHAPTER 21

THE KING'S heart is in the hand of the Lord, as are the watercourses; He turns it whichever way He wills.

2 Every way of a man is right in his own eyes, but the Lord weighs and tries the hearts. [Prov. 24:12; Luke 16:15.]

3 To do righteousness and justice is more acceptable to the Lord than sacrifice. [I Sam. 15:22; Prov. 15:8; Isa. 1:11; Hos. 6:6; Mic. 6:7, 8.]

4 Haughtiness of eyes and a proud heart, even the tillage of the wicked or

the lamp [of joy] to them [whatever it may be], are sin [in the eyes of God].

5 The thoughts of the [steadily] diligent tend only to plenteousness, but everyone who is impatient and hasty hastens only to want.

6 Securing treasures by a lying tongue is a vapor driven to and fro; those who seek them seek death.

7 The violence of the wicked shall sweep them away, because they refuse to do justice.

8 The way of the guilty is exceedingly crooked, but as for the pure, his work is right and his conduct is straight.

9 It is better to dwell in a corner of the housetop [on the flat oriental roof, exposed to all kinds of weather] than in a house shared with a nagging, quarrelsome, and faultfinding woman.

10 The soul or life of the wicked craves and seeks evil; his neighbor finds no favor in his eyes. [James 2:16.]

11 When the scoffer is punished, the fool gets a lesson in being wise; but men of [godly] Wisdom and good sense learn by being instructed.

12 The [uncompromisingly] righteous man considers well the house of the wicked—how the wicked are cast down to ruin.

13 Whoever stops his ears at the cry of the poor will cry out himself and not be heard. [Matt. 18:30–34; James 2:13.]

14 A gift in secret pacifies and turns away anger, and a bribe in the lap, strong wrath.

15 When justice is done, it is a joy to the righteous (the upright, in right standing with God), but to the evildoers it is dismay, calamity, and ruin.

16 A man who wanders out of the way of understanding shall abide in the congregation of the spirits (of the dead).

17 He who loves pleasure will be a poor man; he who loves wine and oil will not be rich.

18 The wicked become a ransom for the [uncompromisingly] righteous, and the treacherous for the upright [because the wicked themselves fall into the traps and pits they have dug for the good].

19 It is better to dwell in a desert land than with a contentious woman and with vexation.

20 There are precious treasures and oil in the dwelling of the wise, but a self-confident and foolish man swallows it up and wastes it.

21 He who earnestly seeks after and craves righteousness, mercy, and loving-kindness will find life in addition to righteousness (uprightness and right standing with God) and honor. [Prov. 15:9; Matt. 5:6.]

22 A wise man scales the city walls of the mighty and brings down the stronghold in which they trust.

23 He who guards his mouth and his tongue keeps himself from troubles. [Prov. 12:13; 13:3; 18:21; James 3:2.]

24 The proud and haughty man—Scoffer is his name—deals and acts with overbearing pride.

25 The desire of the slothful kills him, for his hands refuse to labor.

26 He covets greedily all the day long, but the [uncompromisingly] righteous gives and does not withhold. [II Cor. 9:6–10.]

27 The sacrifice of the wicked is exceedingly disgusting and abhorrent [to the Lord]—how much more when he brings it with evil intention?

28 A false witness will perish, but the word of a man who hears attentively will endure and go unchallenged.

29 A wicked man puts on the bold, unfeeling face [of guilt], but as for the upright, he considers, directs, and establishes his way [with the confidence of integrity].

30 There is no [human] wisdom or understanding or counsel [that can prevail] against the Lord.

31 The horse is prepared for the day of battle, but deliverance and victory are of the Lord.

CHAPTER 22

A GOOD name is rather to be chosen than great riches, and loving favor rather than silver and gold.

2 The rich and poor meet together; the Lord is the Maker of them all. [Job 31:15; Prov. 14:31.]

3 A prudent man sees the evil and hides himself, but the simple pass on and are punished [with suffering].

4 The reward of humility and the reverent and worshipful fear of the Lord is riches and honor and life.

5 Thorns and snares are in the way of the obstinate and willful; he who guards himself will be far from them.

6 Train up a child in the way he should go [and in keeping with his individual gift or bent], and when he is old he will not depart from it. [Eph. 6:4; II Tim. 3:15.]

7 The rich rule over the poor, and the borrower is servant to the lender.

8 He who sows iniquity will reap calamity and futility, and the rod of his wrath [with which he smites others] will fail.

9 He who has a bountiful eye shall be blessed, for he gives of his bread to the poor. [II Cor. 9:6–10.]

10 Drive out the scoffer, and contention will go out; yes, strife and abuse will cease.

11 He who loves purity and the pure in heart and who is gracious in speech—because of the grace of his lips will he have the king for his friend.

12 The eyes of the Lord keep guard over knowledge and him who has it, but He overthrows the words of the treacherous.

13 The sluggard says, There is a lion outside! I shall be slain in the streets!

14 The mouth of a loose woman is a deep pit [for ensnaring wild animals]; he with whom the Lord is indig-

nant *and* who is abhorrent to Him will fall into it.

15 Foolishness is bound up in the heart of a child, but the rod of discipline will drive it far from him.

16 He who oppresses the poor to get gain for himself *and* he who gives to the rich—both will surely come to want.

17 Listen (consent and submit) to the words of the wise, and apply your mind to my knowledge;

18 For it will be pleasant if you keep them in your mind [believing them]; your lips will be accustomed to [confessing] them.

19 So that your trust (belief, reliance, support, and confidence) may be in the Lord, I have made known these things to you today, even to you.

20 Have I not written to you [long ago] excellent things in counsels and knowledge,

21 To make you know the certainty of the words of truth, that you may give a true answer to those who sent you? [Luke 1:3, 4.]

22 Rob not the poor [being tempted by their helplessness], neither oppress the afflicted at the gate [where the city court is held], [Exod. 23:6; Job 31:16, 21.]

23 For the Lord will plead their cause and deprive of life those who deprive [the poor or afflicted]. [Zech. 7:10; Mal. 3:5.]

24 Make no friendships with a man given to anger, and with a wrathful man do not associate,

25 Lest you learn his ways and get yourself into a snare.

26 Be not one of *those who strike hands and* pledge themselves, or of those who become security for another's debts.

27 If you have nothing with which to pay, why should he take your bed from under you?

28 Remove not the ancient landmark which your fathers have set up.

29 Do you see a man diligent *and* skillful in his business? He will stand before kings; he will not stand before obscure men.

CHAPTER 23

WHEN YOU sit down to eat with a ruler, consider who *and* what are before you;

2 For you will put a knife to your throat if you are a man given to desire.

3 Be not desirous of his dainties, for it is deceitful food [offered with questionable motives].

4 Weary not yourself to be rich; cease from your own [human] wisdom. [Prov. 28:20; I Tim. 6:9, 10.]

5 Will you set your eyes upon wealth, when [suddenly] it is gone? For riches certainly make themselves wings, like an eagle that flies toward the heavens.

6 Eat not the bread of him who has a hard, grudging, *and* envious eye, neither desire his dainty foods;

7 For as he thinks in his heart, so is he. As one who reckons, he says to you, eat and drink, yet his heart is not with you [but is grudging the cost].

8 The morsel which you have eaten you will vomit up, and your complimentary words will be wasted.

9 Speak not in the ears of a [self-confident] fool, for he will despise the [godly] Wisdom of your words. [Isa. 32:6.]

10 Remove not the ancient landmark and enter not into the fields of the fatherless, [Deut. 19:14; 27:17; Prov. 22:28.]

11 For their Redeemer is mighty; He will plead their cause against you.

12 Apply your mind to instruction *and* correction and your ears to words of knowledge.

13 Withhold not discipline from the child; for if you strike *and* punish him with the [reedlike] rod, he will not die.

14 You shall whip him with the rod and deliver his life from Sheol (Hades, the place of the dead).

15 My son, if your heart is wise, my heart will be glad, even mine;

16 Yes, my heart will rejoice when your lips speak right things.

17 Let not your heart envy sinners, but continue in the reverent *and* worshipful fear of the Lord all the day long.

18 For surely there is a latter end [a future and a reward], and your hope *and* expectation shall not be cut off.

19 Hear, my son, and be wise, and direct your mind in the way [of the Lord].

20 Do not associate with winebibbers; be not among them *nor* among gluttonous eaters of meat, [Isa. 5:22; Luke 21:34; Rom. 13:13; Eph. 5:18.]

21 For the drunkard and the glutton shall come to poverty, and drowsiness shall clothe a man with rags.

22 Hearken to your father, who begot you, and despise not your mother when she is old.

23 Buy the truth and sell it not; not only that, but also get discernment *and* judgment, instruction and understanding.

24 The father of the [uncompromisingly] righteous (the upright, in right standing with God) shall greatly rejoice, and he who becomes the father of a wise child shall have joy in him.

25 Let your father and your mother be glad, and let her who bore you rejoice.

26 My son, give me your heart and let your eyes observe *and* delight in my ways,

27 For a harlot is a deep ditch, and a loose woman is a narrow pit.

28 She also lies in wait as a robber *or* as one waits for prey, and she increases the treacherous among men.

29 Who has woe? Who has sorrow? Who has strife? Who has complaining? Who has wounds without cause? Who has redness *and* dimness of eyes?

30 Those who tarry long at the wine, those who go to seek *and* try mixed wine. [Prov. 20:1; Eph. 5:18.]

31 Do not look at wine when it is red, when it sparkles in the wineglass, when it goes down smoothly.

32 At the last it bites like a serpent and stings like an adder.

33 [Under the influence of wine] your eyes will behold strange things [and loose women] and your mind will utter things turned the wrong way [untrue, incorrect, and petulant].

34 Yes, you will be [as unsteady as] he who lies down in the midst of the sea, and [as open to disaster] as he who lies upon the top of a mast.

35 You will say, They struck me, but I was not hurt! They beat me [as with a hammer], but I did not feel it! When shall I awake? I will crave *and* seek more wine again [and escape reality].

CHAPTER 24

BE NOT envious of evil men, nor desire to be with them;

2 For their minds plot oppression *and* devise violence, and their lips talk of causing trouble *and* vexation.

3 Through skillful *and* godly Wisdom is a house (a life, a home, a family) built, and by understanding it is established [on a sound and good foundation],

4 And by knowledge shall its chambers [of every area] be filled with all precious and pleasant riches.

5 A wise man is strong *and* ᵖis better than a strong man, and a man of knowledge increases *and* strengthens his power; [Prov. 21:22; Eccl. 9:16.]

6 For by wise counsel you can wage your war, and in an abundance of counselors there is victory *and* safety.

7 Wisdom is too high for a ᑫfool; he opens not his mouth in the gate

p Several other texts, including *The Septuagint* (Greek translation of the Old Testament), so read.
q See footnote on Proverbs 14:3.

[where the city's rulers sit in judgment].

8 He who plans to do evil will be called a mischief-maker.

9 The plans of the foolish *and* the thought of foolishness are sin, and the scoffer is an abomination to men.

10 If you faint in the day of adversity, your strength is small.

11 Deliver those who are drawn away to death, and those who totter to the slaughter, hold them back [from their doom].

12 If you [profess ignorance and] say, Behold, we did not know this, does not He Who weighs *and* ponders the heart perceive *and* consider it? And He Who guards your life, does not He know it? And shall not He render to [you and] every man according to his works?

13 My son, eat honey, because it is good, and the drippings of the honeycomb are sweet to your taste.

14 So shall you know skillful *and* godly Wisdom to be thus to your life; if you find it, then shall there be a future *and* a reward, and your hope *and* expectation shall not be cut off.

15 Lie not in wait as a wicked man against the dwelling of the [uncompromisingly] righteous (the upright, in right standing with God); destroy not his resting-place;

16 For a righteous man falls seven times and rises again, but the wicked are overthrown by calamity. [Job 5:19; Ps. 34:19; 37:24; Mic. 7:8.]

17 Rejoice not when your enemy falls, and let not your heart be glad when he stumbles *or* is overthrown,

18 Lest the *Lord* see *it and* it be evil in *His* eyes *and* displease Him, and He turn away His wrath from him [to expend it upon you, the worse offender].

19 Fret not because of evildoers, neither be envious of the wicked,

20 For there shall be no reward for the evil man; the lamp of the wicked shall be put out.

21 My son, [reverently] fear the Lord and the king, and do not associate with those who are given to change [of allegiance, and are revolutionary],

22 For their calamity shall rise suddenly, and who knows the punishment *and* ruin which both [the Lord and the king] will bring upon [the rebellious]?

23 These also are sayings of the wise: To discriminate *and* show partiality, having respect of persons in judging, is not good.

24 He who says to the wicked, You are righteous *and* innocent—peoples will curse him, nations will defy *and* abhor him.

25 But to those [upright judges] who rebuke the wicked, it will go well with them *and* they will find delight, and a good blessing will be upon them.

26 He kisses the lips [and wins the hearts of men] who give a right answer.

27 [Put first things first.] Prepare your work outside and get it ready for yourself in the field; and afterward build your house *and* establish a home.

28 Be not a witness against your neighbor without cause, and deceive not with your lips. [Eph. 4:25.]

29 Say not, I will do to him as he has done to me; I will pay the man back for his deed. [Prov. 20:22; Matt. 5:39, 44; Rom. 12:17, 19.]

30 I went by the field of the lazy man, and by the vineyard of the man void of understanding;

31 And, behold, it was all grown over with thorns, and *nettles* were covering *its* face, and its stone wall was broken down.

32 Then I beheld *and* considered it well; I looked *and* received instruction.

33 Yet a little sleep, a little slumber, a little folding of the hands to sleep—

34 So shall your poverty come as a robber, and your want as an armed man.

CHAPTER 25

THESE ARE also the proverbs of
Solomon, which the men of Heze-
kiah king of Judah copied: [I Kings
4:32.]

2 It is the glory of God to conceal
a thing, but the glory of kings is to
search out a thing. [Deut. 29:29; Rom.
11:33.]

3 As the heavens for height and the
earth for depth, so the hearts *and*
minds of kings are unsearchable.

4 Take away the dross from the silver, and there shall come forth [the
material for] a vessel for the silver-
smith [to work up]. [II Tim. 2:21.]

5 Take away the wicked from before the king, and his throne will be
established in righteousness (moral
and spiritual rectitude in every area
and relation).

6 Be not forward (self-assertive
and boastfully ambitious) in the presence of the king, and stand not in the
place of great men;

7 For better it is that it should be
said to you, Come up here, than that
you should be put lower in the presence of the prince, whose eyes have
seen you. [Luke 14:8–10.]

8 Rush not forth soon to quarrel
[before magistrates or elsewhere], lest
you know not what to do in the end
when your neighbor has put you to
shame. [Prov. 17:14; Matt. 5:25.]

9 Argue your cause with your
neighbor himself; discover not *and*
disclose not another's secret, [Matt.
18:15.]

10 Lest he who hears you revile you
and bring shame upon you and your ill
repute have no end.

11 A word fitly spoken *and* in due

season is like apples of gold in settings
of silver. [Prov. 15:23; Isa. 50:4.]

12 Like an earring *or* nose ring of
gold or an ornament of fine gold is a
wise reprover to an ear that listens *and*
obeys.

13 Like the cold of snow [brought
from the mountains] in the time of harvest, so is a faithful messenger to those
who send him; for he refreshes the life
of his masters.

14 Whoever falsely boasts of gifts
[he does not give] is like clouds and
wind without rain. [Jude 12.]

15 By long forbearance *and* calm-
ness of spirit a judge *or* ruler is persuaded, and soft speech breaks down
the most bonelike resistance. [Gen.
32:4; I Sam. 25:24; Prov. 15:1; 16:14.]

16 Have you found [pleasure sweet
like] honey? Eat only as much as is
sufficient for you, lest, being filled
with it, you vomit it.

17 Let your foot seldom be in your
neighbor's house, lest he become tired
of you and hate you.

18 A man who bears false witness
against his neighbor is like a heavy
sledgehammer and a sword and a
sharp arrow.

19 Confidence in an unfaithful man
in time of trouble is like a broken tooth
or a foot out of joint.

20 He who sings songs to a heavy
heart is like him who lays off a garment in cold weather *and* like vinegar
upon soda. [Dan. 6:18; Rom. 12:15.]

21 If your enemy is hungry, give
him bread to eat; and if he is thirsty,
give him water to drink; [Matt. 5:44;
Rom. 12:20.]

22 For in doing so, you will ʳheap
coals of fire upon his head, and the
Lord will reward you.

---

r This is not to be construed as a revengeful act intended to embarrass its victim, but just the opposite.
The picture is that of the high priest (Lev. 16:12) who, on the Day of Atonement, took his censer and
filled it with "coals of fire" from off the altar of burnt offering, and then put incense on the coals to create
a pleasing, sweet-smelling fragrance. The cloud or smoke of the incense covered the mercy seat and was
acceptable to God for atonement. Samuel Wesley wrote: / "So artists melt the sullen ore of lead, / By
heaping coals of fire upon its head: / In the kind warmth the metal learns to glow, / And pure from dross
the silver runs below."

23 The north wind brings forth rain; so does a backbiting tongue bring forth an angry countenance.

24 It is better to dwell in the corner of the housetop than to share a house with a disagreeing, quarrelsome, *and* scolding woman. [Prov. 21:9.]

25 Like cold water to a thirsty soul, so is good news from a far [home] country.

26 Like a muddied fountain and a polluted spring is a righteous man who yields, falls down, *and* compromises his integrity before the wicked.

27 It is not good to eat much honey; so for men to seek glory, their own glory, causes suffering *and* is not glory.

28 He who has no rule over his own spirit is like a city that is broken down and without walls. [Prov. 16:32.]

CHAPTER 26

LIKE SNOW in summer and like rain in harvest, so honor is not fitting for a [self-confident] fool. [Isa. 32:6.]

2 Like the sparrow in her wandering, like the swallow in her flying, so the causeless curse does not alight. [Num. 23:8.]

3 A whip for the horse, a bridle for the donkey, and a [straight, slender] rod for the backs of [self-confident] fools.

4 Answer not a [self-confident] fool according to his folly, lest you also be like him.

5 Answer a [self-confident] fool according to his folly, lest he be wise in his own eyes *and* conceit. [Matt. 16:1–4; 21:24–27.]

6 He who sends a message by the hand of a ˢfool cuts off the feet [of satisfactory delivery] and drinks the damage. [Prov. 13:17.]

7 Like the legs of a lame man which hang loose, so is a parable in the mouth of a fool.

8 Like he who binds a stone in a sling, so is he who gives honor to a [self-confident] fool.

9 Like a thorn that goes [without being felt] into the hand of a drunken man, so is a proverb in the mouth of a [self-confident] fool.

10 [But] like an archer who wounds all, so is he who hires a fool or chance passers-by.

11 As a dog returns to his vomit, so a fool returns to his folly.

12 Do you see a man wise in his own eyes *or* conceit? There is more hope for a [self-confident] fool than for him. [Prov. 29:20; Luke 18:11; Rom. 12:16; Rev. 3:17.]

13 The sluggard says, There is a lion in the way! A lion is in the streets! [Prov. 22:13.]

14 As the door turns on its hinges, so does the lazy man [move not from his place] upon his bed.

15 The slothful *and* self-indulgent buries his hand in his bosom; it distresses *and* wearies him to bring it again to his mouth. [Prov. 19:24.]

16 The sluggard is wiser in his own eyes *and* conceit than seven men who can render a reason *and* answer discreetly.

17 He who, passing by, stops to meddle with strife that is none of his business is like one who takes a dog by the ears.

18 Like a madman who casts firebrands, arrows, and death,

19 So is the man who deceives his neighbor and then says, Was I not joking? [Eph. 5:4.]

20 For lack of wood the fire goes out, *and* where there is no whisperer, contention ceases.

21 As coals are to hot embers and as wood to fire, so is a quarrelsome man to inflame strife. [Prov. 15:18; 29:22.]

22 The words of a whisperer *or* slanderer are like dainty morsels *or* words of sport [to some, but to others

are like deadly wounds]; and they go down into the innermost parts of the body [or of the victim's nature].

23 Burning lips [uttering insincere words of love] and a wicked heart are like an earthen vessel covered with the scum thrown off from molten silver [making it appear to be solid silver].

24 He who hates pretends with his lips, but stores up deceit within himself.

25 When he speaks kindly, do not trust him, for seven abominations are in his heart.

26 Though his hatred covers itself with guile, his wickedness shall be shown openly before the assembly.

27 Whoever digs a pit [for another man's feet] shall fall into it himself, and he who rolls a stone [up a height to do mischief], it will return upon him. [Ps. 7:15, 16; 9:15; 10:2; 57:6; Prov. 28:10; Eccl. 10:8.]

28 A lying tongue hates those it wounds *and* crushes, and a flattering mouth works ruin.

CHAPTER 27

DO NOT boast of [yourself and] tomorrow, for you know not what a day may bring forth. [Luke 12:19, 20; James 4:13.]

2 Let another man praise you, and not your own mouth; a stranger, and not your own lips.

3 Stone is heavy and sand weighty, but a fool's [unreasoning] wrath is heavier *and* more intolerable than both of them.

4 Wrath is cruel and anger is an overwhelming flood, but who is able to stand before jealousy?

5 Open rebuke is better than love that is hidden. [Prov. 28:23; Gal. 2:14.]

6 Faithful are the wounds of a friend, but the kisses of an enemy are lavish *and* deceitful.

7 He who is satiated [with sensual pleasures] loathes *and* treads underfoot a honeycomb, but to the hungry soul every bitter thing is sweet.

8 Like a bird that wanders from her nest, so is a man who strays from his home.

9 Oil and perfume rejoice the heart; so does the sweetness of a friend's counsel that comes from the heart.

10 Your own friend and your father's friend, forsake them not; neither go to your brother's house in the day of your calamity. Better is a neighbor who is near [in spirit] than a brother who is far off [in heart].

11 My son, be wise, and make my heart glad, that I may answer him who reproaches me [as having failed in my parental duty]. [Prov. 10:1; 23:15, 24.]

12 A prudent man sees the evil and hides himself, but the simple pass on and are punished [with suffering].

13 [The judge tells the creditor] Take the garment of one who is surety for a stranger; and hold him in pledge when he is security for foreigners. [Prov. 20:16.]

14 The flatterer who loudly praises *and* glorifies his neighbor, rising early in the morning, it shall be counted as cursing him [for he will be suspected of sinister purposes].

15 A continual dripping on a day of violent showers and a contentious woman are alike; [Prov. 19:13.]

16 Whoever attempts to restrain [a contentious woman] might as well try to stop the wind—his right hand encounters oil [and she slips through his fingers].

17 Iron sharpens iron; so a man sharpens the countenance of his friend [to show rage or worthy purpose].

18 Whoever tends the fig tree shall eat its fruit; so he who patiently *and* faithfully guards *and* heeds his master shall be honored. [I Cor. 9:7, 13.]

19 As in water face answers to *and* reflects face, so the heart of man to man.

20 Sheol (the place of the dead) and Abaddon (the place of destruction) are

never satisfied; so [the lust of] the eyes of man is never satisfied. [Prov. 30:16; Hab. 2:5.]

21 As the refining pot for silver and the furnace for gold [bring forth all the impurities of the metal], so let a man be in his trial of praise [ridding himself of all that is base or insincere; for a man is judged by what he praises and of what he boasts].

22 Even though like grain you should pound a fool in a mortar with a pestle, yet will not his foolishness depart from him.

23 Be diligent to know the state of your flocks, and look well to your herds;

24 For riches are not forever; and does a crown endure to all generations?

25 When the hay is gone, the tender grass shows itself, and herbs of the mountain are gathered in,

26 The lambs will be for your clothing, and the goats [will furnish you] the price of a field.

27 And there will be goats' milk enough for your food, for the food of your household, and for the maintenance of your maids.

CHAPTER 28

THE WICKED flee when no man pursues them, but the [uncompromisingly] righteous are bold as a lion. [Lev. 26:17, 36; Ps. 53:5.]

2 When a land transgresses, it has many rulers, but when the ruler is a man of discernment, understanding, and knowledge, its stability will long continue.

3 A poor man who oppresses the poor is like a *sweeping rain which leaves no food* [plundering them of their last morsels]. [Matt. 18:28.]

4 Those who forsake the law [of God and man] praise the wicked, but those who keep the law [of God and man] contend with them. [Prov. 29:18.]

5 Evil men do not understand justice, but they who crave *and* seek the

Lord understand it fully. [John 7:17; I Cor. 2:15; I John 2:20, 27.]

6 Better is the poor man who walks in his integrity than he who willfully goes in double *and* wrong ways, though he is rich.

7 Whoever keeps the law [of God and man] is a wise son, but he who is a companion of gluttons *and* the carousing, self-indulgent, *and* extravagant shames his father.

8 He who by charging excessive interest *and* who by unjust efforts to get gain increases his material possession gathers it for him [to spend] who is kind *and* generous to the poor. [Job 27:16, 17; Prov. 13:22; Eccl. 2:26.]

9 He who turns away his ear from hearing the law [of God and man], even his prayer is an abomination, hateful *and* revolting [to God]. [Ps. 66:18; 109:7; Prov. 15:8; Zech. 7:11.]

10 Whoever leads the upright astray into an evil way, he will himself fall into his own pit, but the blameless will have a goodly inheritance.

11 The rich man is wise in his own eyes *and* conceit, but the poor man who has understanding will find him out.

12 When the [uncompromisingly] righteous triumph, there is great glory *and* celebration; but when the wicked rise [to power], men hide themselves.

13 He who covers his transgressions will not prosper, but whoever confesses and forsakes his sins will obtain mercy. [Ps. 32:3, 5; I John 1:8–10.]

14 Blessed (happy, fortunate, and to be envied) is the man who reverently *and* worshipfully fears [the Lord] at all times [regardless of circumstances], but he who hardens his heart will fall into calamity.

15 Like a roaring lion or a ravenous *and* charging bear is a wicked ruler over a poor people.

16 A ruler who lacks understanding is [like a wicked one] a great oppressor, but he who hates covetousness

and unjust gain shall prolong his days.

17 If a man willfully sheds the blood of a person [and keeps the guilt of murder upon his conscience], he is fleeing to the pit (the grave) *and* hastening to his own destruction; let no man stop him!

18 He who walks uprightly shall be safe, but he who willfully goes in double *and* wrong ways shall fall in one of them.

19 He who cultivates his land will have plenty of bread, but he who follows worthless people *and* pursuits will have poverty enough.

20 A faithful man shall abound with blessings, but he who makes haste to be rich [at any cost] shall not go unpunished. [Prov. 13:11; 20:21; 23:4; I Tim. 6:9.]

21 To have respect of persons *and* to show partiality is not good, neither is it good that man should transgress for a piece of bread.

22 He who has an evil *and* covetous eye hastens to be rich and knows not that want will come upon him. [Prov. 21:5; 28:20.]

23 He who rebukes a man shall afterward find more favor than he who flatters with the tongue.

24 Whoever robs his father or his mother and says, This is no sin—he is in the same class as [an open, lawless robber and] a destroyer.

25 He who is of a greedy spirit stirs up strife, but he who puts his trust in the Lord shall be enriched *and* blessed.

26 He who leans on, trusts in, *and* is confident of his own mind *and* heart is a [self-confident] fool, but he who walks in skillful *and* godly Wisdom shall be delivered. [James 1:5.]

27 He who gives to the poor will not want, but he who hides his eyes [from their want] will have many a curse. [Deut. 15:7; Prov. 19:17; 22:9.]

28 When the wicked rise [to power], men hide themselves; but when they perish, the [consistently] righteous increase *and* become many. [Prov. 28:12.]

CHAPTER 29

HE WHO, being often reproved, hardens his neck shall suddenly be destroyed—and that without remedy.

2 When the [uncompromisingly] righteous are in authority, the people rejoice; but when the wicked man rules, the people groan *and* sigh.

3 Whoever loves skillful *and* godly Wisdom rejoices his father, but he who associates with harlots wastes his substance.

4 The king by justice establishes the land, but he who exacts gifts *and* tribute overthrows it.

5 A man who flatters his neighbor spreads a net for his own feet.

6 In the transgression of an evil man there is a snare, but the [uncompromisingly] righteous man sings and rejoices.

7 The [consistently] righteous man knows *and* cares for the rights of the poor, but the wicked man has no interest in such knowledge. [Job 29:16; 31:13; Ps. 41:1.]

8 Scoffers set a city afire [inflaming the minds of the people], but wise men turn away wrath.

9 If a wise man has an argument with a foolish man, the fool only rages or laughs, and there is no rest.

10 The bloodthirsty hate the blameless man, but the upright care for *and* seek [to save] his life. [Gen. 4:5, 8; I John 3:12.]

11 A [self-confident] fool utters all his anger, but a wise man holds it back and stills it.

12 If a ruler listens to falsehood, all his officials will become wicked.

13 The poor man and the oppressor meet together—the Lord gives light to the eyes of both.

14 The king who faithfully judges the poor, his throne shall be established continuously.

15 The rod and reproof give wisdom, but a child left undisciplined brings his mother to shame.

16 When the wicked are in authority, transgression increases, but the [uncompromisingly] righteous shall see the fall of the wicked.

17 Correct your son, and he will give you rest; yes, he will give delight to your heart.

18 Where there is no vision [no redemptive revelation of God], the people perish; but he who keeps the law [of God, which includes that of man]—blessed (happy, fortunate, and enviable) is he. [I Sam. 3:1; Amos 8:11, 12.]

19 A servant will not be corrected by words alone; for though he understands, he will not answer [the master who mistreats him].

20 Do you see a man who is hasty in his words? There is more hope for a [self-confident] fool than for him.

21 He who pampers his servant from childhood will have him expecting the rights of a son afterward.

22 A man of wrath stirs up strife, and a man given to anger commits and causes much transgression.

23 A man's pride will bring him low, but he who is of a humble spirit will obtain honor. [Prov. 15:33; 18:12; Isa. 66:2; Dan. 4:30; Matt. 23:12; James 4:6, 10; I Pet. 5:5.]

24 Whoever is partner with a thief hates his own life; he falls under the curse [pronounced upon him who knows who the thief is] but discloses nothing.

25 The fear of man brings a snare, but whoever leans on, trusts in, and puts his confidence in the Lord is safe and set on high.

26 Many crave and seek the ruler's favor, but the wise man [waits] for justice from the Lord.

27 An unjust man is an abomination to the righteous, and he who is upright in the way [of the Lord] is an abomination to the wicked.

CHAPTER 30

THE WORDS of Agur son of Jakeh of Massa: The man says to Ithiel, to Ithiel and to Ucal:

2 Surely I am too brutish and stupid to be called a man, and I have not the understanding of a man [for all my secular learning is as nothing].

3 I have not learned skillful and godly Wisdom, that I should have the knowledge or burden of the Holy One.

4 Who has ascended into heaven and descended? Who has gathered the wind in His fists? Who has bound the waters in His garment? Who has established all the ends of the earth? What is His name, and what is His Son's name, if you know? [John 3:13; Rev. 19:12.]

5 Every word of God is tried and purified; He is a shield to those who trust and take refuge in Him. [Ps. 18:30; 84:11; 115:9–11.]

6 Add not to His words, lest He reprove you, and you be found a liar.

7 Two things have I asked of You [O Lord]; deny them not to me before I die:

8 Remove far from me falsehood and lies; give me neither poverty nor riches; feed me with the food that is needful for me,

9 Lest I be full and deny You and say, Who is the Lord? Or lest I be poor and steal, and so profane the name of my God. [Deut. 8:12, 14, 17; Neh. 9:25, 26; Job 31:24; Hos. 13:6.]

10 Do not accuse and hurt a servant before his master, lest he curse you, and you be held guilty [of adding to the burdens of the lowly].

11 There is a class of people who curse their fathers and do not bless their mothers.

12 There is a class of people who are pure in their own eyes, and yet are not washed from their own filth.

13 There is a class of people—oh, how lofty are their eyes and their raised eyelids!

14 There is a class of people whose teeth are as swords and whose fangs as knives, to devour the poor from the earth and the needy from among men.

15 The leech has two daughters, crying, Give, give! There are three things that are never satisfied, yes, four that do not say, It is enough:

16 Sheol (the place of the dead), the barren womb, the earth that is not satisfied with water, and the fire that says not, It is enough.

17 The eye that mocks a father and scorns to obey a mother, the ravens of the valley will pick it out, and the young vultures will devour it. [Lev. 20:9; Prov. 20:20; 23:22.]

18 There are three things which are too wonderful for me, yes, four which I do not understand:

19 The way of an eagle in the air, the way of a serpent upon a rock, the way of a ship in the midst of the sea, and the way of a man with a maid.

20 This is the way of an adulterous woman: she eats and wipes her mouth and says, I have done no wickedness.

21 Under three things the earth is disquieted, and under four it cannot bear up:

22 Under a servant when he reigns, a [empty-headed] fool when he is filled with food,

23 An unloved *and* repugnant woman when she is married, and a maidservant when she supplants her mistress.

24 There are four things which are little on the earth, but they are exceedingly wise:

25 The ants are a people not strong, yet they lay up their food in the summer; [Prov. 6:6.]

26 The conies are but a feeble folk, yet they make their houses in the rocks; [Ps. 104:18.]

27 The locusts have no king, yet they go forth all of them by bands;

28 The lizard you can seize with your hands, yet it is in kings' palaces.

29 There are three things which are stately in step, yes, four which are stately in their stride:

30 The lion, which is mightiest among beasts and turns not back before any;

31 The war horse [well-knit in the loins], the male goat also, and the king [when his army is with him and] against whom there is no uprising.

32 If you have done foolishly in exalting yourself, or if you have thought evil, lay your hand upon your mouth. [Job 21:5; 40:4.]

33 Surely the churning of milk brings forth butter, and the wringing of the nose brings forth blood; so the forcing of wrath brings forth strife.

CHAPTER 31

THE WORDS of Lemuel king of Massa, which his mother taught him:

2 What, my 'son? What, son of my womb? What [shall I advise you], son of my vows *and* dedication to God?

3 Give not your strength to [loose] women, nor your ways to those who *and* that which ruin *and* destroy kings.

4 It is not for kings, O Lemuel, it is not for kings to drink wine, or for rulers to desire strong drink, [Eccl. 10:17; Hos. 4:11.]

5 Lest they drink and forget the law *and* what it decrees, and pervert the justice due any of the afflicted.

6 Give strong drink [as medicine] to him who is ready to pass away, and wine to him in bitter distress of heart.

7 Let him drink and forget his poverty and [seriously] remember his want *and* misery no more.

t It is important to the purpose of this invaluable chapter that one realizes that it is first of all intended for young men. It is the mother's God-given task to provide youth with this information directly from its inspired source, letting them grow up with it in their consciousness.

8 Open your mouth for the dumb [those unable to speak for themselves], for the rights of all who are left desolate *and* defenseless; [I Sam. 19:4; Esth. 4:16; Job 29:15, 16.]

9 Open your mouth, judge righteously, and administer justice for the poor and needy. [Lev. 19:15; Deut. 1:16; Job 29:12; Isa. 1:17; Jer. 22:16.]

10 A capable, intelligent, *and* ᵘvirtuous woman—who is he who can find her? She is far more precious than jewels *and* her value is far above rubies *or* pearls. [Prov. 12:4; 18:22; 19:14.]

11 The heart of her husband trusts in her confidently *and* relies on and believes in her securely, so that he has no lack of [honest] gain or need of [dishonest] spoil.

12 She comforts, encourages, *and* does him only good as long as there is life within her.

13 She seeks out wool and flax and works with willing hands [to develop it].

14 She is like the merchant ships loaded with foodstuffs; she brings her household's food from a far [country].

15 She rises while it is yet night and gets [spiritual] food for her household and assigns her maids their tasks. [Job 23:12.]

16 She considers a [new] field before she buys *or* accepts it [expanding prudently and not courting neglect of her present duties by assuming other duties]; with her savings [of time and strength] she plants fruitful vines in her vineyard. [S. of Sol. 8:12.]

17 She girds herself with strength [spiritual, mental, and physical fitness for her God-given task] and makes her arms strong *and* firm.

18 She tastes *and* sees that her gain from work [with and for God] is good; her lamp goes not out, but it burns on continually through the night [of trouble, privation, or sorrow, warning away fear, doubt, and distrust].

19 She lays her hands to the spindle, and her hands hold the distaff.

20 She opens her hand to the poor, yes, she reaches out her filled hands to the needy [whether in body, mind, or spirit].

21 She fears not the snow for her family, for all her household are doubly clothed in scarlet. [Josh. 2:18, 19; Heb. 9:19–22.]

22 She makes for herself coverlets, cushions, *and* rugs of tapestry. Her clothing is of linen, pure *and* fine, and of purple [such as that of which the clothing of the priests and the hallowed cloths of the temple were made]. [Isa. 61:10; I Tim. 2:9; Rev. 3:5; 19:8, 14.]

23 Her husband is known in the [city's] gates, when he sits among the elders of the land. [Prov. 12:4.]

24 She makes fine linen garments *and* leads others to buy them; she delivers to the merchants girdles [or sashes that free one up for service].

25 Strength and dignity are her clothing *and* her position is strong and secure; she rejoices over the future [the latter day or time to come, knowing that she and her family are in readiness for it]!

26 She opens her mouth in skillful and godly Wisdom, and on her tongue is the law of kindness [giving counsel and instruction].

27 She looks well to how things go in her household, and the bread of idleness (gossip, discontent, and self-pity)

---

u It is most unfortunate that this description of God's ideal woman is usually confined in readers' minds merely to its literal sense—her ability as a homemaker, as in the picture of Martha of Bethany in Luke 10:38–42. But it is obvious that far more than that is meant. When the summary of what makes her value "far above rubies" is given (in Prov. 31:30), it is her spiritual life only that is mentioned. One can almost hear the voice of Jesus saying, "Mary has chosen the good portion . . . which shall not be taken away from her" (Luke 10:42).

she will not eat. [I Tim. 5:14; Tit. 2:5.]

28 Her children rise up and call her blessed (happy, fortunate, and to be envied), and her husband boasts of *and* praises her, [saying,]

29 "Many daughters have done virtuously, nobly, *and* well [with the strength of character that is steadfast in goodness], but you excel them all.

30 Charm *and* grace are deceptive, and *beauty* is vain [because it is not lasting], but *a woman* who reverently *and* worshipfully *fears the* Lord, she shall be praised!

31 Give her of the fruit of her hands, and let her own works praise her in the gates [of the city]! [Phil. 4:8.]

...y daughters have done . . . nobly and well . . . but you excel them all." What a glowing description ... corded of this woman in private life, this "capable, intelligent, and virtuous woman" of Prov. 31! It ... she had done more than Miriam, the one who led a nation's women in praise to God (Exod. 15:20, ... Deborah, the patriotic military advisor (Judg. 4:4-10); Ruth, the woman of constancy (Ruth 1:16); ...annah, the ideal mother (I Sam. 1:20; 2:19); the Shunammite, the hospitable woman (II Kings 4:8-10); ... Huldah, the woman who revealed God's secret message to national leaders (II Kings 22:14); and even ... more than Queen Esther, the woman who risked sacrificing her life for her people (Esth. 4:16). In what ... way did she "excel them all"? In her spiritual and practical devotion to God, which permeated every area ... and relationship of her life. All seven of the Christian virtues (II Pet. 1:5) are there, like colored threads in ... a tapestry. Her secret, which is open to everyone, is the Holy Spirit's climax to the story, and to this ... book. In Prov. 31:30, it becomes clear that the "reverent *and* worshipful fear of the Lord," which is "the ... beginning (the chief and choice part) of Wisdom" (Prov. 9:10), is put forth as the true foundation for a ... life which is valued by God and her husband as "far above rubies *or* pearls" (Prov. 31:10).

she will not eat. [I Tim. 5:14; Tit. 2:5.]

28 Her children rise up and call her blessed (happy, fortunate, and to be envied); and her husband boasts of *and* praises her, [saying],

29 ᵛMany daughters have done virtuously, nobly, *and* well [with the strength of character that is steadfast in goodness], but you excel them all.

30 Charm *and* grace are deceptive, and beauty is vain [because it is not lasting], but a woman who reverently *and* worshipfully fears the Lord, she shall be praised!

31 Give her of the fruit of her hands, and let her own works praise her in the gates [of the city]! [Phil. 4:8.]

---

v "Many daughters have done . . . nobly and well . . . but you excel them all." What a glowing description here recorded of this woman in private life, this "capable, intelligent, and virtuous woman" of Prov. 31! It means she had done more than Miriam, the one who led a nation's women in praise to God (Exod. 15:20, 21); Deborah, the patriotic military advisor (Judg. 4:4-10); Ruth, the woman of constancy (Ruth 1:16); Hannah, the ideal mother (I Sam. 1:20; 2:19); the Shunammite, the hospitable woman (II Kings 4:8-10); Huldah, the woman who revealed God's secret message to national leaders (II Kings 22:14); and even more than Queen Esther, the woman who risked sacrificing her life for her people (Esth. 4:16). In what way did she "excel them all"? In her spiritual and practical devotion to God, which permeated every area and relationship of her life. All seven of the Christian virtues (II Pet. 1:5) are there, like colored threads in a tapestry. Her secret, which is open to everyone, is the Holy Spirit's climax to the story, and to this book. In Prov. 31:30, it becomes clear that the "reverent *and* worshipful fear of the Lord," which is "the beginning (the chief and choice part) of Wisdom" (Prov. 9:10), is put forth as the true foundation for a life which is valued by God and her husband as "far above rubies *or* pearls" (Prov. 31:10).

TO THE
AMPLIFIED
BIBLE

This bibliography has been developed as a companion to the footnotes of the Amplified Bible. Just a quick glance at the sources indexed will reveal the thousands of hours of research that went into the making of the Amplified Bible.

The bibliography is broken down into several categories: Bible Versions; Greek Testaments; Word Studies and Lexical Aids; Commentaries; Other Reference Works; General Resources. In addition, there is a section entitled "Persons Cited", with a brief description of the individual's background.

In spite of rigorous efforts to recover information about the sources used, the Bibliographic material will be incomplete in some cases. However, there is enough in the bibliography to make it a useful tool for understanding the footnotes.

BIBLE VERSIONS
The American Standard Version. New York: Thomas Nelson & Sons, 1901.
Bede, translated portions of the Bible from Latin into Old English, A.D. 735.
The Cambridge Bible for Schools and Colleges. 49 vols. 1878–1952.
Coverdale, Miles, trans. *The Coverdale Bible,* 1535.
Darby, John, trans. *The Bible, A New Translation* N.T., 1871; O.T., 1890.
Jerome, trans. *The Latin Vulgate.* 4th century A.D.
The King James Version. 1611.
Knox, Ronald, trans. *The Holy Bible; A Translation from the Latin Vulgate.* New York : Sheed & Ward, N.T., 1944; O.T., 1948–50.
Lams, George M., trans. *The Holy Bible from ancient Eastern manuscripts.* Philadelphia: A.J. Holman Co., N.T., 1940.
The Old Testament Translated from the Septuagint. 2 vols. London: Skeflington & Son, 1904.
Phillips, J.B., trans. *New Testament in Modern English; Letters to Young Churches; a translation of the New Testament Epistles.* New York: Macmillan, 1951.
Rotherham, Joseph B., trans. *The Emphasized Bible.* New York: Fleming H. Revell Company, N.T., 1872; O.T., 1902.
Tyndale, William, trans. *The Tyndale Bible* (first printing of a New Testament into English). 1526.
Verkuyl, Gerrit, trans. *The Berkeley Version in Modern English.* Grand Rapids: Zondervan Publishing House, N.T., 1945; O.T., 1953.
Way, Arthur S., trans *Way's Epistles: The Letters of St. Paul to Seven Churches and Three Friends.* London: Macmillan, 1901 (revised 1906, Hebrews added).
Wesley, John, trans. *The New Testament.* Londeon: Epworth Press, 1755.
Williams, Charles B., trans. *The New Testament: A Translation in the Language of the People.* Chicago: Moody Press, 1950.

Wycliffe, John, trans. *The Wycliffe Bible* (first translation of the Bible into English). 1380.

GREEK TESTAMENTS

Alford, Henry. *The Greek New Testament, with Notes.* 5 vols. London: Rivingtons, 1857–1861.

Bengel, Johann. *Gnomon Novi Testamenti.* 3 vols. Edinburgh: T. & T. Clark, 1877

Nicoll, W. Robertson, ed. *The Expositor' Greek New Testament.* 5 vols. London: Hodder & Stoughton, 1897–1910.

WORD STUDIES AND LEXICAL AIDS

Abbott-Smith, G. *Manual Greek Lexicon of the New Testament.* Edinburgh: T. & T. Clark, 1937.

Berry, George Ricker. *Greek-English New Testament Lexicon.* Grand Rapids: Zondervan Publishing House, 1966.

Cremer, Hermann. *Biblico-Theological Lexicon of the New Testament Greek.* T. & T. Clark, 1895.

Hickie, W.J. *Greek-English Lexicon to the New Testament.* New York: Macmillan, 1921.

Kennedy, H. A. A. *Sources of New Testament Greek.*

Moulton, James Hope, and George Milligan. *The Vocabulary of the Greek Testament.* London: Hodder & Stoughton, 1952.

Robertson, Archibald Thomas, *Word Pictures in the New Testament.* New York: R.R. Smith Inc., 1930–1933.

Schmidt, J.H. Heinrich. *Synonymik der Grierchischen Sprache.* 1886.

Souter, Alexander. *Pocket Lexicon of the Greek New Testament.* London: Oxford University Press, 1916.

Thayer, Joseph Henry. *A Greek-English Lexicon of the New Testament.* New York: American Book Co., 1889.

Trench, Richard C. *Synonyms of the New Testament.* New York: Blakeman & Mason, 1859.

Vincent, Marvin. *Word Studies in the New Testament.* 4 vols. New York: C. Scribner's Sons, 1887–1900.

Wuest, Kenneth. *Word Studies in the Greek New Testament. Multivolume; Mark in the Greek New Testament; Golden Nuggets from the Greek New Testament; Treasures from the Greek New Testament; Bypaths in the Greek New Testament; Untranslatable Riches from the Greek New Testament; Hebrews in the Greek New Testament* Grand Rapids: Wm. B. Eerdmans Co., 1966.

Young Robert. *Analytical Concordance to the Bible.* New York: American Book Co., 1881.

COMMENTARIES

Barnes, Albert. *Notes on the New Testament.* 12 vols. Grand Rapids: Baker Book House, 1949–1957.

Clarke, Adam. *The Holy Bible with A Commentary and Critcal Notes.* 6 vols.
    New York: G. Lane & C.B. Tippett, 1837–1847.
Gray, James C., and George M. Adams. *Bible Commentary.* 5 vols. Grand
    Rapids: Zondervan Publishing House, n.d.
Henry, Matthew. *Commentary on the Holy Bible.* Philadelphia: Lippincott,
    1856.
Jamieson, Robert, A.R. Fausset, and David Brown. *A Commentary, Critical,
    Experimental and Practical, on the Old and New Testaments.* 6 vols.
    Grand Rapids: Wm. B. Eerdmans Co. 1935.
Lightfoot, Joseph P. *Notes on the Epistles of St. Paul.* London: Macmillan,
    1869. *Saint Paul's Epistle to the Philippians.* London: Macmillan, 1908.
    Saint Paul's Epistle to the Colossians and Philemon. London: Macmillan,
    1886.
Meyer, H.A.W. *Commentary on the New Testament.* 11 vols. Edinburgh: T. &
    T. Clark, 1883–1884.
Speaker's Commentary. 10 vols. London: J. Murray, 1871–1881.
Swete, Henry Barclay. *The Gospel According to Saint Mark.* London:
    Macmillian, 1898
Trench, Richard C. *Notes on the Miracles of our Lord.* London: Parker, 1862.
    Studies in the Gospels. 1867.
Westcott, Brooke Foss. *The Epistles of Saint John.* Grand Rapids: Wm. B.
    Eerdmans, 1955.

OTHER REFERENCE WORKS
Davis, John D. *A Dictionary of the Bible.*: Philadelphia: Westminster, 1936.
Exell, Joseph S., ed. *The Biblical Illustrator.* 28 vols. Grand Rapids: Baker
    Book House, 1956.
Orr, James et al., eds. *The International Standard Bible Encyclopedia.* 5 vols.
    Chicago: The Howard Severance Company, 1930.
Webster, Noah. *New International Dictionary of the English Language.*
    Springfield: G. & C. Merriam Company, 1961.

GENERAL RESOURCES
Farrar, Frederick W. *The Life and Work of Saint Paul.* 2 vols. New York: E.P.
    Dutton and company, 1889.
Lamsa, George M. *Gospel Light: comments on the teachings of Jesus from
    Aramaic and unchanged Eastern customs.* Philadelphia: A.J. Holman Co.
    1936.
Murray, John. *The Sovereignty of God.* Grand Rapids: Zondervan Publishing
    House, 1940.
Warfield, B.B. *Biblical Doctrines.* London: Oxford University Press, 1929.

PERSONS CITED
Aristotle, 4th century B.C. Greek philosopher.
Bengel, Johann, Lutheran Minister and theologian (1687–1752)
Calvin, John, 16th century Protestant Reformer (1509–1564)

Clark, George Whitefield, Scripture harmonist (1831–1911)

Chrysostom, John, 4th century Doctor of the Greek Church.

Doddridge, Philip, British Nonconformist minister, educator, author, and hymn writer (1702–1751).

Godet, Frederic L., Swiss Reformed theologian and exegete (1812–1900).

Gould, Ezra Palmer, Professor of New Testament literature (1841–1900)

Gurnall, William, British theologian and Bible commentator (1617–1679)

Kypke, G.D., Bible scholar (1724–1779)

Lumby, J. Rawson, Church historian and Bible commentator (1831–1895)

Luther, Martin, leader of the German Reformation (1483–1546).

Macknight, James, Church of Scotland minister and Bible translator (1721–1800).

Melanchthon, Philip, German Reformer, theologian, and educator (1497–1560).

Meyer, H.A.W., German Protestant minister and New Testament scholar (1800–1873).

Origen, 3rd century theologian of the early Greek Church.

Richard of St. Victor, 12th century scholar and mystic.

Schmidt, J.H. Heinrich, German classical language scholar (1834- ??).

Taylor, Jeremy, Anglican bishop and writer (1613–1667).

Westcott, Brooke F., New Testament scholar (1825–1901).